Theatre Of Fire

Cornelius Dusart, Dutch, 1660-1704, Woman lighting a rocket, mezzotint
on paper, 1695, 24.7 x 18cm, Stanley Field Endowment, 1964.47.
Photograph © 1995, The Art Institute of Chicago.

Theatre Of Fire

SPECIAL EFFECTS
IN EARLY
ENGLISH AND SCOTTISH
THEATRE

PHILIP BUTTERWORTH

Foreword by Glynne Wickham

THE SOCIETY FOR THEATRE RESEARCH
LONDON

First published 1998
by The Society for Theatre Research,
c/o The Theatre Museum, 1E Tavistock Street,
Covent Garden, London WC2E 7PA

ISBN 085430 0627

General Editor: Dr. Richard Foulkes

Volume Editor: Professor Glynne Wickham

Printed by Woolnough Bookbinding
Church Street, Irthlingborough, Northants
Typeset by Sinclair Scott, Northampton

In memory
of my father
C.B.
1917-1973

Contents

Illustrations

Foreword

IT WOULD be hard to imagine any book planned to appear under the imprint of the Society for Theatre Research to mark its Jubilee year better calculated to appeal to a wide spectrum of readers than Philip Butterworth's *Theatre of Fire*.

It has been meticulously researched from a multitude of unfamiliar and often obscure sources of medieval and renaissance origin, many of them in languages other than English.

These have been delicately pieced together in the manner of a fine patchwork quilt to provide a coherent and highly convincing account of the spectacular aspect of theatrical production that has fascinated audiences for centuries – conflagrations, pyrotechnics of all descriptions and magically contrived illuminations.

When the Cornish Cycle of Mystery Plays was revived in 1969 (for the first time in more than 450 years) in the amphitheatre near Perranporth which originally contained it, nothing excited audiences more than the recurrent appearances of devils from a Hell that belched smoke and flames and which finally hoisted them all on their own petards when Hell was harrowed by Christus Rex in the closing scenes of *Resurrectio* on Day Three.

In explaining how medieval stage-managers and their technicians contrived to make devils, dragons and other apocalyptic beasts seem to breathe smoke and fire while projecting fireworks from their mouths and tails; or how thunderbolts seemed to strike pagan temples, set them on fire and reduce them to smoking piles of rubble without appearing to injure any of the actors, Dr. Butterworth brings not only the fruits of his scholarly research, but his practical experience of theatrical production, to bear on many medieval and renaissance stage directions that have hitherto defied rational explanation.

Taking great care to test the likely veracity of descriptions purporting to have been offered by eye-witnesses by distinguishing between those accounts that merely inform readers of what was intended to happen and those which tell them what spectators present at the time actually saw, and then by submitting all stage-directions within play-texts to equally rigorous scrutiny, he succeeds in separating those that are to be taken literally from those only intended by the playmaker to provide guidelines to skilled craftsmen to assist them in effecting the desired theatrical illusion.

This approach to those spectacular pyrotechnical effects demanded in the texts of medieval and renaissance plays, as also in the many secular dramatic entertainments commissioned to celebrate royal weddings, births, or visits to foreign cities (whether in city-streets in daylight or in roofed banquet halls at night) leads Dr. Butterworth on to seek out the authors of those manuals that were the required reading of those master-craftsmen, their journeymen and apprentices who earned their livings from knowledge of the chemical and minerological skills, or 'secrets', needed to manufacture fireworks and other explosive devices known to startle, intrigue and delight audiences in earlier times as in their own.

This has resulted in a book that, for the first time, enables theatrical directors, actors, designers and dramatic critics to substitute reliable, factual interpretations of fascinating medieval and renaissance stage-effects for their previous, largely imaginative and often erroneous, speculations.

Each chapter is devoted to the means required to provide particular 'special effects' – devils spouting fire, lightning, thunder, smoke, boilings and burnings of living persons; – and finally to those individuals known to be involved in the chain of supply of those ingredients needed to produce these stage-effects. Each of these topics, moreover, is further reinforced by a sequence of Appendices which provide readers with extracts from those manuals and recipe books on which the artificers servicing requests from pageant-masters, masters of Court and Civic Revels and their technicians relied to satisfy their clients.

Many of these recipe books must be regarded as derived from inherited traditions as practised in much earlier times and from Oriental as well as European sources. Since the Society for Theatre Research offers annual research awards, it is thus to be hoped that some young scholar, inspired by Dr. Butterworth's achievements as represented in this book, may venture to emulate his example by following it up with another on the pyrotechnical effects demanded by Greek and Roman dramatists in classical antiquity.

In the meantime, since fireworks of one sort or another have time out of mind been used to mark the climax of many domestic, as well as royal and civic, celebrations, it is fitting that *Theatre of Fire* should be published in conjunction with those other celebrations planned to greet the Jubilee of the Society's inauguration and in honour of its founders, its benefcators, sponsors and the many voluntary Committee members responsible for its achievements through its first fifty years.

Glynne Wickham

President.

PREFATORY NOTE

IN ORDER not to unbalance the work with too many notes, some of the shorter references and quotations have not been directly acknowledged. However, in such instances, the absence of note recognition occurs in a context where the source is clear or can be deduced from existing references.

Substantial appendices conclude the work as a means of presenting significant evidence. Some of this material is previously unpublished and other items are here brought into focus from disparate sources.

ACKNOWLEDGEMENTS

THIS WORK began its existence as a Ph.D. thesis with the title *Fire and Flame as Special Effects in the Medieval and Tudor Theatre* and was supervised by Peter Meredith in the School of English at the University of Leeds. *Theatre of Fire* is a partially re-written and restructured working of the completed thesis from which a number of papers have already been published. Sections of these articles have been fused into the present work and I am grateful to the editors, Meg Twycross, Peter Meredith, Clifford Davidson, David Bergeron and Peter Greenfield for permission to reproduce parts of articles and chapters published in *Medieval English Theatre*, *The Iconography of Hell*, *The Iconography of Heaven and Research Opportunities in Renaissance Drama*.

The growth of the work has occurred over several years and in that time a number of individuals have made significant contributions to it. In particular, I should like to thank Daphne Hale, Lynette Muir and Arthur Pritchard for their generous help with translation. In the early stages of the work, Miklos Menis of the theatre company "Theatre of Fire" was most helpful in sharing his pyrotechnic insight. Others who have been considerate with their knowledge and experience of fireworks are Michael Swisher, *Pyrotechnia* and Chris Philip.

One of the joys of preparing the book has been the opportunity to work amongst scholars who create the industrious atmosphere of the North Library of the British Library. To them and the ever courteous and knowledgeable library staff, my thanks. Similarly, I have spent many productive hours in the "bowels" of the Brotherton Library at the University of Leeds. Here again, the library staff have been enormously helpful. Additional library, archive and museum staff who have offered help are : Patrick B.Nolan, The Hagley Museum and Library, Delaware; David J.Eveleigh, Blaise Castle House Museum, Bristol; Francis Comerford, *The Stage and Television Today* ; Ian Hill, The Scottish Record

Office, Edinburgh; W.M.Kellner, Department of Manuscripts,The British Library; Dieter Kudorfer, Die Bayerische Staatsbibliothek, München; A.Morton, Welbeck College; Rosemary Weinstein, The Museum of London; C. Anne Wilson, The Brotherton Library, University of Leeds; Mary K. Yallop, Allhallows Museum, Honiton; Kate Harris, Longleat House; Karen Hearn, The Tate Gallery; Pamela Stuedemann, The Art Institute of Chicago. Library staff at Bretton Hall have been most reliable and painstaking in their efforts to secure even the most obscure works.

Friends and colleagues at Bretton Hall have offered inspiration, scholarly support and friendly disparagement by referring to this study as "bangers-up-the-bum" work. Also the College management has been most supportive and I would particularly like to thank Tim Stephenson for demonstrating his continued faith in my work.

Other scholars who have offered help and encouragement are : Martin Banham; David Bevington; Inga-Stina Ewbank; A.E.Green; Max Harris; C.Walter Hodges; Alexandra F.Johnston; John Marshall; C.E.McGee; David Mills; Barbara Palmer and Alessandro Vitale-Brovarone.

As might be expected, officers and members of The Society For Theatre Research have been courteous, encouraging and practically helpful. I should particularly like to thank Margaret Collins; Russell Jackson and Chris Baugh. Richard Foulkes has steered the book through its stages of production with appropriate skill and care and Glynne Wickham, as volume editor, has brought his great experience, understanding and scholarship to bear on the editorial process. Thanks are also due to Deborah Brooke who has worked upon the index with her customary diligence.

My gratitude must be further extended to Peter and Greta Meredith. Peter's considerable contribution to my thinking has been generous, scholarly and always stimulating. Among Greta's attributes is the care and skill that is reflected in her "little book" that prevents her from repeating a recipe. Their friendship is also a continued source of sustenance.

Finally, and most of all, thanks must go to Sheila for her forbearance and stock of well-targetted questions designed to keep me on my toes.

Philip Butterworth Kirkburton, September 1997.

INTRODUCTION

WE LIVE in an increasingly safety-conscious age. In Northern Europe and North America promotion of safety issues is dominant in many aspects of life. Legislation that encapsulates aspects of safety grows in scale and scope. In the work place much of our practice is now affected by tightened safety codes or regulation. Any event where the public gathers in large numbers is also subject to intensified safety considerations by ever vigilant local authorities. When we travel, our safe use of the services is conditioned by both law and procedure. Rules that govern sporting activities are now penetrated by safety concerns to such an extent that some sports face severe restrictions or even extinction if, for example, someone is injured or killed. The position of sports such as pistol shooting, boxing, rugby and Grand Prix racing is constantly under review by public organisations. Ritual reaction by some public bodies concerning safety matters is now endemic in our Western societies.

Responses from such organisations towards the use of fireworks serve as an example of this kind of institutional behaviour. The Department of Trade and Industry recently invited submissions from public bodies concerning responses to the D.T.I. discussion paper, "Controls on the Availability of Fireworks". The British Safety Council in its concluding comments to its submission recorded that it was committed to:

> a reversal of the deregulation of the industry; restrictions on the types of fireworks available to the general public; sales of fireworks only on production of Group 1 and 2 or Group 3 and 4 licences; sales only through specialist, licensed retailers; firework displays licensed by Local Authorities and supervised by Local Authorities and the Fire Service; licences for persons in the business of using

professional fireworks; and a formal, national training scheme for display organisers.[1]

The purpose of this description of late twentieth-century safety consciousness is to enable the contrast to be displayed between our societies and those of the Middle Ages where the values, practices and attitudes were clearly so different. The temporal, religious and cultural differences between our own age and those of the Middle Ages are such that any assumptions on which our interpretation of this past is based must acknowledge the filtering of our own perceptions in order to arrive at any accuracy of understanding. Consequently, notions of what constitutes "safety", "danger" and "risk taking" today are clearly based upon different responses, expectations and practice. So, when we perceive danger or risk taking in the realisation of particular special effects, we must be cautious about assessing the danger, risk or effectiveness in its appropriate context. From the relative comfort of our twentieth-century position it may be all too easy to obscure the existence or importance of medieval evidence because of our prevalent preoccupation with safety. The sort of caveat expressed here applies to the stance adopted to the examination of all kinds of evidence.

Appropriate evidence concerning the use of special effects in fire and flame in the medieval and Tudor theatre points to some hazardous, exciting and spectacular theatrical activity. The effects range from the simple use of candles to impressive "set-pieces" for dramatic firework events. Despite the overt theatrical nature of such effects, little has been written about them. A number of works exist that discuss devices, "feintes" and "secrets" in the medieval French theatre,[2] but no substantial research has been undertaken in the area of special effects in English and Scottish theatre. Hence my purpose in this work is a practical one; it is to assemble and analyse available evidence concerning such special effects in the English and Scottish medieval and Tudor theatre and attempt to determine its significance. So, what is the nature of the available evidence?

Five major forms of evidence present themselves for consideration. They are: guild, civic and ecclesiastical records; firework writers' recipes; eye-witness accounts; recipes in Books of Secrets and stage directions in plays. Because these sorts of evidence are dissimilar in form and yield distinctly different information, it is important to examine the value of evidence with considerable care. Although references to pyrotechnic matters occur within various dramatic texts, the reliability of such material is insecure unless it is corroborated, amplified or explained by one of the five major forms of evidence. Since the dramatic text is, by its nature and purpose, a fiction employing imaginative licence, its worth as evidence can not necessarily be relied upon. If a "character" in a play refers to an action that needs to be performed, the implied action does not, of itself, constitute evidence of the action. This kind of fictional requirement is sometimes referred to as an "implicit" stage direction.[3] The weakness of the information contained in this type of direction, in providing evidence, may be illustrated with reference to the Chester *Pageante of Noyes Fludd*. God has commanded Noah to build the ark and specified the animals to be taken on board. When the ark is complete the seven members of Noah's family each offer a stanza describing different animals admitted to the ark. For example:

SEM

Syr, here are lions, leopardes in;
horses, mares, oxen, and swynne,
geates, calves, sheepe, and kyne
here sytten thou may see.[4]

If the information contained within these stanzas is taken as "implicit" stage direction content then it may be supposed that all these animals are present on board the ark. However, all that this detail confirms is that the dramatic narrative requires the animals to be present. This sort of information does not confirm the form in which the animals exist. Are the animals real, representational or imaginary in the theatrical reality? Does the dramatic text contain any evidence that determines the form? Are there any theatrical conventions embedded in the dialogue that help to identify the form? Because these questions cannot be answered with any degree of certainty, the reliability of the evidence provided by the "implicit" stage direction within the dramatic text is weakened. However, clear information of the form and theatrical convention is offered by an adjacent "explicit" stage direction as follows:

Then Noe shall goe into the arke with all his familye, his wyffe excepte, and the arke muste bee borded rownde aboute. And one the bordes all the beastes and fowles hereafter reahersed muste bee paynted, that ther wordes may agree with the pictures.[5]

The function of this kind of direction is essentially practical and refers to the conscious and deliberate construction of the theatrical moment or event. By its very existence the "explicit" direction draws attention to the fact that its expression and function is different from that of the dramatic text. Since the presence of an "explicit" stage direction in a dramatic text presupposes a capacity to implement its practical requirement(s), it may be considered to provide a more reliable form of information than the "implicit" direction in the dramatic text. Even so, the "explicit" direction does not necessarily provide evidence of the instruction having been implemented, but it does offer proof of its requirement.

Evidence contained in each of the five categories outlined above presents itself in different ways which will guide and shape resultant analysis. Any of the five areas may yield evidence which may be used to verify that found in the others.

Information may be culled from civic, guild and ecclesiastical records in the form of account books. Expenses formally entered into account books of organised or official bodies are sometimes capable of providing evidence of practice or procedure. Until the early nineteenth century little attention was given to evidence concerning dramatic activity contained within such records. The first published work, of any significance, to place value upon civic and guild records, as evidence, occurs in the remarkable nineteenth-century work *A Dissertation on the Pageants or Dramatic Mysteries anciently performed at Coventry* by Thomas Sharp, published in 1825.[6] In this work Sharp draws upon a range of guild accounts in an attempt to develop understanding of performance conditions relevant to the mystery plays at Coventry. Additional value may be placed upon the "hitherto unexplored"[7] records published by Sharp since most of the original documents were burned in a fire at the Birmingham Free Reference Library in 1879. Sharp's transcriptions of guild accounts now form a major source of evidence concerning the mystery plays at Coventry.[8] Apart from the exposure of John Payne Collier's records[9] and the often inaccurate compilation of Elizabethan and Stuart records by John Tucker Murray in the nineteenth century,[10] it was not until later in the century that attention was given to records by J.O.Halliwell-Phillipps in his search for Shakespearian evidence.[11] Also in the nineteenth and early twentieth century some local antiquarians began to publish municipal and churchwardens' accounts.[12] In 1851 John Nicholl published *Some Account of the Worshipful Company of Ironmongers* which concerned company accounts from the sixteenth century. These accounts record expenses incurred by the Ironmongers that relate to their contribution to the *Lord Mayors' Show* in London during the latter half of the sixteenth century.[13] E.K.Chambers published *The Mediaeval Stage* in 1903 in which he consulted a wide range of published records concerning liturgical, civic and folk drama.[14] Though Chambers' thinking concerning the evolutionary nature of English drama has been questioned, his work on and in association with appropriate records continues to act as a focal point for the study of records. The first *Accounts of the Lord High Treasurer of Scotland* [*The Accounts*] edited by Sir James Balfour-Paul were issued at the turn of the century and continued to be published until 1970 when volume XII was edited by Charles T.McInnes.[15] These accounts contain a number of references to theatrical events. Albert Feuillerat's *Documents relating to the Office of the Revels in the time of Queen Elizabeth* were published in 1908 and followed up by his *Documents relating to the Revels at Court in the time of King Edward VI and Queen Mary* in 1914.[16]

A significant development in the publication of dramatic records from original documents occurred with the Malone Society *Collection* series, first published in 1911, edited by W.W.Greg, and which continues to be published.[17] An important resource concerning Scottish records is Anna J.Mill's *Mediaeval Plays in Scotland* published in 1924.[18] This study deals with folk plays, minstrelsy, court revels and municipal plays. In 1931 the accounts of the *Lord Mayors' Pageants of the Merchant Taylors' Company in the 15th, 16th & 17th Centuries* were published and edited by R.T.D.Sayle.[19] The accounts of another London company were published in 1933 under the title *Records of the Skinners of London - Edward I to James I* and edited by John James Lambert.[20] These accounts together with those of the Merchant Taylors and Ironmongers offer important evidence in relation to the *Lord Mayors' Show*. In 1955 F.M.Salter published his *Mediaeval Drama in Chester* which provided an analysis and re-evaluation of the Chester mystery plays based upon guild and civic records of the city.[21] This work together with the developing publications of the Malone Society affected a most important event in the publication of records, namely, the inauguration of the project known as *Records of Early English Drama*.

In 1975 the *Records of Early English Drama*, or *REED*, project was launched in Toronto and in 1979 the first two volume edition of the records at York was published.[22] This work amply satisfies the principal aim of *REED*, which "is to locate, transcribe and publish systematically all surviving external evidence of dramatic, ceremonial and minstrel activity in Great Britain before 1642.".[23] The two *York* volumes contain new and previously published accounts which have been systematically organised.[24] Since publication of the *York* records some 14 volumes have appeared from *REED* covering both cities and counties and another 10 volumes, that are editorially complete, await publication. Although Anna J.Mill in her *Mediaeval Plays in Scotland* presents the principal records concerning dramatic activity in Scotland, she does omit some accounts that have been published subsequently in full. Two such publications are the *Accounts of the Treasurer of Scotland*, volume 12, 1566-1574 [*The Accounts*], edited by Charles T.McInnes and published in 1970 [25] and *Accounts of the Masters of Works*, volume 1, 1529-1615, edited by Henry M.Paton and volume 2, 1616-1649, edited by John Imrie and John G.Dunbar and published in 1982 [both volumes referred to as *The Accounts M.W.*].[26] An important attempt to rectify the dearth of continental evidence in English translation is to be found in *The Staging of Religious Drama in Europe in the Later Middle Ages:Texts and Documents in English Translation*, edited by Peter Meredith and John E.Tailby.[27] Another work that presents many records only partially covered by *REED* is Ian Lancashire's *Dramatic Texts and Records of Britain: A Chronological Topography to 1558*, published in 1984.[28] This source of evidence, like the *REED* volumes, is also a useful bibliographical tool.

Clearly, interpretation of the kind of records published by *REED* and others is open to misuse or abuse. Consequently, care must be taken in the evaluation of such records. Recognition of context and purpose of materials, processes and events must condition understanding.[29] Even so, it is still possible to arrive at misleading or wrong conclusions despite appropriate care. A number of studies have been conducted based upon records published by *REED*[30] and understanding of early drama practice is thus being confirmed, questioned or modified.

An example of the way in which publication of records may be used to develop understanding of theatre conditions may be seen in relation to the hitherto cherished notion that the Elizabethan theatre developed from and alongside theatre played in inn-yards. Confirmation of this practice is not borne out by evidence assembled in *REED* volumes.[31] Although a small amount of evidence of this relationship exists in London,[32] a more widespread use of inn-yards as performance venues does not appear to have taken place.[33] Even a location such as the New Inn at Gloucester, frequently said to have been a place where travelling players played, offers no evidence of the use of its yard as a playing area. Nor indeed has *REED* revealed any evidence of the New Inn as host to any dramatic activity. References to musical events occur, but even these take place inside the Inn and not in the yard.[34] Despite the absence of evidence, this does not prove that the New Inn was not a performance venue. It does, however, enable us to question this purpose.[35] It is only when the wider context is considered concerning travelling players at Gloucester in the sixteenth century that performance conditions become clearer. Evidence exists in the records to demonstrate that the common practice concerning travelling players at Gloucester, of which there were many during the late sixteenth century, was to play in the Bothall [Booth hall].[36] The example of travelling players at Gloucester serves to illustrate the worth of emergent records published by *REED*. Some records possess obvious or explicit value and some may be used to question or challenge existing or presumed knowledge.

It may be possible to attach considerable weight to the authenticity and reliability of records, as evidence, but accurate knowledge of the events to which they refer may be incomplete. In which case, interpretation and evaluation of records needs to be considered alongside other forms of evidence in order to seek or establish clearer understanding. Of the other categories of evidence to be examined in this work, the recipes offered by writers on pyrotechnic matters constitute a form of evidence previously unexplored in the service of understanding early theatre.[37] These recipes may be used to explain evidence found in records, eye-witness accounts and stage directions. However, the recipes are themselves sometimes incomplete or ambiguous; terminology can be imprecise or vague. Superficially, the firework writer is seemingly sharing his knowledge and skill with the reader by articulating appropriate techniques and processes. However, it is possible that some writers withhold significant information in order to retain control and apparent secrecy of processes which ironically prevent recipes from working. Like books produced by early writers on magic, some of the pyrotechnic writers do not always complete their recipes. Awareness of this condition needs to operate as a caveat when considering recipes. Even so, coincidence of ingredients and processes in recipes of early writers, together with modern understanding of pyrotechnic processes, enables such sources to be considered as evidence.

Principal sources of information concerning early pyrotechnic production and practice include the works of Vannoccio Biringuccio, Peter Whitehorne, Cyprian Lucar, Robert Norton, Francois de Malthe, John Bate, John Babington and Casimir Simienowicz. Biringuccio's *Del la Pyrotechnia* published in 1540 is concerned primarily with metallurgy, although Book X which consists of eleven chapters deals with "Artificial Combustible Materials and the Procedures Followed in Making Those Commonly Called Fireworks to Be Used in Offensive and Defensive Warfare and for Festivities on Holidays."[38] Whitehorn's *Certaine wayes for the ordering of Soldiours in battleray...*, published in 1573 is concerned with the production of saltpeter, gunpowder and "wildfire" for military purposes.[39] Much, but not all, of this book is a plagiarised translation of Biringuccio's *Del la Pyrotechnia*, Book X.[40] In 1588 Cyprian Lucar translated the *Three Bookes of Colloqvies concerning the Arte of Shooting in great and small pieces of Artillerie...*, by Nicholas Tartaglia and added an appendix referred to as the *LUCARAPPENDIX collected...to show vnto the Reader the properties, office, and dutie of a Gunner, and to teach him to make and refine artificial saltpeeter, to sublime brimstone for gunpowder to make coles for gunpowder....*[41] Distinction between military and recreative use of fireworks is sometimes ambiguous in this work. *The Gvnner Shewing The Whole Practise Of Artillerie...* by Robert Norton, published in 1628, is concerned with information required by gunners and ends with a section on "Extraordinary Artificiall Fireworkes, as well for Pleasure and Triumphes, as for Warre and Seruice.".[42] Francois de Malthe's *A Treatise of Artificial Fire-VVorks both for VVarres and Recreation...*, published in 1629, gives details of the manufacture of "fiery arrowes", "a Petard", "Rockets for the ground", "Serpents", "golden rayne", "Starres giving great Reports", "Saucissons", "fierie boxes", "fierie Lances", "Girondells or fierie Wheeles", "Ballouns" and "flying Saucissons".[43] The English translation refers to the author as Thomas Malthus. This work together with the published works of John Bate and John Babington provide the principal information concerning production of fireworks in England in the early seventeenth century. *The Mysteryes of Natvre and Art: The Second Booke, Teaching most plainly, and withall most exactly, the composing of all manner of Fire-works for Triumph and Recreation* by John Bate (1634), contains useful information concerning firework production, effects and devices.[44] Perhaps the most important source of information concerned with firework making is John Babington's *Pyrotechnia Or, A Discovrse Of Artificiall Fire-works.*[45] This is the first English book to deal excusively with the making of fireworks for public presentation. A later and important seventeenth-century work that was not translated into English until 1729 is *The Great Artillery of Casimir Simienowicz, Formerly Lieutenant-General of the Ordnance to the King of Poland. Translated from the French, By George Shelvocke, Jun.Gent.*[46]

Early firework books may be likened to manuals concerned with informing or instructing the reader in pyrotechnic processes; effectively they are "How to do it " books. The function and purpose of such books therefore creates a different kind of evidence to that contained in records. Books by firework writers exist by virtue of a declared intention to inform. Records, however, do not normally exist in order to describe what happened, although they may inform that the event took place.

Because some recipes are plagiarised, similar care to that required in analysing records needs to operate in assessing the worth and use of recipes.[47] Although recipes may be followed with meticulous care, it is likely that some of the intended effects would require further information to make them work. Even if weights and measures could be relied upon, the purity of ingredients referred to in the recipe may not be the same as those used today. However, the precise relationship between purity and weight is less important, in this work, than the intended effect produced by chemical reaction of ingredients. Modern understanding of the chemical relationship of pyrotechnic materials and their resultant effects is more precise than it was in the sixteenth century and may be used as a means of determining the efficacy of early recipes.[48] Although pyrotechnists of today still need to experiment in order to produce specific effects, understanding of the ways in which individual ingredients function within a firework mixture is more complete.

Other evidence to that which occurs in early pyrotechnic books may be found in generically similar writings known as "Books of Secrets". Such books are concerned with recipes that inform the reader as to how to create and organise materials and processes to fulfil particular effects. The value of the recipes contained in these sources has been underestimated previously because the ideas do not necessarily exist through understanding of scientific principles; they rather reflect the writers' experience. However, some basic, straightforward and workable practices are included in these works. Similar caution to that concerning the interpretation of pyrotechnic recipes needs to apply to these sources.

The principal "Books of Secrets" that are applicable to this work are: *The Secrets of Albertus Magnus. Of the Vertues of Hearbs, Stones, and certaine BEASTS*, by Albertus Magnus, published in 1617. This work contains a variety of recipes concerning the production of flame and fire.[49] Thomas Hyll's *A Briefe and pleasaunt Treatise, Intituled: Naturall and Artificiall Conclusions*, (1586), offers some recipes concerning candles and flame as lighting.[50] Further lighting devices and techniques are presented in Hugh Platte's *The Jewell House of Art and Nature* (1594)[51] and John White's *A Rich Cabinet, with variety of Inventions* (1651).[52]

The form of evidence which would seem least controversial and most valuable in its accuracy is the eye-witness account. However, such reports are often subjective by nature and need to be treated with circumspection. The principal advantage of the eye-witness description exists in the very selection of items or events recorded. These sorts of accounts focus on that which is witnessed. It follows, by implication, that those items or events that are not selected are of less importance to the eye-witness. Even so, eye-witness reports may be valuable in recording the fact that something happened. The authority of such observations exists by virtue of the presence of the witness at the event.

Evidence will be sought from the following historical and eye-witness accounts: John Stow's *The Annales of England...*, (1601) and the later edition *The Annales or Generall Chronicle of England...* of 1615[53]; Raphael Holinshed, *Holinshed's Chronicles of England, Scotland, and Ireland* (1586;

rpt.1807/8)[54]; Edward Halle, *Hall's Chronicle* (1548; rpt. 1809)[55]; *Grafton's Chronicle*, (1569; rpt. 1809)[56]; John Nichols, *The Progresses and Public Processions of Queen Elizabeth* (1823)[57] and *The Progresses, Processions and Magnificent Festivities, of King James the First* (1828)[58]; J.S.Brewer, *Letters and Papers of Henry VIII*, (1862-1918)[59]; *Calendar of State Papers, Domestic Series, Edward VI, Mary, Elizabeth*, (1856-71)[60]; and *Calendar of State Papers Venetian*, (1864-1947)[61]; *The Diary of Henry Machyn, Citizen and Merchant-Taylor of London, From A.D. 1550 to A.D. 1563*, (1848).[62]

A complication arises with some evidence that is presented in the form of eye-witness accounts. Material encountered in **CHAPTER 5**, **CHAPTER 6** and **APPENDIX 1E** concerning the celebrations for Frederick and Elizabeth in 1613 is documented in Nichols and a previously unpublished account in *MS BL Additional 70518*.[63] This material gives the impression of being eye-witness evidence, but on closer examination seems to be statements concerned with that which is intended to happen or should happen. The value of the accounts is brought into question because the titles to the descriptions are written as if the events have happened, whereas the actual accounts are written in the present tense. For instance, Nichols provides the heading "The True Description of such part of the Fire-workes as were devised and accomplished by Mr.John Nodes, Gunner and Servant to the King's most excellent Majestie.".[64] The "True Description...", however, concerns itself with relating the narrative of the event and describing the intended firework effects:

> Now to this aforesaid pavillion, wearyed with toyle and travaile, the great unresistable Champion of the world, and the uncontrolable Patron, Saint George, comes; and seeing so bright and luculent a goddesse, according as his necessitie required, demanded entertainment, whereby he might be refreshed, after his laborious atchievements and honorable endeavours.[65]

The "True Description..." may be a true description of what was intended to happen but not necessarily of one that actually happened. Similar "True Descriptions..." are offered on behalf of "Mr.Thomas Butler, Gunner and Servant to the King's Royall Majestie"; "Mr.John Tindall, Gunner and Servant to the King's Royall Majestie" and "Mr.William Fishenden, Gunner and Servant to his Majestie".[66] The contribution of "William Bettis his invention..." is all recorded in the past tense and gives the impression of being an eye-witness account for this reason.[67] However, the content of this account in relation to the others suggests that it was either written in the past tense before the event or after the occasion in an attempt to describe that which was intended to happen. The purpose of such information may be concerned with statements of intent or possibly publicity material.[68] The narrative terms in which some of the accounts are written, indicates "inside" knowledge of the intention which further reduces the possibility of the descriptions as eye-witness observation. For instance, in Mr. Thomas Butler's description the following is recorded:

> Thirdly, the foure squares of the Tower are fiered with abundance of lights, with rackets flying into the ayre, with fiers dispearsed and scattered divers and sundry wayes, and with reports and blowes, some great and some lesse, according to their making.[69]

It is not surprising that Thomas Butler would know that it was possible to create different effects from fireworks "according to their making". However, the impression given is that the fireworks are yet to be made. This sort of content may still be considered as evidence of intention but should not be mistaken for evidence of events which necessarily have occurred. Clearly, appropriate care needs to be exercised here in order that the narrative is not allowed to misrepresent reality.

I suggested earlier that the "explicit" stage direction is of more value than the "implicit" kind in its capacity to provide evidence. Perhaps even more care needs to be taken in the use and interpretation of stage directions, as evidence, than that associated with other forms. The authority of the "explicit" stage direction, when considered as evidence, stems from a function that is normally concerned with the nature, manner, time and place of stage action or conditions. The direction is addressed to the people who put on, or intend to put on the play. Although "explicit" directions in plays of today usually signal a difference in function from the fictional text, the same cannot always be observed in stage directions in medieval or Tudor plays. Indeed, it may be questioned even whether the stage direction, as encountered today, is always the same concept as that found in medieval texts. The medieval stage direction sometimes presents some apparently confusing information. The use of stage directions, as evidence, must therefore take account of possible and different generic functions from those employed today.

Given that importance is being attached to the "explicit" stage direction, it may be useful to identify some types of "implicit" ones in order to down-grade them in importance as reliable sources of information. Interestingly, stage directions that may be regarded as "implicit" in medieval plays provide most confusion to the modern interpreter. To add to the muddle, these directions unlike their modern equivalents, are not confined to the dramatic text but also appear in the form normally associated with the "explicit" stage direction i.e. they are separated from the text.[70] The qualification of these directions as "implicit" versions exists because the content merely duplicates that found in the dramatic text and does not convey additional practical information of use to those who put on the play.

Another sort of "implicit" stage direction that is sometimes presented in the form of an "explicit" kind is that which relates or links the biblical narrative with the dramatic fiction. The absence of such a direction would leave the sense of the dramatic text incomplete. However, this sort of direction may also present little practical value of the kind associated with "explicit" versions.

The following stage direction occurs in the Towneley play of *Jacob*:

> Hic egrediatur Iacob de Aran in terram natiuitatis sue. (Here Jacob goes out from Harran into the land of his birth.)[71]

This direction is presented in the "explicit" form whilst fulfilling "implicit" functions of creating links in the biblical and dramatic narratives. The essence of the instruction is to inform Jacob that he shall simply move from one place to another. At both locations, before and after the stage direction, Jacob is praying to God. However, in each case the content of the prayer is different since the biblical narrative determines that the first prayer is delivered in "Harran" and the second in the "land of his birth", namely "Caanan". This constitutes a leap in the biblical narrative from *Genesis 28, 22* to *Genesis 32, 9*. If, however, this stage direction (*Genesis 31, 13*) had not been included in the text, knowledge that Jacob had travelled to another country would not be apparent. Clearly, the stage direction used here links different parts of the biblical narrative and serves to inform and focus change of time and place. It seems that the main purpose of the stage direction is to communicate understanding of the text. The practical value of the stage direction is limited unless "Harran" and the "land of his birth" embody specific locations within an unexplained theatrical convention. Even so, an audience would need to know of Jacob's travels from one country to another - for an audience does not read a stage direction.

Similar problems of uncertain evidence are posed by the following type of stage direction found in the Towneley *Conspiracio*:

> Tunc pergent Iohannes et Petrus ad Ciuitatem et obuiet eis homo, etc. (Then John and Peter shall go on to the city, and let a man meet them, etc.)[72]

Superficially, the requirement seems a simple, practical one. The content of the direction is contained in *Luke 22, 10-13* and links and informs the dramatic fiction. From a practical point of view, it needs to be established what is meant by "Ciuitatem". The biblical and fictional sense is clear but what does this word mean from a theatrical standpoint? The term may possess no value at all if the function of the direction is to repeat the biblical narrative or inform the dramatic fiction. If, however, "Ciuitatem" refers to a practical requirement then it must refer to a theatrical convention, the terms of reference of which are not apparent. Does "Ciuitatem" refer to a specific location or setting in the staging?

The uncertainty in separating the respective threads of meaning in this sort of stage direction renders the content unreliable as evidence.[73]

Although stage directions so far identified present a mixture of clearly articulated requirements together with some that are not so clear, the idea that the stipulations exist at all indicates that the respective phenomena contained in each direction were known ones that were capable of being delivered. A similar point may be made in respect of the information contained in records or accounts. Given that the ingredients and materials were paid for at all indicates both need and purpose. However, proof of payment for such items in records does not confirm proof of use. Similarly, practical requirements expressed in stage directions do not necessarily provide verification of their theatrical existence. If it can be shown that the "know-how" or practical/technical knowledge and understanding existed in order to fullfil such requirements in stage directions and itemised payments in records, then the weight of proof as to the practical implementaion of such needs is increased. Not only do appropriate techniques of producing special effects need to be identified, but further understanding of the roles, skill and involvement of likely personnel need to be considered.

What sort of special effects were involved in plays and celebrations and who created them? Who provided the raw materials and expertise to use them? These, and similar questions affect the organisation of this book. **CHAPTER 1** serves to identify and establish the principal special effects that require examination. This chapter also registers known individuals involved in the chain of supply and use of pyrotechnic materials in plays and celebrations. Such identification occurs in evidence provided by stage directions, records and eye-witness accounts. Subsequent chapters analyse, amplify, explain and illustrate the identified special effects in roughly the same order as that encountered in **CHAPTER 1**. Thus, **CHAPTER 2** examines the use of squibs, shooting fire, casting fire, devils on fire and devils spitting fire. The evidence to which reference is made in this chapter exists in approximately equal amounts from stage directions, recipes and records. **CHAPTER 3** examines requirements for light, sound, smoke and heat as determined largely by stage directions. Flashes of fire, lightning, thunderbolts, thunder, storms, smoke, boilings and burnings are the effects discussed in this chapter. **CHAPTER 4** further promotes the sequence of effects identified in **CHAPTER 1** by considering different forms of lighting production. Ingredients, materials and techniques of producing light for illumination, atmosphere and theatrical articulation of the biblical narrative are examined in this chapter. The evidence is drawn mainly from recipes in firework books and Books of Secrets. Content in **CHAPTER 5** is derived from a discussion of larger special effects such as dragons shooting fire, flame and fire at Hell mouth and fireworks as narrative. Evidence in this chapter is drawn from eye-witness accounts, stage directions and records. Further expansion in the dimension of special effect provision is discussed in **CHAPTER 6**. Here, the relationship between pyrotechnic effects and theatre form is discussed via identification of a form of pyrotechnic theatre referred to as the "fort holding". Although some of the evidence discussed in **CHAPTER 6** extends beyond the reign of Elizabeth, I have included it because it illuminates earlier practice and demonstrates a development in understanding of techniques and processes.

The work concludes with extensive appendices. **APPENDIX 1** presents pertinent eye-witness accounts. **APPENDIX 2** records detailed and relevant firework accounts. **APPENDIX 2C** is published for the first time. Although **APPENDIX 3B** has already been published, **APPENDIX 3A** is presented for the first time since the sixteenth century. The recipes offered in **APPENDIX 4** are included as a demonstration of the imagination and practical scope of the specific techniques articulated by Babington.

Many of the ingredients and materials referred to in this work require explanation and some further contextualisation. This concern has guided identification of the content of the **GLOSSARY**. Items exist here because of their original inclusion in one or more of the major forms of evidence utilised in the work.

CHAPTER 1

Principal Effects and their Providers

THE range of effects under consideration, as indicated by stage directions, records and eye-witness accounts, is both substantial and remarkable. Although some of the effects are quite simple in their requirements, others are more demanding and do not immediately suggest ways in which they were or could have been implemented. So, what sort of effects were involved and who enabled them to happen?

Perhaps the simplest and most ubiquitous of effects was that produced by the "squib". Despite the fact that the term possessed currency in the sixteenth century it was used mainly by the layman and not the pyrotechnist. The latter frequently used terms such as "fizgigs", "rockets" or "serpents".[1] Although these terms could and did refer to other types of fireworks, they were also used loosely to refer to the "squib", particularly when they occurred in translation. Nevertheless, the effect required was one of a firework that squirmed erratically to produce a fizzing shower of sparks that sometimes ended in a small report. The unpredictable behaviour of the firework induced a gleeful panic among spectators when thrown among them.[2] A number of mid-sixteenth century accounts of such use occur, for example, in references to the *Lord Mayors' Show* in London.[3] However, squibs were sometimes employed for their fizzing effect in apparently more controllable situations such as the one envisaged by a stage direction in John Heywood's *The Play of Love* of 1534:

> Here the vyse cometh in ronyng sodenly aboute the place among the audyens with a hye copyn tank on his hed full of squybs fyred cryeng water. water/fyre fyre/fyre/water/water/fyre/ tyll the fyre in the squybs be spent.[4]

1

This direction synthesises a strong theatrical moment, but how would the requirement have been achievable? The stream of fizzing sparks produced by the squib is the same or similar to the effect produced by a variety of ignited tubes of gunpowder.

Perhaps one of the crudest and most dangerous uses of this sort of effect may be seen in the well-known requirement expressed in the early fifteenth-century stage plan of *The Castle of Perseverance* where:

> he þat schal pley belyal loke þat he haue gunnepowdyr brennynge In pypys in hys handys and in hys erys and in hys ars whanne he gothe to batayl.[5]
> (he that shall play Belyal look that he have gunpowder burning in pipes in his hands and in his ears and in his arse when he goes into battle).

No doubt the pyrotechnic result of this direction would have been even stronger when dramatically realised, but how could the effect have been achieved? A larger effect of the same pyrotechnic process was produced by the fire club as required by a stage direction in George Whetstone's *Promos and Cassandra* (1578). The direction requires that there should be "Two men, apparrelled lyke greene men at the Mayors feast, with clubbes of fyre workes" [FIG.1].[6] The "clubbes", when activated, would have been expected to produce a powerful pyrotechnic and dramatic effect. So, what were fire clubs and how were they made to work?

The above effects are concerned with the ability to cast fire outside of and away from the body. The requirement to project fire from within the costume or body of the protagonist can be seen in a number of stipulated effects such as one in the late fifteenth / early sixteenth-century *Provencal Stage Director's Book* where a direction requires a devil to eject fire through a mask [FIG.2].[7] The process was clearly dangerous, so could the effect have been achieved with any control? Further "spouting" or "spitting" of fire by devils is alluded to by an implicit stage direction in Ben Jonson's seventeenth century *The Divell is an Asse* when Mere-Craft attempts to disguise Fitz-Dottrel as a devil:

2

THE
SECOND BOOKE,
Teaching moſt plainly, and withall moſt exactly, the compoſing of all manner of Fire-works for Triumph and Recreation.

By *I. B.*

LONDON,
Printed by *Thomas Harper* for *Ralph Mab.* 1634:

1. A wildman with Bate's version of the fire club.
Bate, *The Mysteryes of Nature and Art* , title page.

3

It is the easiest thing Sir, to be done.
As plaine, as fizzling: roule but wi' your eyes,
And foame at th' mouth. A little castle-soape
Will do't, to rub your lips: And then a nutshell,
With toe, and touch-wood in it to spit fire.[8]

Again, production of the effect seems not without risk in terms of the mouth and lips of the performer, yet the effect was seemingly possible.

Not only were devils required to spit, consume and project fire, but they were frequently required to "be on fire". A stage direction in the *Gwreans an Bys:The Creation of the World* (copied from an earlier text in 1611) requires Mychaell and Gabryell to fight Lucyfer "wth swordis and in the end Lucyfer voydeth & goeth downe to hell apareled fowle wth fyre about hem turning to hell and every degre of devylls of lether...".[9] In the fifteenth-century *Origo Mundi* of the *Cornish Ordinalia* a stage direction requires Maximilla's clothing to be set on fire as she sits down.[10] How might the performers of Lucyfer and Maximilla be on fire without being hurt?

Conflagrations or flashes of fire are frequently required by stage directions such as the one in the Chester Drapers' play of *Cain and Abel* (text, sixteenth century), where "a flame of fyer shall descende upon

nota

2. A representation of a devil's mask that attempts to show the means of ejecting fire. Vitale-Brovarone ed. *Il quaderno di segreti*, p.50. Reproduced by kind permission of Edizioni dell 'Orso.

thee sacrafice of Abell".[11] In *The Life of Saint Meriasek* (early sixteenth century) four outlaws are the target of a stage direction which states: "Hic ignis venit super illos" (Here fire comes upon them.).[12] George Peele's *The Old Wives Tale* (1595) contains a stage direction which declares: "A voice and flame of fire: Huanebango falleth downe.".[13] These three directions seem to require the ability to target fire in some sort of controlled way. Robert Greene's *Alphonsus King of Aragon* (1599) gives the following stage direction:

> Let there be a brazen Head set in the middle of the place
> behind the IV.; Stage, out of the which, cast flames of fire,
> drums rumble within, Enter two Priests.[14]

Another stage direction later in the same play instructs: "Cast flames of fire forth of the brazen Head.". In *A Looking Glass for London, etc* (1594) by Lodge and Greene a stage direction informs: "Vpon this praier she departeth, and a flame of fire appeareth from beneath, and Radagon is swallowed.".[15]

Instructions found in stage directions for flames of fire are sometimes the literal or practical descriptions of the effect required. However, the same effect may be referred to by the more theatrically conscious instruction for "lightning". The list of effects required by the *Mystery of the Acts of the Apostles* at Bourges in 1536 contains the following description:

> The Jews try to get hold of the Virgin Mary's body to take it
> from the apostles, and immediately their hands wither and
> they are blinded by the fire the angels throw (**gectent**) at
> them. Belzeray [a Jewish Prince] puts his hands on the
> litter on which the Virgin Mary is being carried, and his
> hands remain attached to the said litter and much fire in
> the form of lightning (**fouldre**) is thrown at them, and the
> Jews must fall to the ground, blinded.[16]

The effect indicated here revolves around the notion that the angels "throw" something which causes simulated lightning. Is it possible that the angels could throw actual fire?

A number of late sixteenth-century plays contain stage directions which stipulate lightning as an effect. In Marlowe's *Dr.Faustus* lightning is sought along with other pyrotechnic effects.[17] In Robert Greene's *Friar Bacon and Friar Bungay* a stage direction requires that "a lightning flasheth forth", as part of a sequence where a "brasen head" is smashed with a hammer.[18] *The Battle of Alcazar* ascribed to George Peele, contains stage directions which indicate the use of pyrotechnic effects including the production of lightning.[19] Stage directions in *Grim the Collier of Croydon* also require the production of lightning as an effect.[20] Even though there are late sixteenth-century stage directions that indicate the need for lightning, earlier use is not so clear. For instance, in *The Conversion of Saint Paul* (early sixteenth century, with later additions) shortly after the arrival of Saul on horseback, the following stage direction indicates:

> Here comyth a feruent, wyth gret tempest, and Saule faulyth down of hys horse; þat done, Godhed spekyth in heuyn:[21]

How is the direction for a "feruent, wyth gret tempest" to be interpreted? Is it the same or similar to the effect described by Abramo, the Russian Bishop of Souzdal of the Florence *Annunciation* in 1439? Abramo indicates the effect as follows:

> In the meantime a fire comes from God and with a noise of uninterrupted thunder passes down the three ropes towards the middle of the scaffold, where the Prophets were, rising up again in flames and rebounding down once more, so that the whole church was filled with sparks.[22]

Although this description appears to be precise, how could it possibly have been enacted? Surely, this is too fanciful?

A number of stage directions in fifteenth and sixteenth-century plays establish the need for thunder. In the Digby *Mary Magdalen* (early sixteenth century) a stage direction reads: "Wyth þis word seuyn dyllys xall dewoyde from þe woman, and the Bad Angyll entyr into hell wyth thondyr.".[23] The requirement for thunder expressed in this direction appears to be similar to that indicated for the entrance of Belyal in *The Conversion of Saint Paul*. In both cases thunder accompanies "entrance" and "exit" movement of the respective devils. The list of effects for the Bourges *Mystery of the Acts of the Apostles* recorded in 1536 requires: "There must be thunder in Paradise...".[24] Two stage directions in Peele's *The Old Wives Tale* refer to the use of thunder.[25] In the anonymous *Famous History of the Life of Captain Thomas Stukeley* (1596) a stage direction suggests the following: "and so both armies meeting embrace, when with a sudden thunderclap the sky is on fire...".[26] *The Battle of Alcazar* contains stage directions that indicate various pyrotechnic requirements together with that of thunder.[27] Several stage directions in *Grim the Collier of Croydon* contain references to thunder.[28]

Instructions for the production of thunder are contained in the text of the Valencia *Assumption Play* and two directions require the thunder to be accompanied by smoke.[29] The synchronised creation of smoke and explosion is the means by which the devil Fergalus is cast out of the body of the "Canaanites daughter" at Mons in 1501:

> Here there comes a smoke and an explosion from under
> the girl and Fergalus comes out. [He speaks briefly.] He
> goes to Hell.[30]

In Robert Wilson's *The Cobbler's Prophecy* (1594) a stage direction records: "Enter the Duke, his Daughter, Priest, and Scholler: then compasse the stage, from one part let a smoke arise: at which place they all stay.".[31]

Smoke may well have contributed to the effects required by stage directions in *The Croxton Play of the Sacrament* (mid-fifteenth century) in order to aid communication of the appearance of a boiling cauldron and a burning furnace. Here the cauldron is required to "byle, [boil] apperyng to be as blood" and later in the play "the owyn must ryve asunder and blede owt at þe cranys, [crevice] and an image appere owt with woundys bledyng.".[32] If smoke was used to create this effect how might it have been employed to such controllable purpose?

In contrast to the murkiness of light produced by smoke, a number of plays require light effects for specific purposes over and above that of producing illumination of the scene. For example, references to bright light at the beginning of the York Saddlers' *Harrowing of Hell* play (fifteenth century) suggest that some physical representation or appearance of light is required, although stage directions to this effect are absent.[33] Stage directions do exist in the Lucy Toulmin Smith edition of this play but these are her interpolations; they do not exist in the York manuscript *(British Library MS Additional 35290)*.[34] The Towneley *Extraccio animarum* (late fifteenth century) contains virtually identical references to the need for bright light.[35] The Chester Skinners' play of *The Resurrection* contains references in the text to a "great light" witnessed by the Roman soldiers when they awake to find Christ risen.[36] These various indications in texts seem to be important as far as adherence to the biblical narrative or the *Gospel of Nicodemus* is concerned. However, some references, albeit vague ones, to the production of light do exist in "explicit" stage directions. For instance, in the *Passio Domini* of the *Cornish Ordinalia* at the point of Christ's death, a stage direction instructs: "Here the sun is darkened".[37] This requirement does not indicate the nature of the sun, the style or method by which the effect is realised. In *The Life of Saint Meriasek* at the point where Silvester baptises Constantine the following stage direction occurs:

> Cum in aquam descendisset baptismatis mirabilis enituit splendor lucis Sic inde mundus exiuit et christum se vidisse asseruit[38]
> (When he went down into the water of baptism there shone forth a marvellous splendour of light. So thence he came forth clean, and declared that he had seen Christ).

Although the purpose of the light is clear the direction does not disclose the theatrical identity of "a marvellous splendour of light". How might this quality of light have been achieved? Other stage directions make similar requirements. At Bourges, for instance, when the angels are required to set free from prison St.Peter and St.Paul there should appear "a great light". A similar direction at Bourges requires:

> St.Michael must present the soul to Jesus Christ. Having done this, they come down from Paradise accompanied by all the angelic hierarchy, and as soon as Jesus Christ reaches the monument there must be a great light at which the apostles are amazed.[39]

Beyond the requirement that there "must be a great light", its nature and means of production is not made explicit. Again, how might "a great light at which the apostles are amazed" have been created? At Mons in 1501 during *The Resurrection* the following direction is recorded:

> And the two angels remove the stone, and Jesus rises and puts his right leg out of the tomb first, and there should issue with him a great brightness and smoke of incense and light.[40]

The need for "a great brightness and smoke of incense and light" is clear enough although any precision as to what constitutes the effect and its creation is not revealed. A late reference to the early seventeenth-century play, *The Second Maiden's Tragedy* contains a similar but more involved direction:

> On a sodayne in a kinde of Noyse like a Wynde, the dores clattering, the Toombstone flies open, and a great light appeares in the midst of the Toombe.[41]

Additional, yet incomplete, information is offered by a stage direction at the start of the Chester Cooks' *Harrowing of Hell* play:

> Et primo fiat lux in inferno materialis aliqua subtilitate machinata, et postea dicat Adam.
> (And at the start let there be material light created by some cunning device and afterwards Adam shall say).[42]

This stage direction refers not only to the kind of light to be produced but to the means of producing it. Even so, a "cunning device" is still a tantalizingly vague description when considering ways of achieving the necessary light. The quality of light required by the above stage directions, whilst imprecise in descriptive terms, is specific enough to be distinguishable from light required to illuminate the theatrical event. These effects are indeed special.

Some of the more demanding and involved effects were those required to give theatrical existence to dragons and hell mouth. In *The Life of Saint Meriasek* a stage direction instructs: "her a gonn yn y dragon ys movthe aredy & fyr".[43] Does this requirement really refer to a gun? Preparations for the Coronation of Henry VII's Queen Elizabeth of York in 1487 involved a dragon of a large dimension. On her way by river from Greenwich to London she encountered many decorated barges "and in especiall a Barge called The Bachelers Barge, garnyshed and apparellede, passing al other, wherin was ordeynede a great red Dragon spowting Flamys of Fyer into Temmys".[44] The reception for Charles V involved the following spectacle when he came to London in 1522:

> aboue this buyldyng was a faire pagiaunt, in the whiche stoode Iason all in harnes, hauing before hym a golden Flece, and on the one side of hym stoode a fiery Dragon, and on the other side stode two Bulles whiche beastes cast out fyer continually,...[45]

Presumably, the term "beastes" refers to all three animals that "cast out fyer continually". To what does "continually" refer and how might this condition have been achieved? The same allusion to the story of Jason is recorded some 25 years later for the coronation procession of Edward VI when "towardes the Chepe behynde the throne the golden fleece was kept by two bulles and a serpent casting out of their mouthes flaming fire, according to the story of Jason.".[46] During the coronation celebrations for Anne Boleyn in 1533, the Lord Mayor's water pageants included:

a Foyst or Wafter full of ordinaunce, in whiche Foyst was a great Dragon continually mouing, & castyng wyldfyer, and round about the sayd Foyst stode terrible monsters and wylde men castyng fyer, and makyng hideous noyses.[47]

The lavish reception that accompanied the Earl of Leicester on his entry into the Hague in 1585 included "fireworks of rockets, squibs, wheeles, and balles of fire, with a dragon that continued casting out of fire an houre, woonderfull artificiallie made." [**FIG.3**].[48] A stage direction in Robert Greene's *Friar Bacon and Friar Bungay* written between 1589 and 1592 indicates the following: "Heere Bungay coniures and the tree appeares with the dragon shooting fire.".[49] The *Revels Accounts* for 1552-3 indicates payment for creating fire in a dragon's mouth:

> **The same** Nicholas [Leveret] for a dragons head and a dragons mowthe of plate with stoppes to burne like fier. v^s. for trymmyng of iiij^{or} boxes with plate for the same. ij^s. ij fyer boxes xij^d. iiij^{or} small cheines of yerne at xij^d the pece. iiij^s. xiiij yardes of ynglish wier great at ij^d the yarde. ij^s iiij^d. and for vj dozen of hookes ij^s....[50]

The dragons so far considered operate from a static position when they project fire. However, some dragons were required to "fly" as well as cast fire. Perhaps the most enigmatic account of a fiery-flying dragon was that said to be observed on the 23rd June, 1520 at the meeting between Francis I of France and Henry VIII of England at the Field of the Cloth of Gold. As is well known, the events which combined to constitute the celebration took place at Guisnes. One account of the proceedings records the following:

> Here mention must be made of a singular circumstance, namely, the appearance in the air of a great salamander or dragon, artificially constructed; it was four fathoms long, and seemed to be filled with fire, very horrible and terrible. It seemed to come from the direction of Ardres. Many were greatly frightened thereby, thinking that it must be a comet or some monster or portent, as nothing could be seen to support it. It passed over the Chapel where Mass was being said, across the camp, with an undulating motion, as fast as a pedestrian could travel, as far as Guisnes, mounting as high in the air as a crossbow would carry an arrow.".[51]

If this description accurately identifies such a fiery-flying dragon, how might the device have operated?

At Warwick in 1572 a dragon was used as part of the pyrotechnic mock battle, or "fort holding", held in honour of Elizabeth I:

> for at the last, when it was apointid that the overthrowing
> of the fort should bee, a dragon, flieing, casting out huge
> flames and squibes, lighted upon the fort, and so set fyere
> thereon, to the subversion thereof;...[52]

Another "fort holding" was held in Edinburgh in 1617 to celebrate the birthday of James I and on this occasion a pyrotechnic fight ocurred between the figure of St.Andrew and a dragon. John Crowe saw the event and he records:

> Thair was a devys maid, that out off the pallace off
> St.Androis cam Sanct Andrew ryding on a hors, with a
> speir off fyr in his hand, and met the dragon midway, that
> came out of the Castle of Envy, and out of hir mouth cam
> fyr spouting, so they foght aspace togither; bot Sanct
> Andrew did overcome the dragon and cam home ryding,
> and was welcomed home by the men of the pallace.[53]

3. Three "set-pieces" used during the reception of Robert Dudley, Earl of Leicester into the Hague in 1585. *Delineatio Pompae Triumphalis*, Strong and van Dorsten, *Leicester's Triumph*, p.48.
Reproduced by kind permission of E.J.Brill.

In 1575 a proposal from an Italian pyrotechnist was offered to the Earl of Leicester in which: "A dragon as big as an ox will be seen, which will fly two or three times higher than the tower of St Paul's, and staying at that height it will be wholly consumed with fire, and then suddenly there will issue from the whole of its body dogs, cats, and birds which will fly about and throw out fire everywhere, which will be a most stupendous thing".[54] If the "tower of St Paul's" refers to St.Paul's cathedral in London, then the height at which the dragon was intended to "fly" was between 978 feet and 1467 feet, given that the spire of St.Paul's was apparently heightened in the fourteenth century by 489 feet.[55] This is a considerable height and may be exaggerated. Even so, how might it have been possible to create such an effect?

Extensive accounts exist of the firework celebrations to mark the marriage of Frederick and Elizabeth *(Heaven's Blessing and Earth's Joy)* in 1613. "John Taylor, the Water Poet" offers the following description of the work of "Mr.Thomas Butler, Gunner and Servant to the King's Royall Majestie":

> Saint George, being mounted on horseback, makes towards the Castle of Brummond;... having in his helmet a burning flaming feather, and in one hand a burning launce, and in the other a fiery sword, with which weapons he assailes the dreadfull Dragon with such fury and monster-quelling stroakes, as if the Cyclops had bin forging and beating thunder-bolts on Vulcan's anvile;...[56]

The business of depicting a dragon in fire or projecting fire from its mouth is echoed by requirements for fire at Hell mouth. In the Bourges Parade of 1536 account is made of "a great serpent whistling and spitting fire from throat, nostrils, and eyes".[57] A similar effect is indicated in the Hell mouth of the Rouen *Nativity* play in 1474 when "flames of fire are thrown out from the nostrils, the eyes, and the ears".[58] Between Hell's tower and limbo in the Paris *Resurrection* of 1419 is the pit of hell from which " shall come forth flaming sulphur,...".[59] In the *Anglo-Norman Adam* (twelfth century) a stage direction informs: "et in eo facient fumum magnum ex[s]urgere," (and in Hell they shall make a great smoke arise,).[60] The records at Coventry concerning the Cappers and their play of *The Resurrection and Descent into Hell* and the Drapers and their pageant of *Doomsday* refer to their respective Hell mouth properties. Payments occur in the accounts of both guilds towards the building, refurbishment and maintenance of Hell mouth.[61]

12

Further records exist of payments made to individuals for items to be used in the creation of special effects and public celebrations. Given that appropriate materials for the construction of special effects could be obtained, who bought them and who made use of them?

The providers of pyrotechnic materials are frequently named individuals whose roles in the chain of supply are sometimes uncertain. However, some patterns of trade are discernable. For instance, the buying and selling of gunpowder was largely conducted by grocers or merchants. Why should grocers or merchants be connected with trade in gunpowder?

The *York House Books* for 1587-8 record "dyvers of our merchants have latelye made their adventure to Hambrough [Hamburg], and have ordere to their servants to buye both powder and matche, which, God willinge, will be at this Cittye shortlye.".[62] Expenses for the provision of gunpowder for the *Midsummer Show* at York in 1584 are recorded "to mr brooke sherife for one dosen corn powther [corned gunpowder] for the shott with the pagiante xiiijs". During the period 1563-4 "Parcivallus Brooke, marchant" was made a freeman of the city of York and became the pageant master of the Mercers in 1570. By 1571-2 "mr brooke" was a Chamberlain of the city. In 1587 it was "Agreed that this Cittye shall beare the adventure of two barrells of powther weighinge about tenne hundrethe and three quarterons weight shipped for this Cittyes use in the Elizabetha of Hull and that Mr.Alderman Brooke shalbe payd for the same. Also it is agreed that a foote post shall go to Hull to Mr.Brookes man to buy certane corne powther so that the same be provided at xij^d a pound or under.". Upon receipt of the gunpowder it was "Agreed that Mr.Percivall Brooke and Mr.Moseley shall consyder of some convenyent place for lyinge of powther.". In 1573-4 "Thomas Mooselay, marchant" was made a freeman of the city of York and a Chamberlain in 1577. He was twice made Mayor of York; once in 1588-9 and again in 1600-1.[63]

Also at York in 1584 another payment was made for the *Midsummer Show* to "Bryan byrkhead merchant for 30li. of corne powther at 13d the pound delivered to the shew xxxijs vjd". Brian Birkhead was made a freeman of the city of York in 1579 and pageant master of the Mercers' Guild in 1580. By 1587-8 he was made a Chamberlain of the city.[64]

A similar record of payment occurs for 1585 for "the shew & play on mydsomer even & mydsomer day" to "Iohn fisher for xlli. of corne powder at xijd. ob. the li./ xl s [xl] viij d". Fisher was made a freeman of the city of York in 1571 and pageant master of the Mercers' Guild in 1578.[65]

The *Chamberlains' Accounts* at Norwich for 1584-5 record payment to "Mr Thomas Layer Maior for ⌄ ⌐xxiiij li. of⌐ goo*n*nepoulder wh*i*ch his seruant had at A shew vpon the water that night when he tooke his chardge at x d the li. xx s". Thomas Layer was the son of William Layer, a Norwich "grosser". Thomas was apprenticed to William Bathcom in 1546 and served his apprenticeship for 7 years as a grocer. In 1557 he was created a freeman of the city of Norwich.[66]

At Bristol in 1574 payment is recorded to "William Newton grocer for certeign corne powder delyvered to John Sachefield j li. x d.". This payment was made in respect of the "fort holding" held to honour the visit of Elizabeth to Bristol. Further payments for the same event are recorded "to dyverse Grocers for vij^{C}lij$^{lbs.}$ ¹/₂ of corne powder as by their bill amounteth 752 lbs. ¹/₂ xlix li. ixs. xd.[67]

The *Churchwardens' Accounts* for St.Martin Coney Street, York record payment to "Thomas Porter for gonnpooder and matche at the first muster viij d".[68] Thomas Porter was not a merchant or grocer but a locksmith. He was created a freeman in 1577. As can be seen, this payment was not one towards an entertainment.

In 1567 the *Ironmongers' Registers* for the Ironmongers' Company of London record the following payments for gunpowder at the Lord Mayors' Show:

> Item, to John Donne, Iremonger, for ij^{C}lb. of gonne powder, at vj^d lb   v^{li} - -
>
> Item, more ij. hundredth weight at liij^s y^C C.   v^{li} vj^s -
>
> Item, more one hundreth weight at   lj^s iiij^d
>
> Item, more ij^C weight of powder at   iiij^{li} xvj^s j^d
>
> Item, to a porter for carrying ye powder iiij^d [69]

The same accounts record payment to "Mr.Morley, for one that kept the powder in the foyste xviij^d".[70] Richard Morley was the son of Robert Morley and was apprenticed to Laurence Greene, cutler in 1547.[71] The cutlers were one of the constituent trades of the Ironmongers' Company in London.

Payments of "xx d" are recorded to "peter Gose" and "Arnolde fremer" for each providing "ij lib & di' of gunpouder" to a show or play at Canterbury on "seint Thom^{a}s Night" in 1505-6.[72] In the records at Chester for 1563-4, Thomas Yeaton was paid "xiiij s" for "gonne poulder at the trivmthe by master mayres apoyntment...". Further payment is recorded at Chester to "Raymond Stockton for the gunpowder, £40. And paid for cartage thence, 2s...".[73] At Maidstone in 1589 for the *Coronation Day Celebration*, "Simō ellis"was paid for "xiij pound of powder xiij ^{s}".[74]

Further named individuals are recorded as being paid for other pyrotechnic materials such as pitch, tallow and rosin. At "the playe of New Romney" in 1560 payment was made to "m^r Baylif iij^d of three iij^d of pytche & rosen j^d ob...".[75] Records concerning "Money Laid owt one the Coronatiō Daye" celebration at Maidstone in 1589 detail payment to "willm Plūmer & Richard Maplesdē for browĕ pap [brown paper] whyt pap [white paper] & Rosine iiij^s viij^d".[76] *The Watch and Play Society* accounts for Wymondham, Norfolk for 1537-8 record the following payments to William Kett and William Kedell:

> It. paid xvjd. to Willm̄ Kett for xvj li. of talow to the cresset light.
> It. paid viijd. to the same Will. for piche and rosen to the same light.
> It. paid vjd. to William Kedell makyng the same light.[77]

The provision of tow and the making of "quickmatch", albeit for military purposes, is recorded at York for 1588. It was agreed:

> that the Chamberlains shall forthwith provid and buye fyve hundrethe weight of towe; and that spinners shall presentlye be provided to spynn the same, with all expedicon and that then the yarne shalbe delyvered to John Devowe to make matche on.
> ...
> And now John Devowe beinge called, towchinge the provision of matche for this Cittye; the sayd John Devowe haithe promised to provyd and make redye one C weight of matche against tewesdaye next before none.[78]

The *Drapers' Repertory* for June 1541 records payment for "3s. 8d. for a gallon of 'aqua vyte' to burn in the dragon's mouth; 16d to him that kept fire in the dragon's mouth;". The "him" to which reference is made here is 'Thom^as palm' as recorded in the *Wardens' Accounts* for 1540-1.[79] A similar payment is recorded in the *Revels Accounts* for 1552-3 as "one pottle of aquavite for the pageaunt of ma[r]ce and to burne in other properties. ij ^s.". In this instance the aquavitae was bought by Thomas Bocher and seems likely to have been used to fire the dragons mouth provided by Nicholas Leveret, wyerdrawer.[80]

Firework ingredients were paid for by John Howard, Duke of Norfolk to "Garard of Sudbury" in 1483 for "all suche stoffe as folewyth, that he bowgt for the Dysgysing":

Fyrst, for iiij. dos. of golde paper, and silver rowche (roche)
clere and verte   viij. s.
Item, for viij. qayeres (quires) paper   ij. s.
Item, for ij. b. of arsowde.(arsidue)
Item, for iiij. schetes of golde paper, and silever   xv. d.
Item, for j.lb. of glew   ij. d.
Item, for ij. doss. of golde foyle   xxij. d.
Item, for iiij. qayres of paper   xij. d.
Item, for iiij. qrtrs of a lb. of arsowde   xviij.d.
Item, for sursuphuryfe (sulphur?)   j. d.
Item, for iiij. callis (coals)   iiij. d. ob.
Item, for a pownde of gounpowder   x.d.
Item, for halfe a doss. of golde paper   xij. d.
Item, for packe threde   j. d.
                    Summa totall xxj. s. ob.[81]

For the *Entry of Marie of Lorraine* (second wife of James V) into
Edinburgh in July 1538 "expensis maid upone the munitioun eftir the
quenis grace hame cumming..." record payment:

> to Peris for certane expensis maid be him eftir the schippis
> returnyng and quenis grace entray to Edinburgh in
> saltpeter brunstane (sulphur) ule petroll (oil of petrol)
> tarpantyne (turpentine) aquawite (aqua vitae) quik silver
> (mercury) hardis (course flax or hemp) pak threid and
> quheill rymmis (wheel rims) conforme to his compt sene be
> Maister Henry Bennavis and me iiii lib. iiis. vid.[82]

Some more detailed payments made to gunners in the service of the
Crown are contained in *The Accounts* for 1538-41:

> Item, gevin at his command to Maister Wolf and Cristopheir,
> Frencheman, gunnaris, for expens debursit and maid be
> thame upoun quik silver, aqua vite, salmoniakill (sal
> ammoniac), canis (canes), vermenioun ule (vermillion oil),
> petrolle, ule de olive (olive oil), wannat ule (walnut oil),
> turpatyne (turpentine), bristane (sulphur), lynt, hemp,
> talloun (tallow), and utheris expens maid and debursit be
> thame upoun vj dosane fyr sparris (fire spears), twa dosane
> fyr gannis (fire arrows), xv fyre ballis, and viij fyre perkis
> (poles, stakes), witht utheris fyre werk schot devisit be the
> Kingis grace, as thair compt particulary beris,. lvij li. vj s. j d.[83]

Similar payments to "Maister Wouff, gunnar" were made in 1536 "for fire speris, fire ballis, fire arrowis, and uther fire werk, as in his bill of compt proportit x frs. vj s. iij d."[84]

There are also recorded instances of gunners who operated as gunpowder makers. *The Accounts* record payment to "Michaell Gairdner, gunnar and poulder maker in the castell of Edinburgh" for his services at the celebrations to mark the baptism of James I [*Baptismal Celebrations*]. *The Exchequer of Receipt, Auditors' Patent Book* for 1566 records the "Patent for Francis Lee, gunpowder maker, to have the office of one of the 4 master gunners in the Tower of London, lately occupied by Christopher Gold, deceased, with a fee of 12d. a day.".[85] In June 1563 the same Francis Lee was granted a 21 year lease "of one tenement and mill, with the buildings thereto adjacent, called the 'gonpowder myll' together with the wharf opposite the said tenement (100 feet by 42 feet) together with a large pond called 'the Gonpowder myll ponde,...' ". The land and premises occupied by Lee were initially granted by Henry VII in 1536 to Lee's father, Thomas Lee, for "the only use of making gunpowder".[86] As one of the four master gunners in the Tower of London, Francis Lee was paid "for gunshot on land and water" and "for fireworks within the city on 4 wheels" as part of the *Merchant Taylors' Pageant* in the *Lord Mayors' Show* in 1568.[87]

The *Records of the Skinners* of London for 1551 outline payment to "William Harris, gunner" for his contribution to the *Lord Mayors' Show* whereupon he:

> faithfully promised and himself bindeth to have at three sundry places a hundred "dubble throwrowlye" furnished, to wit, at the "nashe" 40, at Bridwell 30, at "parrish garden" (Paris Garden) by the waterside other 30, with squibs for the wild men and also to provide a great "boate or foyste" with mast and topcastle and all things with ordnance fully furnished for the worship of this Company, and the said William to have for the well doing and furnishing of the aforesaid business the sum of 4li.[88]

The Accounts concerning the *Baptismal Celebrations* at Stirling in 1566 contain references to expenses "payit to Johnne Chisholme, comptrollar of the said artailyerye, for his awaitting and extraordinar service making in the dressing and overseing and causing to mak this triomphe of fyrework above speciffyit be the space for fourtye dayis, to wit xxx dayis in Leyth and ten day in Stirviling for his panis and extraordinar waigis, ilk day vj s. viij d., summa xiij li. vj s. viii d.". An extensive list of firework materials for which Johnne Chisholme and his team of gunners were responsible is contained in *The Accounts* for 1566[89] **[APPENDIX 2A]**.

A similar series of detailed payments is recorded for firework materials at the "fort holding" to celebrate the birthday of James I in Edinburgh in 1617 [*Birthday Celebrations*] **[APPENDIX 2B]**. On this occasion "The expenses maid upoun the fyirwarkis within the castell of Edinburgh and in the utter clois of the palace of Halyruidhous 19 June" were paid to "Johne Prat for his paynes taken in the saidis warkis be the space of sevin dayes haifing daylie xxiiiis. inde viii lib. viii s.". Additional payments were made to individuals within his team which included Johne Schort, Thomas Smyth, Anthony Achesone, Robert Dickesone, Johne Ewnes and Elias Pratt.[90]

Such comprehensive lists of firework ingredients invite investigation into their identity, purpose and function. What were the materials and their likely uses?

Further to the trade in gunpowder, grocers dealt in other pyrotechnic ingredients. Two sources of evidence that signify this range are recorded in the Tariff of Charges detailed in **APPENDIX 3B** and secondly, in the right bestowed upon the Grocers' Company in London by Henry VI in 1447 which granted the "Privilege of Garbling and Examining Drugs, Spices, etc.":

THE KING, to all whom, &c. greeting,- know ye that we, considering how much it will be for the general good and advantage of all the subjects of our kingdom of England, that all sorts of spices and merchandizes as well annis, cummin, wormseed, wax, alum, kermes,— as pepper, ginger, cloves, mace, cinnamon, rhubarb, scammony, spikenard, turpentine, senna, almonds, dates, rosin, treacle, electuaries, syrups, waters, oils, ointments, plasters, powders, and all conserves and confections, — as gum, ginger, succades, cardamums, and all sorts of merchandizes, spices, and drugs, in any wise belonging to medicines, and whatsoever shall by sufficient officers skilled in the premises of this kind whom we are pleased to depute and appoint, duly and justly to supervise, garble, search, examine, and prove, to the purpose and intent, that none of our subjects aforesaid may in future be deprived of benefit in buying any of the aforesaid merchandizes, spices, and drugs,... [91]

The sale of impure or imperfect goods was the concern that this "privilege" was intended to rectify. The process of "garbling" refers to the searching out of impurities among goods in order to maintain quality and dependability. These concerns were particularly important in relation to items used in food and medicine.

John Hestor's stock-list, contained in **APPENDIX 3A**, indicates an extensive range of items that could be obtained from him. There is evidence to suggest that many of these items could have been obtained also in earlier times from spicers and apothecaries.[92]

Records occasionally itemise payment to individuals for creating a named special effect. For instance, at Cambridge in the *King's College Mundum Book* for 1552-3 a series of payments occur that represent costs towards the production of thunder and lightning in a presentation of *Hippolytus* at King's College:

Item in gunne powder	xiiij d
Item for shootynge of	iiij d
...	
Item soluti Thorpe pro factura fulminis tempore Ludorum [Item paid to Thorpe for the making of lightning at the time of the plays]	iij d
...	
Item paid to Thorppe for makynge thunder agaynst the plays	iiij s
Item paid to Burwell for a drye ffatte [cask or barrel] to make the thunder on	xx d
Item payd to Ames the cowper for ij gret howpes [hoops]	xij d[93]

John Burwell was an apothecary and it might therefore seem appropriate that he was able to provide a "drye ffatte" by virtue of his profession. However, Burwell is also recorded as having been paid for items which may not be strictly related to his work. He was paid "for gere fetched at him to ye plaie...vj s viij d". In addition, payment is recorded in the *Queens' College Magnum Journale* for a large chest in which materials for a comedy were stored. Similarly, Thorpe is also recorded in the *Queens' College Magnum Journale* as having performed other roles "for the tragedy publicly put on by him 6s 8d" and the provision "for three beards 4 s" and "one coller 4 d".[94] One of the roles played by Thorpe at King's College may well be the same as that performed by Iohn Izarde when he was paid "for his device in counterfeting Thunder & Lightning in the playe of Narscisses" at Court in 1571.[95]

Clearly, the evidence concerning the need for special effects is considerable, even though the means of producing them is not always immediately apparent. Records itemising copious amounts of firework materials exist and a working presumption might be that these ingredients possessed purpose and function. So, how were these items used to create special effects?

CHAPTER 2

Fireworks, Wildmen and Flaming Devils

NOTIONS of hell and hellfire act as powerful points of focus in the biblical narrative that require theatrical consciousness in their pyrotechnic interpretation. The principal mechanism for this practical expression is the devil. Although devils, by their very identity, are frequently seen as conveyors, consumers and projectors of fire, they are not the only figures who operate in this way. Other characters are also noted as producers of fire and a number of devices are recorded for such purposes.

The *Drapers' Repertory* for 1521 concerning the *Midsummer Show* in London records that the guild paid for "iij pagentę that is to say/the Castyll of Werr'./the Story of Iesse. & Saynt Iohn Euñgelist/And also they had. A King of Moorę & 1 moryans in the stede of an oþ^r pagent".[1] Iohn Wakelyng was paid "v ^S" for playing the "king of the Moorę" for two nights and the guild was responsible for "fynding hym his apparell his stage & wyldfyre".[2] Another item in the same accounts records payment to "Willm kyng for xlv reedę of wyld fyr' for bothe nyghtę about þe king of Moorę Sm^a. vij ^S viij ^d". Two possible techniques suggest themselves in attempts to explain the nature of "xlv reedę of wyld fyr'": one may refer to fire arrows fired from bows[3] and the other may refer to reeds filled with a gunpowder mixture required to burn but not explode.[4] Of these, the latter explanation seems more likely since payment is recorded in the same accounts for a "dymy lawnce that the kyng of the Moorę pavillion was born vppon over his hede.". These "reedę of wyld fyr' " may have been fixed to the "pavillion" or held in the hand.

"Wildmen", "woodmen", "woodwards", "woodhousys", "greenmen" and "ivemen" are examples of terms used to describe characters who operated fire devices such as fire clubs. As indicated earlier, the stage direction in Whetsone's *Promos and Cassandra* requires "clubbes of fyreworke" to be provided for "Two men, apparrelled lyke greene men at the Mayors feast".

One form of fire club ejected a stream of sparks in much the same way as that implied by the "reede of wyld fyr" and Bate describes its construction:

> you must fill divers canes open at both ends (and of a foot long, or more, or lesse, as you think fit) with a slow composition, and binde them upon a staffe of foure or five foot long; prime them so that one being ended, another may begin: you may prime them with a stouple or match (prepared as before) make an osier basket about it with a hole in the very top to fire it by, and it is done. [**FIG.4**].[5]

According to Bate the canes need to be left "open at both ends" in order to insert the connecting stouple. The effect produced by this fire club is one of intermittent streams of sparks produced by burning "slow composition" in each cane. The interval between each stream of sparks is governed by the length of time taken to burn the linked stouple. The term "slow composition" refers to the burning rate of the gunpowder. The principal means of changing the burning rate of a mixture is to vary the proportion of charcoal in the composition. By adding more charcoal to the mixture, the burning rate is slowed down. Bate

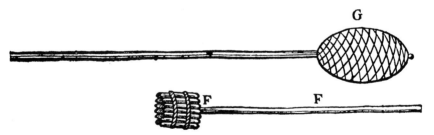

4. A fire club of "divers canes open at both ends" showing the "canes" fastened to the "staffe" and another drawing showing the "osier basket" over the "canes". "The figure F, F, representeth the staffe, with the canes bound upon it. The figure marked G, representeth the staffe having a basket wrought over it.". Bate, *The Mysteryes of Nature and Art*, pp.92-3.

acknowledges the principle with reference to compositions for rockets: "if it be too strong [gunpowder] let him adde more charcoale untill hee finde them flie according unto his desire. Note that the charcoale is only to mitigate the violence of the powder...".[6]

An item in the *Revels Accounts* for 1551-2 records: "Two turned clubbes with pykes - ij ˢ / one hollowe clubb to burne squibbes in - ij ˢ".[7] The type of club that contains squibs could be a variation of the one described above or a version of another one also described by Bate:

> you must make an ovall ball of pastebord, canvasse, or parchment glewed together, which you must first fill with a slow composition, ram it in, and then bore divers holes round about it, and put therein serpents, fire bals, or what you will: fasten it upon a staffe, and prime it in the top with a cane filled with a slow composition: [**FIG.5**].[8]

The "slow composition", once ignited, burns down the length of the "ovall ball" igniting the inserted fire balls, serpents or squibs. The stream of sparks issued by the fire club, the "reede of wyld fyr" and the squib were effectively the same.

The squib normally consisted of a strengthened-paper tube or "coffin" and contained two kinds of mixtures: roughly two thirds of the coffin contained "slow composition" or mealed powder and the smaller section of the tube held corned powder which provided the final report. The coffin of the squib (or serpent), according to Bate, was "not much thicker than a goose quill, and about foure inches long".[9] A division was created between the two powders by "choaking" the coffin with packthread. The basic powder mixture created the shower of sparks which in turn ignited the corned powder to produce the report.

Another device that seems to require timed ignition of squibs is that, referred to earlier, in the stage direction in John Heywood's *The Play of Love*. The order of firing of these squibs clearly affects the amount of

5. Another fire club of "pastebord, canvasse, or parchment" with "serpents" inserted : "this is represented by the figure A,A.". Bate, *The Mysteryes of Nature and Art*, pp.92-3.

time available to complete the action. If the squibs are fired at roughly the same moment then this dictates the shortest amount of time possible to fulfil the requirement of the stage direction. To extend the time, successive firings using connected stouple or quickmatch would have been necessary.

The act of throwing squibs or as it is sometimes described, "casting fire", may be seen in the stage directions in *The Conversion of Saint Paul* and *Dr.Faustus*.[10] Further illuminating references to this process, its purpose and use by devils and wildmen, are contained in the records of the Skinners, Ironmongers and Merchant Taylors of London in respect of the *Lord Mayors' Show* in the sixteenth century. The *Records of the Skinners of London* for 1551 detail payment to "William Harris, gunner", for providing "squibs for the wild men".[11] The *Merchant Taylors' Books* for 1556 record the following provision for the *Lord Mayors' Show*: "to devise other conceits such as 'woodwards', and other pastimes with men casting squibs of fire.".[12] The same records for 1556 indicate the need "to fynde ij men to be woodhousys wch shall cast squybbe w^t fyre y^t day & they to haue [cote] & clubbe accordyngly as hath bene done in tymes past/...". Records contained in the *Merchant Taylors' Books* for 1561 empower Iohn Shutte "⌐also he to fynde ij men to be¬ woodhouses to cast sqwybe or wildefyer the morrowe aft' the seid feaste of S & Iude next ⌐& also to fynde ye seid wildefyer¬".[13] *The Ironmongers' Court Books* for 1566 record that "Hugh Wattes and Christopher Beck agree to find 2 woodmen, with clubs, squibs, and powder, and all other necessaries, for 33 s. 4 d.".[14] The same records also demand that the quantity of squibs required are "sufficient for the tyme,". Another item in the *Merchant Taylors' Books* for 1568 offers further information on the process of "casting fire":

> Itm̃, it is aggreed and concluded to and wth Hughe Wattes and Chrystopher Beck, That they shall serve for woodhousis or Ivie men the morrowe after Symonde and Jude next and they to fynde appell (apparel) for them selfe as also vyssers squybbe and powdre and they to shote of Fyer wth the seid squybbes contynually.[15]

This record is helpful in that it more firmly identifies the process of shooting fire with that of casting squibs. "Hughe Wattes and Chrystopher Beck" also provided the Ironmongers with their services for the 1569 accounts record the following: "Paid to Xp'ofer Becke, and Hewe Wattes, Iveman, that 0 vid (served) my lorde mayre wth wilde fyar...xxxiij ^{s} iiij^d".[16] Further information concerning the function

24

of the "wylde men" is offered by the *Merchant Taylors Books* for 1575: "And to make waye in the streetes, there are certayne men apparelled lyke devells, and wylde men, with skybbs, and certayne beadells…". So "devells" as well as "wylde men" performed the act of "casting fire". Henry Machyn's observation supports this function in respect of devils: "and ther was a dullvyll shuting of fyre, and won was lyke Deth with a dart in hand.".[17] The *Chamberlains' Account Books* for 1568 at Newcastle record payment for the *hoistmans playe* to "A man that kest (cast) fyer vj d Soma".[18] In 1572 the "ryght honorable Henrye erle of derbye" was welcomed to Liverpool by "Mayster Maior his bretheren with the bailiffes" on his way to the Isle of Mann. A feature of the entertainment provided for the Earl on "the same evening at after supper one Raphe Powell gonner by Mayster Maiors appointment being readie with squybbes to make pastyme was commaunded by my Lord to staye tyll yt was A litle darker whoe afterwardes when yt was darke in ye eveninge caste the said squibbes abroade very trymlye wherat his honor toke great pleasure…".[19] As part of the celebrations on the Thames in honour of Queen Elizabeth, Henry Machyn records: "sqwybes horlyng on he to and fro, tyll x at nyght, or her grace depertyd, and all the water-syd st… with a M. pepull lokyng one here grace.".[20]

The process of "casting fire" in the form of squibs as well as hand-held devices, such as fire clubs, seems to be only part of the potential armoury employed by wildmen and devils. The direction contained within the well-known stage plan of *The Castle of Perseverance*, provides graphic instructions as to the pyrotechnic accoutrements of the devil, Belyal. The effect of "gunnepowdyr brennynge In pypys…", referred to earlier, is likely to be the same as that of the "reede of wyld fyr'" required by the "king of the Moore" as outlined above. The gunpowder composition indicated by this instruction appears to be that which was frequently used for "golden" or "silver rain" which produced a shower of sparks but not an explosion.[21] Although the "pypys…in hys erys and in hys ars" seem to have been fixed to the body in some way, the "pypys in hys handys" would thus be capable of exaggerated movement. It is of course possible that the hand-held "pypys" were scattered like squibs. If the "pypys in hys handys" were not thrown then their use as threatening weapons may be seen to complete the formidable warlike image. Presumably, Belyal's costume/mask contained some sort of framework, possibly of wicker or wire, built into it in order to secure the "pypys" in his "erys" and "hys ars".[22] It is possible that another figure dressed Belyal with his "pypys" and ignited him, for the text gives some indication of such readiness:

Gula. Lo, Syr Flesch, whov I fare to þe felde,
Wyth a faget on myn hond for to settyn on a fyre.
Wyth a wrethe of þe wode wel I can me welde;
Wyth a longe launce þo loselys I schal lere.
Go we wyth oure gere.
þo bycchys schul bleykyn and blodyr;
I schal makyn swyche a powdyr,
Boþe wyth smoke and wyth smodyr,
þei schul schytyn for fere.[23]

If these words by Gula (Gluttony) may be interpreted as an implicit stage direction, then Gula together with other Sins may be required to carry lighted faggots, "match" or "tow" to set off Belyal when battle was engaged.[24] The need for such timed and safety conscious preparation of Belyal is supported, perhaps somewhat negatively, by the accident during the *Mystery of St.Martin* at Seurre in 1496:

> Then Lucifer began to speak, and during his speech the man who played Satan, when he prepared to enter through his trapdoor (**secret**) underground, his costume caught fire round his buttocks so that he was badly burned. But he was so swiftly succored, stripped, and reclothed that without giving any sign [of pain] he came and played his part, then retired to his house.[25]

Presumably, Satan was ignited moments before his "entrance" when the accident occurred and his rescue was perhaps effected by those who set him alight. This incident from the *Mystery of St.Martin* quite possibly represents an unsuccessful version of the requirement in *The Castle of Perseverance*. Pater, in the anonymous fragment *The Prodigal Son* of 1530 exclaims: "The deuyll cast wylde fyre in thy tayle" and the same allusion occurs in stage directions of early seventeenth-century plays.[26] It is possible that the accident at the *Mystery of St.Martin* may refer to the unfortunate result of another method that required devils to be set on fire. The technique or trick was clearly dangerous and represents another possibility with regard to the "entrances" and "exits" of Belyal and Mercury in *The Conversion of Saint Paul*. Belyal's "entrance" with "thunder and fyre" and Mercury's "entrance" "with a fyeryng" and their respective "exits" "with fyrye flame" may have been achieved using the method outlined below. The technique is clearly documented in *Il quaderno di segreti d'un regista provenzale del Medioevo* (The Volume of Secrets of a Provencal Stage Director's Book), written sometime between

the end of the fifteenth century and early sixteenth century. The process
is outlined as follows:

> Finta a far
> un diable tot ple
> de fuoch: pren tre-
> mentina e bota-
> ne ab escho sus
> lo diable, e pueis [..]
> agone de quoto
> banat an d'aigo ar-
> den e fais-lo tene
> an la trementina;
> bota-i fioch, pueis
> bota-li un quano
> de podro a quado
> pe e mai a qua-
> do mo, e un au-
> tre diable li vo[l-]
> ra bota fuoc as
> quanos e mai al qu[...]
> <...>[27]

(A trick to make a devil completely full of fire: he takes
turpentine and throws [casts? smears?] some of it with a
fuel [fuse? igniter?] on to the devil, and then adds cotton
soaked with spirit [aqua ardens] and makes it remain
[stick?] with the turpentine; he gives it fire and then puts a
reed of powder in each hand and foot and another devil
will see to setting fire to the reeds and also to...[cotton?]).

The "quano de podro" (reed of powder) recorded here and placed in
each hand and foot is a similar requirement to that made by the
direction in *The Castle of Perseverance*. These reeds may have been larger
than goose quills and of a size more like canes. The resin "trementina"
(turpentine) [**GLOSSARY**] exists as a waxy solid which is smeared or
pasted on to the devil's costume. The turpentine would have been used
to produce the principal smoke and flame of the effect whereas the
cotton soaked in "d'aigo arden" (aqua ardens) [**GLOSSARY**] would
have primed the effect.[28] Although the turpentine would burn, it would
not ignite at the low temperature of the aqua ardens; hence the
impregnated cotton would have been fired in order to raise the
temperature and ignite the turpentine. It is not clear how much cotton

or how many pieces of it were used but it would easily stick to the waxy turpentine. Timing of ignition and suffocation of the flame seems critical to the success of the effect and the well-being of the performer. Information as to how the actor was protected from the flame is not contained in the account, but protection of some kind would have been essential.[29]

An account referring to a similar trick occurs in a chronicle describing life in the Household of Miguel Lucas de Iranzo for 1461:

> In front of the place where the Countess was seated, there then appeared the head of this huge dragon (**serpiente**). It was made of painted wood, and a device inside it (**su artificio**) propelled the boys out through its mouth one by one, and it breathed huge flames at the same time. And the pages, whose tunics, sleeves, and hoods were soaked in spirits (**aquardiente**), came out on fire, and it seemed that they were really being burned up in flames.[30]

Although the dragon breathing flames is of interest, the principal concern here is with the pages who are ejected through the mouth of the dragon. Their clothes soaked in "aquardiente" (aqua ardens) would be set on fire to give the appearance of being consumed by flame. The important concern here is that when aqua vitae or aqua ardens is set on fire, the resultant flame does not burn the host material that is soaked in the spirit [**CHAPTER 4** and **GLOSSARY**]. The flame is fed by the spirit which is thus consumed. The phenomenon is referred to in *The Sectret Miracles of Nature* in 1658 as follows:

> wet a Table-cloath or linnen Towel with that liquor [aqua vitae], and put it to the flame; if it burn presently and do not touch nor hurt the linnen, it is pure and unmixed. For linnen wet in this water will flame and not be consumed. For the flame will but gently lye upon the finest linnen, and not take hold of it, but licks up all that is next of kind to it,...[31]

The pretence referred to in the description concerning the Household of Miguel Lucas de Iranzo indicates theatrical deception of the kind suggested in *Il quaderno di segreti*....Again, the means of conducting the trick in terms of timing and safety is not recorded.

The need to protect the performer's body is again negatively illustrated by the well-known accident at the French court in 1393.[32]

28

Hugonin de Guisay "devysed syxe cotes made of lynen clothe, covered with pytche, and thereon flaxe lyke heare,..." as part of a "mummery agaynst nyght" during a wedding celebration. When Charles VI and his nobles put on these costumes and were "sowed fast in them, they seemed lyke wylde wodehouses, full of heare fro the toppe of the heed to the sowle of the fote.". The King appears to have been aware of the inherent fire risk to the costumed men since he ordered "all varlettes holdinge torches to stande up by the walles, and none of them to aproche nere to the wodehouses that shulde come thyder to daunce.". These instructions had been delivered prior to the late arrival of the "duke of Orlyance" and his retinue. The duke's curiosity as to the identity of the "wodehouses" made him take a torch "so nere, that the heate of the fyre entred into the flaxe, wherin if fyre take there is no remedy, and sodaynly was on a bright flame, and so eche of them set fyre on other; the pytche was so fastened to the lynen clothe, and their shyrtes so drye and fyne, and so joynynge to their flesshe, that they began to brenne and to cry for helpe. None durste com nere theym; they that dyd, brente their handes, by reason of the heate of the pytche.".[33] The king escaped, as did one man who raced to the buttery and doused himself in a "vessell full of water", but four men died of their burns.

Although this account does not deal with an attempted trick that went wrong, it does suggest the need to protect the performer's body in order to successfully complete the trick in *Il quaderno di segreti...*. The principal purpose of the "pytche" in the French account was that of an adhesive, although the accident occurred because it functioned as a fuel. The primary use of "trementina" in the Provencal method was as a fuel, even though it also functioned as an adhesive. The effects appear to be unintentionally similar.

Protective undergarments, possibly made of thick wool, may have afforded some safety to the performer, although other means of protecting the body are suggested in an account offered by Thomas Hyll:

> How to make a man to appeare on a flame burning without any harme.
>
> TO doo this, take Brimstone, Orpiment, and common Oyle, of these make an ointment, with the which anoint thy garment all about, & thy head and handes, and after light the same & it wil burne all at once without harme. Also take iuice of Adders tongue, ye iuice of March Mallowes, or

other Mallows, & the white of an Egge, these mixe together, annointing therewith all about thy body, and then cast the fine pouder of Brimston on the same, setting it ouer a fire, & it wil strangely burne, and neither harme hands nor garment annointed therewith.[34]

This account contained in Hyll's *A Briefe and pleasaunt Treatise, Intituled: Naturall and Artificiall Conclusions:...* (1586) appears to contain two recipes that function in a similar manner. In both instances the "Brimston" [sulphur][**GLOSSARY**] acts as the fuel that ignites at a low temperature. The "Orpiment" [**GLOSSARY**] also works as a fuel. The other ingredients when mixed and applied to the body and clothes act as a barrier to the burning sulphur. The efficacy of these recipes may be doubted, but the purpose of Hyll's book is to demonstrate how such recipes may operate as tricks. This book is generally considered to be the earliest one, written in English, on conjuring. A similar recipe intended to fulfil the same purpose is contained in *The Book of Secrets* attributed to Albertus Magnus. The earliest versions of this book began to appear towards the end of the thirteenth century and were first translated into English circa 1550.[35] This recipe contains significant differences from Hyll's account and may be more authorative:

> When thou wilt that thou seem all inflamed, or set on fire from thy head unto thy feet and not be hurt.
>
> Take white Great Mallows or Hollyhock, mix them with the white of eggs; after, anoint thy body with it, and let it be until it be dried up, and after anoint thee with Alum, and afterward cast on it small Brimstone beaten unto powder, for the fire is inflamed on it, and hurteth not, and if thou do thus upon the palm of thy hand thou shalt be able to hold the fire without hurt.[36]

Although some of the components are the same as those in Hyll's recipe, the significant additional ingredient here is alum which is a fire-retardant and frequently used in tricks involving fire [**GLOSSARY**].[37] Of additional significance in this recipe is that "the fire is inflamed on it,...". This description seems to refer to the notion that the burning sulphur consumes itself without burning the host surface that is previously coated with alum. This combustive property is similar in effect to that already referred to with burning aqua vitae or aqua ardens in respect of the Iranzo pages who were "ejected" from the mouth of the dragon.

The dramatic use of *The Legend of the Holy Rood* in the *Origo Mundi* of *The Cornish Ordinalia* includes the episode concerning the burning clothes of Maximilla. A stage direction indicates the requirement:

> Et tunc orent et murmurabunt quasi dicendo orationes et veniet maximilla in templo et sedet super stuppam et vestes ejus concremantur a stuppa et ipsa clamat dicens [38]
> (And then they shall pray, and speak low, as if saying prayers; and Maximilla shall come into the temple, and she sits upon a stove; and her clothes are set on fire by the stove; and she cries out, saying:)

This stage direction seemingly changes the incident contained in *The Legend of the Holy Rood* by requiring Maximilla to sit on a "stove"; in the legend, Maximilla sits on a beam of wood that is to become Christ's cross. However, the translation of "stuppam" as a "stove" by Norris in his edition of *The Cornish Ordinalia* is not only baffling but wrong. "Stuppa" refers to hards or oakum [**GLOSSARY**]. Other writers have not referred to this meaning which either suggests that they have taken Norris' interpretation at face value or that they have not realised the significance of the correct definition. The oakum or hards is clearly used as tinder to light the clothes of Maximilla. "Hardis" were also used in the pyrotechnic operations at the *Baptismal Celebrations*. Maximilla clearly sits on the "stuppa" and is lit from below in such a way that the flames are intended to spread to the rest of her clothing.[39] Any of the techniques outlined by Hyll, Magnus and *Il quaderno di segreti...* might be applicable to the requirement of this stage direction. The advantage of these approaches over one which simply makes use of brandy (aqua ardens or aqua vitae) is that better defined flames are possible. In daylight or bright lighting conditions, brandy flames are almost colourless and invisible. The stipulation contained in the direction requires that the clothes are actually set on fire and that their burning does not seem to be simulated by the use of fireworks. Again, timing and precautions taken to extinguish the flames are essential prerequisites to the operation of any of the techniques outlined above. Similarly, protective underclothing appears to be necessary. Additional protective clothing may not be essential with the recipes of Hyll and Magnus since the very concoctions both burn and protect.

In the *Gwreans An Bys:The Creation of the World* Mychaell and Gabryell fight Lucyfer "wth swordis and in the end Lucyfer voydeth & goeth downe to hell apareled fowle wth fyre about hem turning to hell and every degre of devylls of lether...".[40] The precise meaning of "voydeth" is unclear for Lucyfer may "exit" out of sight of the audience or simply retire from the focus of the action.[41] He may still be visible to the audience although he is in hell. Clearly, a withdrawal from the action of a figure surrounded by fire requires a more deft manipulation of the effect than does the "entrance" of such a figure.[42] The "entrance" of a devil who carries fireworks or is "alight" may be timed by him and others to create the maximum visual and aural impact. However, the timed "exit" of a figure such as Lucyfer in the above stage direction suggests that he sets himself "alight" on his withdrawal. The use of organisational personnel to set alight Lucyfer reduces the power of any illusion - should it be required. A fire source, such as a torch, needs to be within the acting space ready to be used by Lucyfer. Reference in the stage direction to "devylls of lether" is consistent with use of the same material to costume Adam and Eva. However, the use of leather to costume a devil, such as Lucyfer, who is required to be "wth fyre about hem" affords a suitable means of protecting the actor from both flame and heat. The meaning of this requirement in the stage direction suggests that Lucyfer is seemingly on fire. A further implication offered by this direction is that the actor playing Lucyfer does not play the scene leading up to his "exit" "wth fyre about hem"; he is only fired at the point of "exit". Whether Lucyfer "enters" "wth fyre about hem" is not clear. Presumably he does not "enter" in this fashion because the pyrotechnic technique is not repeatable unless a change of clothing or re-setting of the device is carried out.

Another technique that may be used by Lucyfer in the *Gwreans An Bys:The Creation of the World* or by Belyal and Mercury in *The Conversion of Saint Paul* is that of spitting fire. A number of similar techniques exist with regard to the projection of such fire.[43] The appropriateness of these seems to relate to the nature of the masks worn by devils. If a devil wore a half-mask or a mask with a large mouth opening then the method advanced by Hyll might be appropriate:

> And also if thou wilt spit fier out of thy mouth without paine, and to doo thee no harme, take the powder of the willowe sticke, finelye beaten and searsed [sieved], with the which ioyne a little new Silke, making it rounde vp lyke vnto a ball, into which put this powder, wrapping the Silke well about it, and after put it within with the powder a little fine Flaxe, and then properly stiche it vp rounde about, which so doone, then cut it open a little on the one side, putting a quicke coale or a light Candle vnto it, to set it on fire a little, then put it againe into thy mouth, holding the

same softly with thy teeth, and turning also the parte cut inward in thy mouth, and when thou wilt spit fier out, then halde the ball strongly in thy mouth and blowe, and the lookers on shall see then a great flame issue foorthe of thy mouth, and doo there no harme at all.[44]

This account is one of the most detailed of the early records of this effect. Even so, it cannot be relied upon as being complete. Hyll assures that the effect will "doo there no harme at all" yet does not offer the means by which the mouth is protected from the flame.[45] Interestingly, the method suggested by Merecraft in his attempt to disguise Fitz-Dottrel as a devil in Ben Jonson's *The Divell is an Asse*, and referred to in **CHAPTER 1**, makes use of "castile soap" as a means of protecting Fitz-Dottrel's lips. Additional protection to the inside of the mouth may be inferred by the use of a "nutshell" to contain the "toe"(tow). In his recipe Hyll records the fuel for the effect as "powder of the willowe sticke, finelye beaten and searsed"(sieved). Jonson corroborates the nature of such fuel as "touch-wood".[46] Effectively, fine sawdust is ignited on its expulsion from the mouth. The same principle is at work when sawdust or iron filings are used to create the shower of sparks as rockets explode in the sky. Later accounts of this trick warn of the necessity to breathe in through the nose to avoid choking.[47]

Hyll offers another recipe for spitting fire:

> Take Towe, and wet the same in Aqua-vitae, and after put fire to it, and blowe the same away, which after will flie vp in the ayre and burne.[48]

The ambiguity of this account may be resolved if the interpretation of "blowe the same away" refers to more aqua vitae, as fuel, blown from the mouth. The principle is the same as that employed by modern fire eaters who spit paraffin over a torch flame.[49] Clearly this method of spitting fire is different from earlier Hyll and Jonson methods in that the source of ignition is outside the mouth. As a consequence, this latter method is less likely to be employed by masked devils unless a concentrated and directed stream of air/fuel can be targeted through the mask to an external flame. A means of creating such directed fuel is contained in a revealing account in *Il quaderno di segreti...*:

> Las caretas d[els]
> diabbles qual que a[go]
> una causa ala boqu[a]

coma aquesta quareta; aqu[e-]
lses que volron fa sa-
li lo fuoc per la
boqua he per las
aurelas he pel
nas.

nota

lo fuoc
salira per
aisi

il fuoco
uscirà per
qui

[E] mai hon a[ura]
pus bel deduch
a fa lor gita [lo]
fuoc per la boqu[a;]
qual que las quar[etas]
ho porto que qual [que]
entre la boqua e [la]
facha de aquel q[ue]
la portara ago u[na]
retreta de fuoc que [pu-]
esco quabe.ii. ho [.iii.]
carbos e que aquel[a]
retreta qual que s[ia]
tota bardegada d[e-]
part dedins affin [del]
fuoc que no cremes [la]
quareta.
Et qua[l...]
.xxx.^ta ho qu[anels]
de aqua to[s]
ples de solpre
mout de dedins
an d' ayga arden,
e quant volras
fa sali lo fuoc

34

no qual mas que
prengos un qua-
nel de auqua
ala boqua e que
lo bufes afin que
vengo contra lo fuoc,
e salira
la flama tota
blava delas lia-
bras del fusser h[...]
del diabble,
e no qual pas q[ue]
[...]es affin que no
[...]onbesso ala boq[ua.][50]

(The devil's masks must have something in the mouth as in the drawing, for those which want to make fire come out of the mouth, ears and nose. Then it can be even more entertaining to make them blow fire out of their mouths. These masks must include between the mouth of the mask and the face of the person wearing it a place separated off to hold the fire of a dimenson adequate to hold 2 or 3 coals, and this area must be all covered with mud on the inside so that the fire does not burn the mask. And there must be 30 or 40 goose quills filled with powdered sulphur inside and aqua ardens and when you want to make the fire come out you do no more than take a quill in the mouth and blow so that the sulphur comes on to the fire and the flames come, all blue, out of the lips of the devil's mask. And not so...in the mouth...[Text incomplete. Probably warning against breathing in the sulphur]).

Unlike earlier examples this technique neither makes use of an ignition source within the performer's mouth nor outside of the mask, yet the means of producing the effect would still not be seen by the audience. Both "solpre" (sulphur) and "d'ayga arden" (aqua ardens) ignite at relatively low temperatures and are mixed to ensure ignition. The lower ignition point of the "d'ayga arden" indicates its function as a combustion agent to the ignition of the mixture. The technique of blowing the contents of the goose quills over the coals and out through the nose and mouth offers a concentrated and targetted method of shooting flame out of the mask. It would be important for the open end of the goose quill to be positioned as near to the exit hole as possible in order to prevent the flame blowing back into the performer's face. Because of such danger to the actor, it may be interpreted that the place separated off to hold the coals would enable a barrier or shield to be part of the construction in order to protect the face. In this event the actor would need to insert the open end of the goose quill into a hole in the shield in order to blow the contents across the coals and out through the mouth and nose. Additional protection of the performer's face may have been still necessary, perhaps in the form of a woollen balaclava type of head covering with holes for eyes and mouth.[51] It is difficult to appreciate how the flame might have been projected through the ears if the coals were placed forward of them in the snout. One possibility is that some sort of truncking from the snout, forward of the coals, would lead back to the ears and and be capable of re-directing the thrust of the mixture. Another possibility might be that the ears were placed forward of the supposed shield and thus any "blow-back" of the flame would fly out through the ears. The use of mud to protect the inside of the mask from flame and heat is most illuminating and similar in its purpose to the protection afforded hell mouth at Mons.[52]

CHAPTER 3

Fireworks as Light, Sound, Smoke and Heat

SPECIAL effects involving light, sound and smoke are real and experienced as such by an audience, whereas the communication of heat as an effect is essentially concerned with illusion. Effects dealing with heat frequently exercise theatrical sleight of hand. References to the need for and nature of such cunning exist among stage directions in plays of a number of European countries.

Sound and light developed by fireworks or firework ingredients is perhaps most skilfully employed in the simulated or representational production of thunder and lightning and one of the simplest methods of producing an effect of lightning is to cast a powder such as rosin into or over a flame to produce a flash of fire. Similar effects can be obtained through the use of other powders that come into contact with flame. Such an effect is implied by payment for "rosyn to the resurrecyon pley" at Reading in 1507.[1] E.K.Chambers is probably correct in his assumption that the rosin associated with this payment is concerned with the flash of fire witnessed by Pilate's soldiers who "are all afraid and fall downe...". As cited earlier, reference to the same moment is made in the Mons and Chester *Resurrection* plays. Porta in his recipe "To cast flame a great way", records the following:

> Do thus: Beat Colophonia [rosin], Frankincense, or Amber finely, and hold them in the palm of your hand, and put a lighted Candle between your fingers; and as you throw the Powder into the Air, let it pass through the flame of the Candle; for the flame will fly up high.[2]

Although different powders are involved this method of producing a flash of fire is virtually identical to the one suggested by Serlio as a means of creating "lightning":

> Lightning must be made in this maner, there must be a man placed behind the Scene or Scaffold in a high place with a bore in his hand, the couer whereof must be full with holes, and in the middle of that place there shall be a burning candle placed, the bore must be filled with powder or vernis or sulphire, and casting his hand with the bore vpwards the powder flying in the candle, will shew as if it were lightning.[3]

This technique as advocated by Porta and Serlio may well have taken place in the Coventry Drapers' pageant of *Doomsday* (sixteenth century) as an effect in or relating to the property of hell mouth. Payments exist in the *Drapers' Accounts* towards the construction, refurbishment and maintenance of hell mouth together with payments for the maintenance of fire.[4] Typically, such records refer to "kepyng of hell mowthe & the fyer.". Payments for rosin also occur in many of the Drapers' accounts and it seems likely that the two demons of the Drapers' *Doomsday* pageant and/or the person who kept the fire threw quantities of powdered rosin on to the fire, enabling more spectacular "entrances" and "exits" to be made.[5] The same technique is also implied by payment for "vj li. of rossell" (rosin) to the *hoistmens playe* at Newcastle in 1568 for what is thought to have been a Harrowing of Hell or Doomsday play.[6] Payment for "di li of rosset [rosin] iiij d" in another list of firework ingredients is recorded for use in hell at New Romney in 1560.[7] Further support for such use of rosin (albeit from an implicit stage direction) occurs in a reference to its devil-like use in *The Bugbears* of 1564 where Biondello makes the following comment:

> O how horribly thie are clad wth visars
>   like develes, what sort of lightes they
>   had.
> what store of squibbes & firworkes, and
>   of rosen punned (powdered) fine,...[8]

The separate devices listed here are likened to those possessed by stage devils and "rosen punned fine" is just one weapon in the armoury. Another implicit stage direction contained in Act 1 of *A Warning for Faire Women* (1599) offers further tentative support for this sort of use of rosin: "With that a little rosin flasheth forth, Like smoke out of a tobacco pipe, or a boy's squib.".[9]

A different requirement, yet similar in effect, is made by some stage directions for "flames of fire". Stage directions referred to earlier, in the Chester Drapers' play of *Cain and Abel* , *The Life of Saint Meriasek*, George Peele's *The Old Wives Tale*, Robert Greene's *Alphonsus King of Aragon* and Lodge and Greene's *A Looking Glass for London etc* all require "flames of fire" to be produced. The "flames of fire" indicated by these stage directions are not necessarily of the same kind and in order to identify the possible means of production both context and purpose need to be considered.

The function of the "flame of fyer" in the Chester Drapers' play is that of a signal from God. If the action of the play was confined to the pageant wagon, then the "flame of fyer" would need to have appeared from the top or top corner of it. Similarly, the "flame of fyer" appears to have been directed towards "thee sacrafice of Abell" and thus would need to cover only a short distance. An appropriate technique to produce such directed flame is to blow combustible powder through a tube and over a flame. As already noted, powdered rosin or collophone [**GLOSSARY**] would have been a suitable powder, as would powdered sulphur mixed with aqua ardens as directed in the account in *Il quaderno di segreti*.... Other powders were also used and a detailed account, together with an authorative illustration, occurs in Giovanni Isacchi's *Inventioni...nelle quali si manifestano varij Secreti, & vtili auisi a persone di gverra, e per i tempi di piacere...*(Inventions...in which are revealed various secrets and useful information for military use and in times of peace.). The account reads:

> VOlendo far il sudetto Vapore bisogna hauer quattro, ò seicauezzi di torze, e porlitutt' insieme, e poi vna tromba picciola fatta à tornio à modo d'vn zuffolo, e fatto in dua pezzilong a vn braccio, nel mezzo di cui far à vna palla buca in cui sarà Vernice in grana macinata con rasciatura di mascare, e limatura di ferro, ma poca, & volendo far la fiamma pigliarete detta tromba in bocca, & soffiarete lentemente, versoli stupini de cauezzi de torze, che vedrete vn vapor grande, che parrà vn baleno di quei che si vegon l' estate ne igran caldi, che precede la saetta, & se voi starete arcosi come in vna grotta, ò in vna scena per esser ciò cosa di piacere...[**FIG.6**].[10]

(If you want to produce the above mentioned vapour you will need to have four or six halters of torches and put them all together and afterwards make a little trumpet on a lathe in the form of a pipe and made in two pieces, a braccio in length, in the middle of which is a hollow ball in which varnish in powdered form is ground with the scrapings of mascare, and iron filings, but a little, & if you wish to create flame take hold of the trumpet accordingly in the mouth & blow slowly, towards the wicks of the halters of torches, so that you make a great vapour, to produce a flash of lightning such as one sees in the summer in the great heat that precedes the thunder and you will see an arc like in a cave, or in a scene that is a thing of pleasure,...).

The purpose of the fire that "comes upon" the Outlaws in *The Life of Saint Meriasek* is that of a warning from God and may refer to a similarly directed flame of fire. The same technical observations may be made in

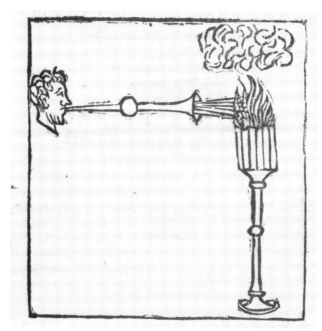

6. The means of producing a flash of fire or "lightning" using powdered varnish, the scrapings of mascare and iron filings.
Isacchi, *Inventioni*, p.111.
BL 5894 Inventioni Isacchi 1579.
By permission of The British Library.

respect of the "flame of fire" required by the stage direction in Peele's *The Old Wives Tale*, although the instruction that "Huanebango falleth down" as a result of the "flame of fire" may indicate that he is intended to be struck by lightning or a thunderbolt. The "flame of fire" referred to in Lodge and Greene's *A Looking Glass for London etc* may well have been achieved by use of the powder and tube method in order to establish the necessary projection of the flame from beneath the stage.

The instruction to "cast flames of fire" in Greene's *Alphonsus, King of Aragon* does not seemingly refer to directed flame. It is possible that the technique of blowing powder through a tube may be appropriate here, if the device is concealed, although the flames produced by any number of the combustible materials referred to earlier, fired inside the "brazen Head", would be sufficient to fulfil the requirements of the stage direction.

Other techniques of projecting fire are referred to in stage directions in their requirements for "lightning". The *Mystery of the Acts of the Apostles* at Bourges in 1536 required angels to "throw" lightning at the Jews in an attempt to stop them removing the body of the Virgin Mary. If, as suggested earlier, the angels actually "throw" something, then some material of substance must be fired first. For example, pieces of tow or oakum dipped in tallow and fired may have fulfilled the task, providing that the angels were able to protect their hands with suitable covering. Claude-Fortuné Ruggieri writing in 1821 refers to this method of creating lightning by saying: "Every means of imitating lightning has been tried, whether by using flammable oils, or tow soaked in the same oils and which was thrown by hand or carried on cords run from below the stage.".[11] Various recipes exist for concoctions capable of being pasted on to the hands in order to afford appropriate protection.[12]

Stage directions that determine the need for lightning occur in a number of sixteenth-century plays such as Marlowe's *Dr.Faustus*, Greene and Middleton's *Friar Bacon and Friar Bungay*, George Peele's *The Battle of Alcazar* and *Grim the Collier of Croydon*.

The stage direction referred to earlier in *The Conversion of Saint Paul* that states "Here comyth a feruent, wyth gret tempest..." is unclear in its meaning. Although part of the action referred to by this stage direction is that contained in *Acts IX, 3 & 4*, the instruction "wyth gret tempest" is confined to the play and is thus an interpretation of the biblical narrative. The source of the direction has consequently influenced writers as to the meaning of the word "feruent". F.J.Furnivall in marginal notes to his edition of the play writes that Saul is "struck by lightning, and falls off his horse.".[13] Mary del Villar regards "feruent" as a "blaze of light" and Darryll Grantley interprets the word as a "flash".[14] Baker, Murphy and Hall suggest that "there would have been simple devices of gunpowder for the divine light...".[15] Thus the "lux de coelo" of *Acts IX, 3* is variously interpreted. So, what is likely to have been the effect and how might it have been created?

It is not clear from the stage direction whether the "feruent" produces the sound of the "gret tempest" or if the latter is produced by other means and timed to accompany the former. The implication is that the "feruent" and "the gret tempest" are different yet contributory aspects to the overall dramatic effect. Although the term "tempest" is primarily associated with wind, accompanying sound is also typical.[16] The word "feruent" may well refer to the provision of bright light as determined by *Acts IX, 3*, but derivatives of the word also refer to heat.[17] If the "feruent, wyth gret tempest" is the cause of Saul falling from his horse then the moment must be one of intended dramatic impact. The speed with which the effect is completed seems to be important. Such instantaneous effect could certainly be produced by either of the methods advanced earlier concerning powders like rosin, varnish or sulphur. The technique concerned with blowing powder through a tube might satisfy the requirement of implied movement and speed by the words "Here comyth a feruent...", but other methods applicable to stage directions which suggest "thunderbolts" may also be relevant. Although the thunderbolt may be regarded as a streaking flash of light, it does not appear to be the same effect as that of lightning created by "rosen punned fine". Nor does the thunderbolt produce the sound of thunder; this needs to created by other means.

Typically, thunderbolts are used as a signal or statement from God or Heaven to an earthly recipient. The eye-witness account referred to earlier and offered by Abramo, the Russian bishop of Souzdal of the Florence *Annunciation* in 1439 indicates one method of creating the effect in his description of the "noise of uninterupted thunder" that "passes down three ropes". It is unlikely that the rope itself is the conductor of the fire even though it is seen to pass "down the three ropes". Rather like the "feruent, wyth gret tempest" it is also unlikely that the fire which "passes down the three ropes" is the source of the thunder. The "noise of uninterupted thunder" which accompanies the fire seems to be produced by other means. The technique employed appears to be the one referred to as "fireworks on lines"; "rockets on lines"; "squibs on lines"; "runners on lines"; or "swevels". A number of seventeenth-century plays record the use of fireworks on lines in both implicit and explicit stage directions.[18] Bate describes how to make "swevels":

SWevels are nothing else but Rockets, having instead of a rod (to ballast them) a little cane bound fast unto them, where through the rope passeth. Note that you must be carefull to have your line strong, even & smooth, and it must be rubd over with sope that it may not burn. If you would have your Rockets to returne againe, then binde two Rockets together, with the breech of one towards the mouth of the other, and let the stouple that primeth the one, enter the breech of the other [**FIG.7**].[19]

Bate is only one of the early firework writers to promote this technique and the main features are well illustrated by this account.[20]

7. Swevels or "rockets on lines".
"A B signifieth the Rocket; D E, the cane bound unto it, through which a rope passeth. The lowermost representeth the double Rocket; A B signifieth one Rocket, and C D another; E the stouple that primeth the one, and entreth the breech of the other; the cane that the rope passeth thorough is supposed to be behinde the two Rockets.".
Bate, *The Mysteryes of Natvre and Art*, pp.76-7.

Such rockets were also capable of being made of different sizes in order to match the distance covered.[21] Bate's method, outlined here, offers a partial means of achieving the effects described by the Bishop of Souzdal for the Florence *Annunciation.*. If the term "feruent" as used in the stage direction in *The Conversion of Saint Paul* may be regarded as synonymous with the term "thunderbolt", then Bate's description of the operation of "SWevels" also provides a partial method of realising the instruction in the stage direction; the technique presupposes the use of a suitable wire or rope.

A description of the entertainment for Elizabeth I at Elvetham in 1591 records: "there were many running rockets uppon lines, which past between the Snail Mount and the castle in the Fort."[22] During the performance of the Modane play of *Antichrist* in 1580 it is recorded that "they shall project fireworks in the air and along the cord (**par la corde**) whenever necessary for the said mystery..."[23] As part of a comprehensive series of effects for thunder and lightning Serlio suggests that:

> you must draw a piece of wyre ouer the Scene, which must
> hang downewards, whereon you must put a squib couered
> ouer with pure gold or shining lattin which you will: and
> while the Bullet is rouling, you must shoote of some piece
> of Ordinance, and with the same giuing fire to the squibs, it
> will worke the effect which is desired.[24]

The "squib" of Serlio's account performs the same function as the "Rocket" in Bate's description. Reference to the "Bullet is rouling" in Serlio's account indicates one of the known methods of producing thunder indoors. The technique of rolling cannon balls (or equivalent) down a wooden trough is known to have existed in the sixteenth century and later evidence concerning this practice is well established.[25] The co-ordinated shooting of "some piece of Ordinance" is yet another example of how more than one effect is often required to create an accumulative effect.

In appearance the thunderbolt is essentially a fizzing or flaming streak of fire delivered at rapid speed. The use of rockets or squibs to create thunderbolts was not the only means available, for a similar yet simplified technique is indicated by the following nineteenth-century account:

> When a thunderbolt is to strike an object, a wire is run
> from the flies to the object which is to be struck. A rider
> runs on the wire. The rider consists of a section of iron

44

pipe. Around it is secured asbestos by means of wire. The asbestos is soaked with alcohol, and is lighted just at the instant when it is to be projected upon the object. It is usually held by a string, which is cut. It rushes flaming through the air, and produces the effect of a ball of fire striking the object.[26]

The simplicity of this technique invites speculation as to its practicability in the sixteenth century. A piece of cane may have worked instead of a section of iron pipe. Tow fastened to the cane and soaked in aqua vitae would have been capable of providing the combustible material of the thunderbolt. Although cane is lighter than iron, gravity would still have allowed the technique to work.

Payments recorded and referred to earlier in the *King's College Mundum Book* for 1552-3 concerning the production of thunder and lightning in a production of *Hippolytus* suggest that the "shootynge of " the "gunne powder" may have contributed to the effect of thunder produced by the "drye ffatte" in a similarly accumulative manner to that suggested by Serlio; the "gunne powder" is also likely to have been used in the production of lightning. Other pyrotechnic ingredients to create lightning are not itemised in the accounts.

The use of gunpowder in ordinance of various kinds for the purpose of producing thunder is also evident. Use of the rolled cannon ball as referred to by Serlio and others and the thunder barrell or "drye ffatte" of the *King's College Mundum Book* provide two other methods of producing thunder. A fourth, yet often complementary method, occurs with the use of drums. Any of these four approaches or permutations of them are capable of producing the desired effect of thunder.[27]

Another technique is indicated by further consideration of stage directions in *The Conversion of Saint Paul*. Despite the difficulty of interpreting the phrase "feruent, wyth gret tempest" another stage direction in the same play is explicit in its requirement of thunder:

> Here to enter a dyvel wyth thunder and fyre, and to avaunce hymsylfe, sayeng as folowyth, and hys spech spokyn, to syt downe in a chayre: [28]

It is not clear from this direction whether the "dyvel" himself creates the "thunder and fyre" or if it is created for him. If the effects are created for the "dyvel", Belyal, then one or more of the previously considered techniques may be appropriate. If on the other hand, the "dyvel" himself creates the "thunder and fyre" then he presumably controls the device or devices to produce the effects. A technique that may be contollable by Belyal is that of "casting fire". This process involves the straight-forward act of throwing fireworks such as squibs, serpents or fiz-gigs.[29] These fireworks typically issue a shower of sparks, meander unpredictably and end in a small explosion. Most of the firework contains a basic gunpowder mixture with a small section in the end filled with another mixture, usually corned powder, which creates the final report. Using this type of firework Belyal would be capable of timing and controlling his entrance, delivering his three stanza speech and sitting "downe in a chayre" as indicated by the stage direction. It is of course possible that the "feruent, wyth gret tempest" is also a squib that is thrown by "Deus".

The act of "casting fire" is indicated by a stage direction in Marlowe's *Dr.Faustus*. Mephistophilis and Faustus "beat the Friars, and fling fireworks among them; and so exeunt.".[30] This mischievous or malevolent behaviour by Mephistophilis is intended to create alarm and confusion among the Friars and possibly seeks the same sort of response provided by Robin and Vintner when a stage direction informs that "Mephistophilis, sets squibs at their backs, [and then exit.] They run about.". Whether the "Thunder and Lightning" required later in the play is produced by this method is unclear. If such a technique is employed it appears to be concerned with the representation of thunder and lightning rather than the simulation of it.

An intriguing payment in the *Smiths' Accounts* at Coventry records the following: "item, paid for starche to make the storme in the pagente, vj d".[31] Like the term "tempest" as used in the stage direction in *The Conversion of Saint Paul*, the meaning of the word "storme" needs to be determined. Does it refer to sound or light or both? If the "storme" is expressed by sound then the "starche" would seem to be the cause of it. How might "starche" create sound? W.J.Lawrence seems certain about its use: "This needs no great speculation: evidently the starch was used to make pellets of hail.".[32] By this suggestion he presumably requires the "starche" to be mixed with water, formed into pellets and dried. No doubt the sight and sound of such pellets was intended to create the "storme". If, on the other hand, the "starche" was required to create light, how might this have worked? Starch is an organic compound and as such it will burn. It is used in some firework mixtures as a low temperature combustion agent, particularly for smoke compositions; when heated it burns without melting.[33] It is possible that starch, which is a white powder, may be used in contact with flame or fire in order to simulate lightning by either of the methods described for rosin. The production of thunder as a separate effect in this pageant may be inferred by the following payments in the same accounts:

> paid to Hewette for fetchynge of
> the hoggesheaddes,   vj d;
> ...
> paid to ij drumme-players,   x d;
> ...
> paid to Christofer Dyglyne for hys
> ij drummes,   vj s viij d;[34]

The barrels and drums may have been used to create thunder in conjunction with the "starche" to produce lightning.

The effect of thunder in the Lucerne *Passion Play* is created by the combination of thunder-barrels and gunpowder: "Paid to Caspar Thürmgen the powder-maker, for 12 lbs. of powder for the guns and the thunder,...".[35] The eye-witness account of Abramo, the Russian Bishop of Souzdal records the following observation concerning the Florence *Annunciation* play:

> Then the curtains of the upper scaffold open and from there comes a volley of shots imitating Heaven's thunder, and the Prophets with their scrolls are not seen again.[36]

As noted earlier, the text of the Valencia *Assumption Play* requires the production of both thunder and smoke.[37] The task of creating smoke for different effects is sufficiently demanding in the Lucerne *Passion Play* for there to be designated "Smoke-Makers (**Roucker**)". Smoke effects of different colours are indicated in various parts of the play:

> Paid for the powder for the smoke in the Mount of Olives and the eclipse to Master Niclaus Schyterberg, without the gunpowder.[38]

Another instruction contained in the Lucerne MSS informs that "they are again to make black smoke in the Mount of Olives for the eclipse".[39] So the "black smoke" is to be produced "without the gunpowder". In the same MSS "when God the Father is about to give Moses the Ten Commandments on the mountain, they are to set the smoke mechanism working so that a cloud is produced.". Elsewhere in the MSS "smoke-makers are to make a cloud" for the Ascension and for Pentecost where "thunder, smoke, and shots" are stipulated. An interesting note in the Lucerne MSS suggests the following:

> Note: In Milan they have artificial fire in the plays which goes up quickly (**gäch uffgat**), produces much smoke, and yet neither burns nor stinks.[40]

It appears that the compositions to produce smoke do not consist of gunpowder and that the stipulation of "black smoke" is not the same requirement as that to "make a cloud" for the Ascension or "when God the Father is about to give Moses the Ten Commandments". The implication derived from the references to the method of producing smoke in Milan is that the Lucerne technique not only produced much smoke but also unwanted smell. Black smoke is likely to have been caused by carbon particles produced by the imperfect combustion of a carbon-rich compound.[41] Brown smoke is capable of being produced from pitch or tar: "Hard pitch is ground to a powder and mixed with potassium nitrate [saltpetre] and sulphur. Glue is frequently added to control the reaction.".[42] Ronald Lancaster suggests that "A better method is to use liquid tar which is absorbed into sawdust. The mixture has better burning characteristics and can be used in thick-walled paper tubes.".[43] The production of white smoke may be achieved by burning a mixture of sulphur and saltpetre.[44] Since sulphur and saltpetre are two of the three ingredients of gunpowder, the reference to "powder for the smoke...without the gunpowder" may be explained by this reaction. In this instance the sulphur would be vapourised by the heat produced by combustion which then condenses into fine particles to produce smoke. Yellow smoke may be produced in the same way by burning a mixture of realgar (arsenic disulphide) and saltpetre.[45]

The production of smoke as determined by the preceding stage directions and instructions is essentially concerned with the development of atmosphere. Additionally, smoke is capable of contributing to the development of illusion. Smoke as a special effect may communicate a particular kind of light which is real and witnessed as such. However, the use of smoke to communicate sensation and/or statement concerning heat deals with illusion.

Stage directions in *The Croxton Play of the Sacrament* contain information concerning the creation of theatrical deception.[46] Few studies of this play have been attempted and earlier twentieth-century writers have been largely dismissive of its dramatic strengths.[47] Some stage directions that require special effects and/or sleight of hand in order to produce blood or false limbs are of interest but not strictly relevant to the use of flame or fire.[48] The pertinent directions are concerned with boiling and burning illusions employing a cauldron and a furnace. The cauldron and its supposed contents is used in an attempt to separate the Host wafer stuck to Jonathas' hand. The stage direction at l.660 requires:

> Here shall Jason pluck owt the naylys and shake þe hond
> into þe cawdron [49]

During the next three stanzas the text makes much macabre play of the effort to separate hand and Host: Jasdon stirs the cauldron and its contents and Masphat blows up the fire. At this point another stage direction at l.672 requires:

> Here shall þe cawdron byle (boil), apperyng to be as
> blood.[50]

The importance of this stage direction is that it is one of the few to be found among English medieval texts that explicitly refers to the creation of theatrical illusion.[51] The communicated appearance of boiling is the principal concern. Other references to this sort of requirement exist among some European texts and evidence concerning methods of theatrical deception is sometimes explained in accompanying records.[52] The instruction invites speculation on a number of interesting issues. Assuming that timing is important, how do the contents of the cauldron manage to "byle" at the appropriate time i.e. on cue? What does the word "byle" mean in this particular context? Do the contents of the cauldron actually boil? What are the contents of the cauldron "apperyng to be as blood"? To whom is such "apperyng" apparent? Since the creation of the fire under the cauldron and the subsequent boiling happen within eight lines of the text, the need expressed by the stage direction occurs within shortened theatrical time and appears to be relatively instantaneous. Although Masphat and Malchas refer to the preparation and subsequent boiling of the cauldron, it is the stage direction that explicitly refers to the creation of theatrical illusion. An initial assumption might be that the cauldron contains a liquid that appears to boil on cue. After all the text does inform us that "thys oyle waxyth redde as blood".[53] It has been suggested that such an effect might have been created by the use of a fountain placed inside the cauldron.[54] Normally the action of a boiling liquid requires that bubbles are seen as evidence of this state. However, for theatrical purposes accompanying steam, vapour or smoke is also suggestive of this condition. Thus the action of the cauldron "apperyng" to boil need not refer to the sight of boiling or bubbling liquid. The use of smoke to create an appropriate effect seems a distinct possibility. Consequently, reference to the contents of the cauldron "apperyng to be as blood" may refer to red smoke. Even if the audience is placed above the action of the play, as has been suggested,[55] the sight of a boiling liquid appearing on cue might be difficult to communicate. An effect of greater dimension might be achieved with red smoke. The possibility of smoke being the conductor of this effect could be more precisely identified if fireworks or firework materials were involved. The creation of red smoke is likely to have been possible through the use of a constituent such as vermillion or vermillion oil mixed with other pyrotechnic ingredients.[56] The trade in "Vermelion" at "ye lof iiij" is recorded in the tariff of charges made by the Worshipful Company of Grocers, London in 1453 [**APPENDIX 3B**]. *The Accounts* record payment for "vermenioun ule" as a pyrotechnic ingredient for celebratory purposes in 1538.[57] However, the reference to "vermenioun ule" does not automatically determine its use in the production of red smoke for its function may be alternatively that of a binding agent in other firework compositions to produce, for instance, red stars for aerial use. Even so, vermillion has certainly been used in the production of red smoke.[58]

The use of fireworks to contribute to the illusion of a boiling cauldron is recorded in a stage direction in the Majorca *SS Crispin and Crispinian play*:

> The official is to go away with two or three men, and they are to bring a piece of lead and a cauldron. They are to put the two youths into a cauldron and a little fire is to be made with straw. They are to put a firework (**coet**) beneath the cauldron, and when the youths have stopped singing, they are to set fire to the firework.[59]

As noted earlier, the communicated effect required of special effects is sometimes realised by the careful and timed execution of two or more techniques that are juxtaposed or superimposed. The effect sought by the direction of the Majorca play offers such an example. Even though the direction does not specify the effect to be achieved, it seems likely that the "firework (**coet**)" and the "little fire" are required to act in concert to produce the overall impact. The resultant effect is more likely to have been one of fire and/or smoke than one of noise. Smoke would produce the necessary dimension to the effect and at the same time remain relatively contollable and safe. The effect intended by the Majorca play does not require the cauldron to contain liquid, although a stage direction from the Modane play of *Antichrist* in 1580 indicates the following:

> Then they shall make water boil in the cauldron in which the seneschal is put and do it with fireworks (**fusées**) without heating the water in the best possible way. [60]

The suggestion here is that the cauldron actually contains water that is artificially made to boil by the use of fireworks. In effect, the water is required to seethe "without heating the water". Because fireworks create their own supply of oxygen by virtue of the inclusion of an oxidising agent such as saltpetre in the mixture,[61] they are capable of operating under water. Even so, some early pyrotechnic sources contain directions for firework mixtures and devices that are specifically designed to operate under water.[62] Such underwater fireworks certainly create violent effervescence and smoke. In the main, underwater devices exist as ballasted fireballs. Typically, this sort of firework consists of a canvas ball filled with a gunpowder mixture "armed" or bound with "marling" cord and daubed with pitch, rosin, tallow or other wax. In order to fire the ball, vents are left in the canvas case and stone or lead is used to ballast them.[63] The cauldron in which the "seneschal" is put in the Modane play of *Antichrist* is preumably large enough to contain him and the fireworks. Some sleight of hand is likely to have been necessary in placing this kind of firework into the cauldron of water, for it needs to be fired before immersion. Nevertheless, the effects of bubbling water accompanied by clouds of smoke would be relatively immediate and capable of occurring on cue.

Either of the above techniques may have been technically capable of fulfilling the requirement of the stage direction in *The Croxton Play of the Sacrament.*. However, it is the possible use of smoke that is likely to give the effect its necessary dimension and perhaps displace the importance of a real or simulated boiling liquid.

When the boiling of the Host in the cauldron is unsuccessful in *The Croxton Play of the Sacrament*, resort is made to sterner measures. Seemingly, another fire is lit in order to heat up an oven in which the host is to be placed. The stage direction at l.695 stipulates: "Here þei kyndyll þe fyre". Further pyrotechnic skill is suggested by this direction in that the effect sought is again required instantly. Although the text requires Masphat to produce "straw and thornys kene" and Malchas is required to "bring on fere", caution must be exercised in determining whether these conditions are observed literally. Even if the fire actually consists of "straw and thornys kene", some insurance of ignition may be sought by impregnating or coating the materials with flammable substances. If the text is not to be taken literally, then the use of spirit such as aqua vitae or bundles of rags or oakum, soaked or smeared with tallow, pitch or rosin would provide suitable means of creating relatively rapid fire. The following stage direction occurs at l.712:

> Here the owyn must ryve asunder and blede owt at þe cranys, and an image appere owt with woundys bledyng.[64]

The image to which the stage direction refers is that of Jesus and the following direction at l.716 requires:

> Here shall þe image speke to the Juys saying thus:

The first of these two directions requires that the oven must "ryve asunder and blede owt at þe cranys". Whether the instruction to "ryve asunder" refers to an explosion, a disintigration or a collapse is not immediately obvious. Clearly, some parts of the oven must remain in order that it may "blede owt at þe cranys", so disintigration does not appear to be the objective. The collapse of the sides and surfaces of the oven does not of itself suggest that it is strong enough to contain and destroy the Host. The sound and sight of fireworks as special effects may well help to complete the action and imagery. Out of the remains of the wrecked oven, the second stage direction requires that "þe image speke to the Juys". How does an image of Jesus "appere owt" of the riven oven? It is possible that a person is concealed inside "þe image" as indicated by the records of the *St.George* play, Turin: "Item: another idol in which is hidden a person who speaks:".[65] If "þe image" is not an actual person or someone concealed in "þe image" then something or somebody must manipulate the action.[66] One possibility is that the image is a mechanical one, whether in two dimensional form, as a painted figure, or three-dimensional form, as a painted dummy. Alternatively, the appearance of the image may be manipulated by someone inside the oven, or at least, out of sight of the audience. Again, the image could be a two-dimensional painted figure or a three-dimensional dummy. If the appearance of the image is effectively stage managed by someone inside the oven, then the size must be large enough to conceal such a person or persons even after the oven splits. Such a possibility seems to have operated at the Modena *Corpus Christi*

Play in 1556, for a description contained in the city records informs us of "how Nebuchadnezzar set up the gold statue forcing everybody to adore it":

> Behind the statue was a furnace ingeniously (**misteriosamente**) constructed and painted in which there were fireworks and people to make them burn at the appointed time.
> ...The king was angry and commanded that they should be forthwith seized and bound and led to the furnace, which very appropriately sent forth flames in several places in such a way that they harmed the others but not the three youths, who right in the middle of the fire began to praise and bless their true God...They finished their singing while the furnace continued to burn, but the flames were so carefully arranged that they harmed no one. [67]

The above action takes place on a cart which is "framed all round by an alabaster frame and at the corners were some heads in relief, all gilded.". Reference to the furnace being "ingeniously constructed" seems to relate to the capacity of the device and its operation to enable the simulated burning of Shadrach, Meschach Abednego.[68] Presumably the use of fireworks and their careful positioning by the "people to make them burn at the appointed time" also contributes to the ingenuity of the effect. One implication involved here is that the firework operators are concealed in the furnace; this possibility may support the notion that the furnace is "ingeniously constructed". Another possibility would involve the "people to make them burn" being stationed behind the action of the play and possibly out of sight of the audience in order to fire the devices by quickmatch.

The conditions implied by *The Croxton Play of the Sacrament* could be achieved by the use of red smoke made to "blede owt of þe cranys". Indeed, smoke produced by a firework would provide a strong theatrical atmosphere out of which the image could "magically" emerge. A firework to produce an explosion which enables the oven to "ryve asunder" is not likely to be one that creates a smoke effect. Clearly, the required impact created by such an explosive firework is likely to be dangerous to anyone inside the oven. It appears that the oven is designed and constructed in such a way as to burst apart at the appropriate moment and may be activated by one or more people inside the oven who would themselves need to be concealed before and after the break up. Fireworks to produce smoke and/or explosion do not seem to be directly responsible for splitting the oven, but timed as contributory special effects. A hidden person within the oven could not only manipulate the image into position but also provide the necessary ventriloquism for Jesus' voice when the image addresses the Jews. Since the list of Dramatis Personae at the end of the play records Jesus as one of the protagonists, it is possible that the voice of Jesus comes from within the oven. Jesus may operate the special effects.

CHAPTER 4

Flame as Light

ALL FLAME produces light. The intensity, illumination, range, colour and atmosphere produced by such light is determined by the nature of the fuel, the method of its supply and the context in which it operates. The means of securing the lighting requirements expressed in stage directions in **CHAPTER 1** must have involved flame in some way. Unless such requirements for "great light" could be satisfied by the multiple use of candles, torches, flambeaux or cressets, then some additional devices, processes or techniques are likely to have been employed in supplementing the flame to produce the necessary power of light. Because the different materials used to create flame possess distinctive properties that affect its nature, it might be useful to identify them and their effects before considering ways of increasing the influence of such flame.

Perhaps the simplest of the flame effects is that produced by the candle. The conventional fuels used in candle making were tallow [animal fat] and beeswax.[1] The combustible qualities of tallow enabled a wider use of the substance beyond that of candle production for it was frequently used in other pyrotechnic processes such as the construction of fireballs "as wel for service in warre, as for pleasure or triumph,...".[2] When used for lighting purposes the mutton variety of tallow was considered to produce the clearest light and least smoke.[3] A mixture of mutton and beef tallow was sometimes used as a means of improving the quality of light produced by the beef variety. Pork tallow was generally avoided since it produced poor light and thick, acrid smoke. However, tallow did not create the brighter flame associated with beeswax. Candles composed of tallow produced more smoke than those made of beeswax.[4] Tallow was also used in the production of rushlights.[5] These consisted of meadow rushes cut to about eighteen inches and partially stripped of the outer green skin. Sufficient skin remained in order to support the pith of the rush which was then alowed to soak in a vessel containing melted tallow. When dried, the rushes could be carried by hand or held in stands made for the purpose.

Not all candles were made of tallow or beeswax and built up around cotton wicks, for cheaper candles and some rushlights were dipped into a variety of molten rosin known as colophone or Greek Pitch.[6] Colophone is produced as a residue when turpentine is distilled with water [**GLOSSARY**]. Several kinds of rosin exist, each consisting of different chemical compositions and burning characteristics; they are also capable of being reduced to powder form [**CHAPTER 1**]. The *Churchwardens' Accounts* at Ludlow, Shropshire record the use of "rosene to make lyght" in church in the 1540's.[7] Rosin was also a constituent ingredient in the production of torches.

Most torches were constructed around resinous sticks or lengths of twisted hemp and daubed with combinations of wax [beeswax], tallow, pitch, rosin, and gum. At Coventry in 1515, the *Carpenters' Account Book* records the following payments:

> [Item payd for iij lb wax to dobbe the torchis þat was
> bowght of hary patison at vj d þe lb]   [xviij d] ⌐xx d.⌐
> Item payd for rosyn & gom to þe same   viij d
> Item payd to nycholas barbur for dobbyng of v torchis
>   xij d[8]

In this account it is not clear whether the "iij lb of wax" refers to beeswax or tallow, for the former was more expensive, cleaner in operation and thus an appropriate fuel for use indoors.[9] If the "wax" was beeswax then its value as a replacement for tallow would have been to reduce the amount of smoke otherwise produced by unburnt carbon. The "gom" could have been one of a number of resinous gums obtained as exudations from various trees and included to ensure ignition.[10]

References exist to another version of the torch, namely, the staff torch.[11] Manuscript illuminations indicate staff torches as being some six to eight feet in length.[12] The upper half of the staff torch was layered with combustible material in the same way as other torches. *Minutes of the Ironmongers' Company* concerning its contribution to the *Lord Mayors' Pageant* record the following:

Item, it is agreed that Richarde Sharpe, wax chaundelo[r], shall deliu[r] viij. dozen staff torches, eùy torche to be of waxe, an elle in lengthe, and att xv [s] the dozen. [13]

Although this reference does not clearly state the length of the staff torch, it suggests that the "elle in lengthe" refers to the wax section and not the total length.

The link was different from the torch in that the combustible part consisted of rags or ends of rope dipped in combinations of pitch, rosin or tallow and wrapped around the ends of staves or sticks.[14]

The gimbal-like metal cradle which was suspended on a pole characterised the appearance of the cresset [**FIG.8**].[15] Records at Coventry refer to materials and processes involving the cresset. The fuel for cressets is referred to as "podyngs" or "puddyngs", "cressyt lyght" and "bettyngs" [**GLOSSARY**]. The terms are not entirely interchangeable although it seems clear that "podyngs" and "cressyt lyght" refer to the same thing, despite the fact that the two terms sometimes occur within records of the same guild; in such cases the references are normally to different years.[16] Use of the term "cressyt lyght" occurs elsewhere in the country [**GLOSSARY**]. "Podyngs" were also referred to as "pvdyng Roppes" and this difference draws attention to the nature of "podyngs".[17] Lengths of rope smeared with rosin were coiled around the central spike of the cresset and set on fire [**FIG.9**].[18] When this fuel was consumed, replenishment was achieved from a bag or panier containing "podyngs" and carried by a boy who followed the cresset bearer.[19] John Stowe observed that "euery Cresset had two men, one to beare or hold it, an other to beare a bag with light, and to serue it,..." [**FIG.10**].[20]

Some records refer to the use of pitch and rosin as fuel in cressets. Pitch is produced as a residue in the distillation of tar. It is brittle when hard yet viscous when heated [**GLOSSARY**]. Pitch is not recorded as an ingredient of "podyngs" at Coventry, but is recorded as an ingredient of "bettyngs". Although "bettyngs" were fuelled by pitch and rosin they were clearly not the same as "podyngs", for payments to both items occur in the same accounts.[21] It seems that "bettyngs" consisted of bundles of hemp or flax which were used to kindle or re-kindle the "podyngs" or "cressyt lyght".[22] Presumably, loosely-bundeled "bettyngs" would ignite more quickly than the densely-packed fibres of rope. Payments were made for the bearing of "bettyngs" in much the same way as "podyngs".[23] The functional difference between "podyngs" and "bettyngs" at Coventry was not made elsewhere. At Exeter in 1433 payment is recorded as follows: "Item in vno homine locato ad

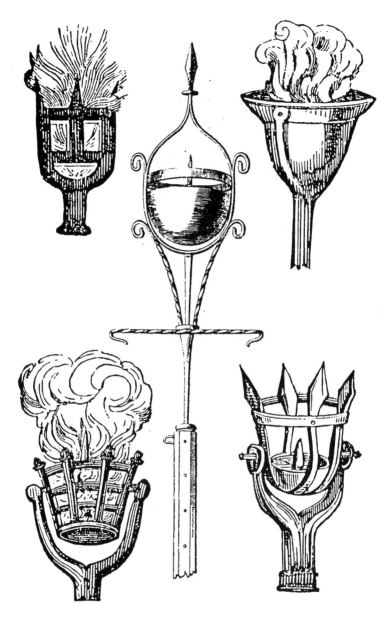

8. Cressets of different designs. The centre cresset is said to be one
preserved in the Tower of London.
Hone, *The Every-Day Book*, I, p.416;
Nicholl... *Ironmongers*, p.62.

9. A Cresset. 19¹/₂ inches long.
Sharp, *A Dissertation on the Pageants*, opp.p.51.

10. Cresset Bearer and Attendant.
Sharp, *A Dissertation on the Pageants*, opp.p.51.

portandum Balles de talwe roson & ocom pro dictis cressantibus eadem nocte j d." (Item, for one man hired to carry balls of tallow, rosin, and oakum for the said cressets on the same night 1d).[24] It is not immediately clear whether the "Balles de talwe roson & ocom" fulfilled the function of the Coventry "podyngs" or "bettyngs". However, the density of rolled up balls of oakum implies the same function as that of "podyngs" i.e. the principal fuel.[25] Lucar offered the following recipe in respect of "cressyt lyght" which may well have functioned in the manner of the Coventry "bettyngs":

> THrust lynnen ragges into oyle of hempsede, and after dippe them in melted tallowe, then putting them into Cressets giue fire to them, & you shall see that they all burne and giue a great light.[26]

The chemical process governed by Lucar's recipe is presumably the same as that offered by Hyll in his recipe to produce candle wicks.[27] Tallow, pitch and rosin appear to have been the main ingredients used to impregnate or smear rope, oakum or hemp as fuel in cressets. As detailed in **CHAPTER 1**, the use of these materials is also recorded at Wymondham by *The Watch and Play Society* in 1537/8.

Clearly, the illumination offered by "cressyt lyght" was greater than that of the candle or torch and was the principal means of lighting outdoor events in the evening.[28] The accompanying smell and smoke produced by the organic concoction of tallow, pitch and rosin did not preclude the use of the cresset at indoor celebrations.[29]

Other materials, when ignited, were also capable of producing different kinds of light. Knowledge of aqua-vitae and its creation is recorded in thirteenth and fourteenth-century treatises.[30] The name aqua-vitae or "water of life" frequently refers to the same liquid described as "aqua-ardens" or "spirits of wine".[31] An explanation of the synonymity of aqua-ardens and aqua-vitae is offered by the name given to the cooling tube used in the distillation of aqua-ardens, namely, the "vitis"; this may be translated as "vine branch" and is presumably named because the tube was twisted like a vine.[32] If any difference existed between aqua vitae and aqua ardens, it is likely to have been as a result of the process of rectification i.e. repeated distillation.[33] In the simplest of extant recipes, aqua vitae was produced as the distillate when wine was heated.[34] Other recipes for aqua vitae and aqua ardens are extant which make use of additional ingredients.[35] To heat the wine in a stillhead beyond the boiling point of alcohol (78°C), produced vapour that condensed as a distillate. The rate at which the wine was heated helped to determine the relative alcoholic content of the aqua vitae and thus the resultant characteristics on ignition. Slow heating was preferable. It was found that the distillate was capable of being set alight and if the alcoholic content was less than 35% then cloth, hair and even flesh, when wetted, would burn without causing damage to the host material. This latter characteristic, referred to in **CHAPTER 2**, was the one frequently utilised as a means of creating theatrical effect. Serlio suggested that:

> Sometime it may chance that you must make some thing or other which should seeme to burne, which you must wet throughly with excellent good Aquauite; and setting it on fire with a candle it will burne all ouer:[36]

Although other references exist to burning aqua vitae, some records clearly refer to its use in pyrotechnic mixtures to ensure ignition.[37] Another function of such mixtures would have been to enable the flaming aqua vitae to be seen. As indicated in **CHAPTER 2**, aqua vitae, when ignited on its own, burns with a relatively colourless flame and when it is mixed with another element, or its salt, the resultant flame is a coloured one. For example, if crystals of any copper salt are dissolved in aqua vitae then the resultant flame will burn with an emerald-green flame. If any of the following salts are mixed with aqua vitae and ignited then coloured flame will result: sodium chloride (common salt) and aqua vitae will produce a yellow flame: saltpetre (potassium nitrate) and aqua vitae will deliver a pale violet flame and calcium chloride mixed with aqua vitae will produce an orange flame. Additional salts that were not known to have existed before the nineteenth century will produce different colours when mixed with aqua vitae.[38] Other accounts, including those identified in **CHAPTER 1**, refer to the capacity of aqua-vitae to burn independently. *The Revels Accounts* for 1578/9 record the use of aqua-vitae as follows: "Ivie and holly for the Rock in the play enacted by the Earle of warwickes servaunts- iiij ^{s} ij ^{d}. Aquavite to burne in the same Rock- iij ^{s}".[39] The *Christ's College Accounts* for 1553-4 record payment "for aqua vite &c ix d" used in a play seemingly produced by a "mr stephenson".[40]

The principal ingredients used to produce white light or fire were camphor and orpiment (arsenic trisulphide) [**GLOSSARY**]. Serlio refers to the quality of light produced when camphor is set alight:

> You may also place certaine candlestickes aboue the Scene with great candles therein, and aboue the candlesticks you

may place some vessels with water, wherein you may put a
piece of Camphir, which burning, will show a very good
light, and smell well.[41]

"Camfer", together with "gonne poudor" and "salt peter" for
dramatic use is recorded at Shrewsbury in 1525-6.[42] *The Accounts* for the
years 1566-1574 record the use of camphor as a firework ingredient at
the *Baptismal Celebrations*.[43] Bate includes orpiment in his recipe for
"Aqua Ardens" although its function is not clear.[44] Hyll requires
orpiment to be mixed with sulphur and oil to produce a form of
quickmatch to light a succession of candles.[45] At Stirling in 1566 "ten
unce of orpyment" were required in conjunction with other firework
materials for the *Baptismal Celebrations*.[46] Lucar also records orpiment as
a constituent in a number of his recipes.[47]

Antimony and amber [**GLOSSARY**] were two ingredients used to
produce a white light that inclined towards yellow.

The introduction of sal-ammoniac as a colour-producing agent has
been attributed to the nineteenth-century writer, Claude-Fortuné
Ruggieri.[48] Yet sal-ammoniac (ammonium chloride) [**GLOSSARY**]
appears as an ingredient among other firework materials in *The Accounts*
for 1538-41.[49] This record establishes the use of sal-ammoniac as a
firework ingredient in the sixteenth century. The colour of flame
produced by sal-ammoniac is green. Lucar used the salt in some of his
recipes, although he did not appear to understand its purpose since its
incorporation was "to make gunpowder more stronger...".[50] Serlio made
use of sal-ammoniac, not as a firework ingredient, but as a means of
colouring water contained in a glass vessel, through which passed
candle light.[51] The resultant light was not only coloured green but
intensified in its effect.

Another means of creating green pyrotechnic effects was by the use
of verdigris, which is a blue/green salt produced by the action of
acetic acid on copper; it is thus an acetate of copper [**GLOSSARY**].
Although Jean Appier (alias Henzelet) has been credited with the
introduction of verdigris in the production of green coloured flame
in the seventeenth century,[52] use of the salt along with other
pyrotechnic ingredients is recorded in the *Chamberlains' Account Book*
concerning the New Romney play of 1560.[53] It appears that the
firework effects implied by these accounts were employed in a
presentation of Hell. Further use of verdigris is recorded by Hyll in
order to contribute to "licour" in which a "weecke" [wick] is dipped
and set alight in order to produce light of which the effect is both
"black and greene".[54]

As indicated in **CHAPTER 3**, the use of "vermenioun ule" (vermillion oil) recorded in *The Accounts* for 1538-1541 indicates the production of a red-flame colour-producing agent.[55] The existence of such a record has not previously been known to pyrotechnic historians.

Although it may be seen that the range of colour-producing agents is limited and relatively crude, by contemporary standards of pyrotechnic practice, awareness of the coloured effects made possible by the inclusion of specific ingredients is evident. Lack of chemical understanding did not necessarily inhibit the use or effect of such materials. However, to increase the scope, influence and impact of light produced by ignition of the above elements, substances, salts, "waters" and oils, some means of reflecting and/or intensifying the resultant flame would have been necessary.

Reflectors in the form of polished metal mirrors were known in Celtic times and lead-backed mirrors existed in the thirteenth century.[56] The different properties displayed by concave, flat and convex mirrors were known in the sixteenth century, even if the principles by which they operated were not clearly understood.[57] At Revello in 1483 the folowing direction was given for the Transfiguration:

> And when Jesus is on the mountain let there be a polished bowl (**bacillo**) which makes the brightness of the sun striking the bowl reflect on Jesus and towards his disciples. Then Jesus shall let fall his crimson garment and appear in white garments. And if the sun is not shining, let there be torches and some other lights.[58]

This instruction clearly demonstrates understanding of the principle of reflection to increase illumination. The "polished bowl" effectively operated as a concave mirror or "sphere", as Biringuccio called the device, and thus concentrated the available light, whether from the sun or torches, on to Jesus and the disciples.[59] The depth of the bowl in relation to its diameter would have affected its capacity to converge or spread light.[60] Similarly, the rim of the bowl would have enabled the rough limits of direction to be determined. The bowl was presumably hand-held in order to accomodate movement of Jesus in relation to the light source. Of particular interest in this instruction is the notion that the effect would still work even without the power of the sun. The use of "torches and some other lights" was also capable of producing a desired effect and would seemingly work because the artificial light source would operate in a relatively darker context.

An account describing the entry of Robert Dudley, Earl of Leicester to the Hague on the 6th of January, 1586 records the following:

> against my lords gate, a barbar had on a wall placed three score or more basons of bright copper, and in the middest of euerie one a wax candle burning was placed, in the middest of all was painted a rose and crowne: this made a faire shew, and was a pretie deuise.[61]

The description alone does not indicate whether the "basons" were placed horizontally or vertically on the wall or if light was reflected towards the viewer. However, confirmation of the vertical disposition of the "basons" is offered by the *Delineatio Pompae Triumphalis* (1586) as shown in **FIG.11.**[62] The "basons" surrounded the "rose and crowne" and reflected light above the heads of people in the procession. The extent to which the light produced was convergent or divergent is unclear. Even so, the accumulative effect must have been impressive. A similar arrangement of the candle/basin relationship exists in accounts concerning the marriage festivities of Francesco dei' Medici and Bianca Capello in Florence in 1579. Here the palace courtyard was converted into a tiltyard with an enclosure, the fence of which was encircled by "a row of decorated basins standing on the ground and containing candles".[63] The reflected light would presumably be scattered.

11. The "basons of bright copper" used during the reception of Robert Dudley, Earl of Leicester into the Hague in 1585. *Delineatio Pompae Triumphalis*, Strong and van Dorsten, *Leicester's Triumph*, p.42. By kind permission of E.J.Brill.

The use of basins to reflect light in order to create greater illumination operates on the same principle as that used by mirrors. Again, for the entry of Robert Dudley to the Hague in 1586, the following account is recorded:

> At the entrance of the fairest street, being also somewhat narrow, there was on ech side of the same gallorie, raised a mans height, ech against other, all hoong with blacke baies, on both which gallories on each side stood fifteene virgins all clad in white, with branches of palme or box wreathed about wax candels light in their hands, euerie of which did reuerence vnto the earle; these stood a speares length distant ech from other. Betwixt euerie one hoong a looking glasse, and betwixt euerie glasse vpon a pretie antike pearch stood a wax candle burning,...This shew was verie proper, but these had no speeches.[64]

The account seems to indicate that thirty "virgins all clad in white" (fifteen each side of the street) each held a candle and the light produced was supplemented by that from a further twenty-eight candles held in front of twenty-eight mirrors (fourteen each side of the street). A total of fifty-eight candles was thus available to reflect and re-reflect light across the street. The illuminated "virgins" must have created a vivid contrast with their background of "black baies". In *The Dialogues of Leoni di Somi*, thought to be compiled between 1556 and 1565, the use of mirrors is advocated in order to "make the set more gay and bright". di Somi writes:

> I should like to point out also that the small mirrors which some managers set at appropriate places in the perspective settings and the far sides of the wings are very effective. They reflect those concealed lights which the architects cleverly place behind columns and in the openings between the wings, thus serving to make the set more gay and bright. Not only can these reflections give no annoyance to the eyes; they have the further advantage that here we obtain light without smoke - a great consideration.[65]

Although the principle of reflected light as suggested here is the same as previous examples, the effects are likely to be different. If the unspecified number of "small mirrors" were "set at appropriate places in the perspective settings" in such a way as to be visible to the audience, then depending on the number, a "glittering" type of effect may have resulted. If, on the other hand, the "small mirrors" were placed out of sight of the audience on "the far side of the wings", then the audience would see the reflected light but not its source. The position of the "small mirrors" may therefore be determined by the ability to direct reflected light in a way which would enhance the "perspective settings". The "small mirrors" do not appear to have been positioned in such a way as to create concerted reflected light towards the audience, since di Somi seems pleased with the notion that "these reflections give no annoyance to the eyes".

A possible and similar use of mirrors is recorded in the *Revels Accounts* for 1612: "Looking glasses xl^{ty} dozen to sett vppon the Braunches at xviij^d. the dozen lx^s".[66] A total of 480 "Looking glasses" were thus available for use on the "Braunches". In the same accounts payment is also made for "Braunches xxxvj each conteyninge xv^{en} lightes at xl^s the pece lxxij^{li}". If the "Braunches" referred to in these two items are the same, then 480 "Looking glasses" would have been available for use in relation to 540 candles in the 36 "Braunches". If all the "Looking glasses" were used then only 60 candles would not have possessed appropriate reflectors. The effect must have been quite stunning, irrespective of which hall was used.[67] It is possible that the "Looking glasses" were arranged in such a way as to reflect light randomly throughout the hall and perhaps achieve the sort of effect produced by a stationary mirror ball. Equally, the potential illuminative power might have been harnessed and directed by placing the "Looking glasses" at similar angles to enable convergence of light.

Another use of mirrors to produce light of a greater illumination is suggested by Hugh Platte in his description of a lantern:

> What light a Candle woulde shewe if it were placed in a large Cilinder like vnto a halfe Lanterne, all of Latten kept bright and glistring, the same being inwardly garnished with diuerse steele Looking-glasses, so artificially placed as that one of them might reflect vnto an other [**FIG.12**].[68]

The angled arrangement of the "diuerse steele Looking-glasses" effectively enables more lighting sources to be created that are in turn reflected and re-reflected in order to produce greater illumination. The principle involved here is the same as that of the faceted reflector of the modern fresnel lantern.

66

John Baptista Porta in his description of "How to make an Amphitheatrical Glass" offers two versions of lighting devices based on the same principle [**FIG.13**]. In the first of these two methods he suggests that a "circle" is made "on a Table" of "what largeness you desire,....". An octagonal shape is created within the circle and on 7 of the 8 lines of the octagon:

> let Looking-glasses be raised perpendicularly; for the face that shall be against the Looking-glass, placed in the middle, will fly back to the beholder of it, and so rebounding to another, and from that to another, and by many reflections you shall see almost infinite faces, and the more the Glasses are, the more will be the faces: If you set a Candle against it, you shall see innumerable Candles.[69]

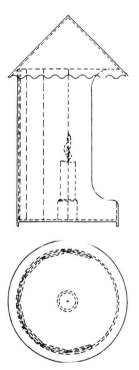

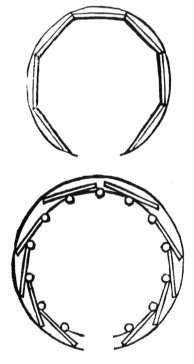

12. Platte's "halfe Lanterne". (My interpretation).
Platte, *The Jewell House of Art and Nature*, p.32.

13. Porta's plan drawings of his versions of the "Amphitheatrical Glass".
Derek J.Price ed. *Natural Magick*, pp.359-60.

In his second version of an "Amphitheatrical Glass", Porta declares that he "will now make one that is far more wonderful and beautiful. For in that the beholder shall not see his own face, but a most wonderful, and pleasant, and orderly form of pillars, and the basis of them, and variety of Architecture.". With regard to the size of the device, Porta indicates his preference:

> I hold the best to be where the diameter is two foot and a half: divide the circumference into equal parts; as for example into fourteen; the points of the divisions shall be the places, where the pillars must be erected. Let the place where the spectator must look, contain two parts; and take one pillar away, so there will be thirteen pillars:...then raise Looking-glasses upon the lines of space between, not exactly, but inclined: ...Hence by the reciprocal reflection of the Glasses, you shall see so many pillars, basis, and varieties, keeping the right order of Architecture, that nothing can be more pleasant, or more wonderful to behold... If you set a Candle in the middle, it will seem so to multiply by the Images rebounding, that you shall not see so many Stars in the skies, that you can never wonder enough at the Order, Symmetry, and the Prospect.[70]

Such ability to reflect light may be the simplest way of increasing illumination, yet the principal means of increasing intensity and controlling direction of light is through the use of a lens. The purpose of a lens is to create convergence or divergence of light. Eye-glasses and lenses were known in the thirteenth century, although the construction of lenses for lighting purposes was not always from a solid piece of glass.[71] Lenses were often created from round glass vessels containing liquid. Hugh Platte suggests the following method of creating a lighting device that operates as a lens:

> CAuse a round & double Glasse to bee made of a large size, & in fashió like a globe, but with a great rounde hole in the toppe, and in the concaue part of the vppermost Glasse place a Candle in a loose socket, and at some hole or pipe which must bee made in the side thereof, fill the same with spirite of Wine or some other cleare distilled water that will not putrifie, and this one Candle will give a great and wonderfull light, somewhat resembling the Sun beames [**FIG.14**].[72]

This vessel consists of a double skin of glass that contains "spirite of Wine" [aqua-vitae] or "cleare distilled water" as a medium through which the light from the candle flame is focused by the convex outer surface. The description given by Platte of the "wonderfull light, somewhat resembling the Sun beames" is not a fanciful exaggeration, but an attempt to describe an effect of slim vectors of intensified light that radiate from the vessel. Confirmation of this technique and commensurate effect is offered by the more complex device known as the "Glory Box" developed by Furtenbach in the seventeenth century.[73] The apparatus was used at dramatic moments such as the appearance or intervention of God; the kind of moment as required by the stage directions cited in **CHAPTER 1**. Furtenbach suggests: "With very little expense a powerful light can be placed behind a round double glass filled with water and put at the very center of the *glory*,...". The *glory* is a specially designed box some 3 feet square and 2 feet deep which is lined with reflecting materials, some of which represent the sun's rays. The glass vessel is a crystalline globe 5 inches in diameter. Furtenbach writes:

> This globe must be carefully made by the glassmaker from two pieces of crystalline glass set two fingers' distance apart. It is filled with water to which a little bit of red coloring is added. It must be made with a neck or hole the width of a finger to put the water in by, and also with a peg (**Zapfen**). By the peg and the neck it is made fast to the box. Or if no better can be had, a glass flask with a curved side can be used.[74]

14. Platte's "round & double Glasse". (My interpretation).
    Platte, *The Jewell House of Art and Nature*, pp.31-2.

The effect produced by the water filled glass is said to produce light "like an eye that sends out sunbeams towards the spectators to cause great wonder by its shimmering...a shimmering and shining splendor that the man who looks at it too closely would lose his sight".[75] The basic detail concerning the "crystalline globe" as described by Furtenbach is almost identical to the instruction made by Platte some seventy years earlier. There are, however, some significant differences between the requirements of Platte and Furtenbach. In the former, a candle flame produced the light source which is placed in the centre of the "double glass". The light source required here seems to be a more powerful source than a candle flame. It is possible that a torch or a number of closely arranged candles might have been used. A light source powerful enough to qualify for Furtenbach's description of "a powerful light" seems to have been too big to fit into the middle of his 5 inch "crystalline glass". Given that the effect of the "glory" is a two dimensional one, it does not matter that the light source is placed behind the glass rather than in the middle. In the event that a "crystalline glass" could not be obtained, Furtenbach suggests that "a glass flask with a curved side can be used". Platte also describes a similar liquid-filled vessel which acts as a lens:

> I knewe an expert Ieweller, dwelling (whilest he liued) in the Blacke-friers, who had a Glasse with a round bellie, and a flat backe standing vpon a foote, with a Lampe placed so at the backer part thereof, as that the light thereof, was iust opposite to the center of the bellie through which (the Glasse being first filled with spirite of Wine) there would so brim and glittering light appeare, as that by the helpe thereof he would graue anie curious worke in golde as well at midnight as at the noone day.[76]

It is the convex outer surface of such a glass that enables the resultant light to be focused. The critical position of the light source in relation to the "bellie" of the "Glasse" would have been the means of focusing the emergent intensified light. In this instance the light source is recorded as a "Lampe". The size and power of this "Lampe" is unrecorded although Serlio made a similar requirement which might have been on a greater scale:

> And behind the glasses you must set great Lampes, that the light may also be stedfast: and if the bottels or other vessels of glasse on the side where the light stands were flat, or rather hollow, it would show the clearer...[77]

When Serlio suggests that the light "would show the clearer", he seems to be referring to focused light. The principle of focus is clearly illustrated with reference to the lacemaker's lamp, which consists of a globe of water suspended on a base. Attached to the base is a moveable candle holder which is capable of being moved up or down in order that the flame of the candle might be positioned opposite the "bellie" of the globe. The light produced when the candle is in this position is a slim vector of focused, intensified light that falls on to the lacemaker's work. The size of the globe of a lacemaker's lamp is usually 4-8 inches in diameter. This sort of device is also known as a condenser [**FIG.15**].[78]

A liquid-filled globe of a slightly different design is recorded by John White:

> Goe to the Glasse-house, or Glasse-shop, and let them blow
> you a thin round Globe glasse, bigger then a penny Loafe,
> (the bigger the better) with a short neck like a Bottle, they
> know how to make them. When you have this Glasse, with
> Glew or Wax bind a piece of Tape or Packthread about the
> neck or top, making a little loope therewith to hang by;
> Then fill your Glasse with the purest Conduit or Spring-
> water you can get, (putting some Aqua-vitae therein to

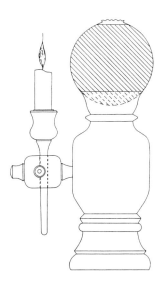

15. A Lacemaker's Lamp.

keepe it from freezing) stopping it close to keepe the dust out; having thus done, if you will use it at a Table or Bench, knock a Tenter-hooke or Naile into the Seeling or Shelfe, and with a Tape or Packthread fasten it to the loope and hang it up; (but a round stick were better to hang it on, putting it into a poast or hole in the wall, that you may let it higher or lower at your pleasure in turning the stick:) Then behind your Glasse set a Candle lighted upon the Table and you shal have a glorious light through the Glasse, and water for your purpose; [**FIG.16**].[79]

A common feature of these globes or condensers is that they consist of relatively thin glass in relation to their overall size. If the light produced by the globe of the lacemaker's lamp is compared to that delivered by an equivalent sized glass fish bowl consisting of thicker glass, the light produced by the latter is poorer in intensity, illumination and focus. White is careful to suggest that his "round Globe" should consist of "thin" glass. **FIG.16** confirms the basic intention, although the candle would have needed to be nearer to the globe in order to produce focused light. Typically, the distance of a candle flame from the surface

16. John White's version of a condenser.
White, *A Rich Cabinet, with variety of inventions*, B[r].

of a lacemaker's lamp is between 1 and 3 inches. The relative height of the "bellie" of the globe to the candle flame would have been the means of creating an appropriate angle and "throw" of light. The relationship between the flame and the "bellie" would have needed adjustment to keep the light on the book. White refers to this condition when he says "you may let it higher or lower at your pleasure in turning the stick".

Most of the evidence so far considered dealing with water filled vessels as lenses occurs on a relatively domestic scale. However, the principles to which Platte refers were applied to stronger light sources in the form of torches or lanterns and larger glass vessels were capable of producing greater intensity and illumination. Larger condensers appear to be suggested by the description given by John Rovenzon:

> For such of the workes as require light to worke by in the night, being distant from the places where the Furnaces are, there is a new-deuised luminary of glasse, or glasses filled with water, & a candle placed to giue light through it, which giueth a very great light a great distance off, with small charge; and may be conuerted to excellent vse, being placed in high places, in crosse-wayes, and streets of Citties and Townes, to the sauing of lanthorne, and candle-light, and the auoyding of inconueniences happening by darknesse.[80]

Although the light source in this instance is still the candle, it does seem that the "glasses filled with water" need to be larger than the ones so far considered, if the intended application is to take place in the street.[81] Rovenzon's reference to "the sauing of lanthorne, and candle-light" seems to refer to the notion that one candle or lantern could be placed in the centre of a number of symmetrically arranged globes "placed in high places" in order to light each street of the "cross-wayes". This is not a fanciful suggestion if later lacemaker's practice is considered. The lacemaker's lamp was sometimes arranged in a group of four such lamps known as a "candle block" or "flash".[82] The wooden stems or bases of the individual lamps were secured to the top of a wooden stool. A candle was placed in the middle of the four globes and the work of four lacemakers, sitting around the "candle block" could be illuminated. In some instances it was possible to tilt the wooden stem holding the globe in order to direct the light on to the lacemaker's work [**FIG.17**]. The illumination produced by Rovenzon's device would have been greater if the light source had been a lantern or torch.[83] Such an elaboration took place at the nuptials of Cosimo I and Eleanora of Toledo in Florence in 1539. Vasari records the following:

Appresso ordinò con molto ingegno una lanterna di
legname a uso d'arco dietro a tutti i casamenti, con un sole
alto un braccio, fatto con una palla di cristallo piena
d'acqua stillata, dietro la quale erano due torchi accesi, che
la facevano in modo risplendre, che ella rendeva luminoso
il cielo della scena e la prospettiva in guisa, che pareva
veramente il sole vivo e naturale; e questo sole, dico,
avendo intorno un ornamento di razzi d'oro che coprivano
la cortina, era di mano in mano per via d'un arganetto
tirato con sì fatt'ordine, che a principio della comedia
pareva che si levasse il sole, e che salito infino al mezzo
dell'arco scendesse in guisa, che al fine della comedia
entrasse sotto e tramontasse.[84]

(Nearby he set up with great ingenuity a lantern of timber
by means of an arc [or arch] behind all the appartments,
with a sun above, a braccio across, made with a crystal
sphere filled with distilled water, behind which two torches
were lighted which somehow made it glow so that it
rendered the sky luminous of the scene and the stage
picture in such a way that it appeared to be truly the living,
natural sun; and this sun, I say, having round about a
decoration of golden rays which covered the curtain was
drawn little by little by means of a winch so that at the
begining of the performance it appeared that the sun rose,
and that having finally climbed to the middle of the arc, it
descended in the same way, that at the end of the play it
entered underneath the set.)

The description seems to suggest that the lantern consists of a
wooden frame or cradle that holds two torches and the crystal sphere in
a fixed relationship. The cradle is set just behind the arc or arch and
presumably placed on a track of a circumference which is effectively the
same as the arc or arch. A winch manoeuvres the cradle from the base of
the arc or arch, over the top and back down the other side. One winch,
if suitably geared, could have moved the whole cradle. If the winch was
not geared then two winches may have been necessary: one to pull the
cradle up to the top of the arch and another to control the descent. The
size of the crystal sphere is recorded as a "braccio" across, which is a
measurement of just under two feet.[85] This globe represents a
considerable difference of scale to the ones considered earlier. The
flickering flames of the two torches seem to have provided greater
strength as the light source and the effect is likely to have been one of

shimmering radiance rather than still, focused light as produced by the relatively constant candle flame of the lacemaker's lamp. The effect of this sphere representing the sun is enhanced by "avendo intorno un ornamento di razzi d'oro che coprivano la cortina..." (having round about a decoration of golden rays which covered the curtain...). Presumably the curtain was in some way attached to the frame of the globe in order that the globe and the "razzi d'oro" could move together. Perhaps the "razzi d'oro" were capable of reflecting light in the same way as those in Furtenbach's "Glory box". The idea of decorative rays or beams to support and complete the light effect produced by a condenser is suggested by the list of properties of the Lincoln Cordwainers and their *pageant of Bethelem*:

> Item a great hed gildyd sett w^t vii Beamez & vii glassez for
> y^e sam And on long beame for y^e mouthe of y^e said hed
> Item iij^{re} greatt stars for y^e sam w^t iij^{re} glassez And a cord
> for y^e sam steris [86]

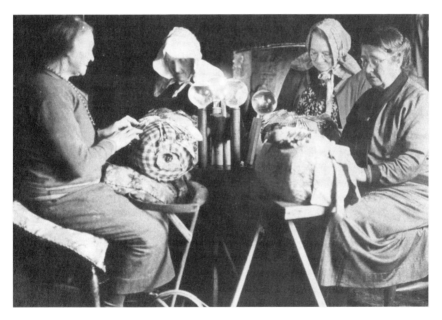

17. Lacemaker's work illuminated by the "candle block".
Blaise Castle House Museum, reg.no.TD.1940.
Courtesy of City of Bristol Museum & Art Gallery.

It seems likely that the purpose of the "vii glassez" was concerned with contributing to the effect of the "vii Beamez" which seem to have been an integral part of the "great hed". The function of the "vii glassez" seems to be concerned with the production of light that is intended to coincide with the "vii Beamez" or produce sufficient illumination to be reflected by the "vii Beamez". The assumption to be made is that the "great hed" is effectively a two-dimensional representation consisting of "vii Beamez" painted or fashioned with reflective material to contribute to the light produced by the "vii glassez". The "vii glassez" were presumably filled with liquid and lit from behind. Each of the "vii glassez" would have been positioned opposite appropriate holes at the narrow ends of the "vii Beamez" towards the centre of the "great hed". Candles, lanterns or torches may have produced the light source. Like the "gret hed" the "iij^re greatt stars" seem to have been large, two dimensional, painted or gilded stars, possibly with radiating points or beams and openings at their centres to accommodate the "iij^re glassez". If the *pageant of Bethelem* centred around a nativity scene, then the light of the "iij^re grett stars" would perhaps have needed to appear or disappear or even change position. The "cord for ye sam steris" seems to have been the means of alligning the "iij^re glassez" with holes at the centre of the "iij^re greatt stars". Whether the cord pulled the "iij^re greatt stars" or the "iij^re glassez" into their respective positions is not clear. Presumably the "iij^re greatt stars" might have been more manipulable than "iij^re glassez" filled with liquid.

A description of a French banquet contained in *Hall's Chronicles* records that "the roofe was set full of starres gilt furnished with glasses betweene the fretes:".[87] It is possible that the glasses were intended to reflect light from below in the hall, although it is equally possible that the "stars" were intended to emit light and may have done so in the manner suggested by the accounts of the Lincoln Cordwainers.

The principal means of achieving focus and direction of light with condensers depends upon the height and distance of the flame relative to the "bellie" of the globe. Vertical down light is suggested by the Serlio recipe referred to earlier in which a piece of burning camphor, placed in water, is lit by a candle from below. The burning camphor as the light source was presumably intensified through the base of the glass vessel. Another example of the use of vertical down light is given in *The Dialogues of Leoni di Somi* as part of a description concerning a pastoral feast:

> still greater splendour was provided by several great globes
> filled with water, cleverly set in the middle of each archway.

Above these, lamps had been placed in such number that each arch seemed lit up by a blazing sun. Indeed, it seemed brighter than at high noon.[88]

Again, the use of "great globes" implies vessels of a dimension greater than those used in lacemaker's lamps and may have been as large as the one used by Aristotle San Gallo.

Lenses and reflectors are separately capable of producing light of greater intensity and illumination. If lenses and reflectors are used in conjunction, then even greater luminosity is possible. Serlio was well aware of such technique:

> But if you need a great light to show more then the rest, then set a torch behind, [a glass vessel filled with coloured water] and behind the torch a bright Bason; the brightnes whereof will shew like the beames of the Sunne.[89]

It is clear that the descriptions of light required by stage directions appear similar to the effects described by eye-witnesses and other writers on the production of light. The need for "a marvellous splendour of light", "a great light" and "a great brightness" as expressed by stage directions is not essentially different from the descriptions of light produced by various vessels. Platte's descriptions of his "round & double Glasse" lamp suggests that the device "will give a great and wonderfull light,...".[90] Furtenbach, in translation, suggests that the "powerful light" of his "Glory Box" would create "great wonder by its shimmering... a shimmering and shining splendor that the man who looks at it too closely would lose his sight.".[91] The light produced by the "Glasse with a round bellie" belonging to the jeweller of Platte's acquaintance is described as a "glittering light".[92] White refers to the light produced by his condenser as a "glorious light".[93] Rovenzon in his account of the condenser describes the emergent light as "a very great light".[94] The point concerning these descriptions is that they are apparently as vague as the requirements of the stage directions. This should be not too surprising given the absence of an appropriate technical vocabulary and/or the technical means of measuring light. Then, as now, light as perceived by the onlooker is a relative phenomenon. Even though a late twentieth-century person may have experienced greater extremities of artificial levels of light than a medieval counterpart, he or she would still need relative terms to describe observed light. The witness of today may still describe lighting in a production as "great lighting" or "ingenious lighting effects".

Although the terms are similar, the meaning is clearly different. Lighting in the theatre of today tends to make use of specially designed lanterns with a power consumption typically between 500 and 3,000 watts. The witness who observes such power is aware of this capacity when he or she describes "great lighting". If modern electrical ability to produce artificial light determines the darkness/light scale, it would easily subsume another scale of that determined by flame.

If the "sun" referred to in the *Passio Domini* of the *Cornish Ordinalia* was a light source, then a form of condenser might have been used. The removal of a flame or the covering of the globe might have fulfilled the requirement of the direction. Given the significance of the baptism of Constantine in *The Life of Saint Meriasek* the "marvellous splendour of light" would presumably need to fall on Constantine as a symbolic gesture. The technique as described by the Revello direction with the basin as a reflector seems an appropriate means of creating the necessary light, particularly if a relevant amount of space was available. Similarly, the "great light" required by the Bourges directions may well indicate the use of reflectors since the light is presumably required to fall upon St.Peter and St.Paul. The apostles would have been able to "perform" their "amazed" response to the reflected light. The "great brightness" required to accompany the *Resurrection* at Mons and the tombstone "great light" of the *Second Maiden's Tragedy* are effects likely to have employed lanterns. The effect could have been intensified if the respective tombs were lined with reflective material. The effects required at such moments seem to require relatively constant light. Flickering torches would not have produced this quality. If light sources such as Platte's "halfe Lanterne" with "steele Looking-glasses" or either version of Porta's "Amphitheatrical Glass" were used, then the effect may have been further intensified. It is this latter type of light source which might be offered as a possible means of fulfilling the needs of the stage direction in the Chester Cooks' *Harrowing of Hell* play. This lantern seems to satisfy the intensity demand as permitted by the relatively confined space of a pageant vehicle positioned in a Chester street. Such an embellished lantern might also have qualified as a "cunning" or "ingenious device".

CHAPTER 5

Hell Mouth and the Dragon

A<small>LTHOUGH</small> there are a number of references to fired projectiles such as fireballs, fire spears and fire arrows for celebratory purposes,[1] the same items are not recorded in stage directions in plays. The principal pyrotechnic effect referred to by stage directions is flame itself. Other than projected flame to simulate effects like lightning or devils casting fire, the main projected fire effects are those from animal heads such as Hell mouth and dragons.[2]

Two stage directions concerning *The Life of Saint Meriasek*, one of which was referred to in **CHAPTER 1**, record the following "stage management" awareness:

[her y dragon aredy in ye place

[her a gonn yn y dragon ys mouthe aredy & fyr[3]

The content of the play is woven out of three separate stories concerning the legend of Meriasek, the legend of Saint Silvester and Constantine and the story of the Virgin's rescue of the *filius mulieris*. The scene is set in Italy where two heathen dukes become the intended prey of a huge dragon. Earlier in the play Constantine has been converted and it is this process which is regarded by the heathen Bishop of Pola to be the cause and continuing reason for the existence of the dragon. The dukes escape to Constantine and promise to become Christians if he can kill the dragon. It is Pope Silvester, encouraged by Saint Peter, who finally vanquishes the dragon and brings about the baptism of the two dukes.

Clearly the effect sought is one of the dragon breathing fire and the "gonn" appears to be the means by which fire is projected. Whether the "fyr" indicated by the direction is that projected from the "gonn" or a separate source is not clear. Interpretation of the phrase "& fyr" and its function is therefore important in relation to the involved pyrotechnic technique. Use of the word "gonn" does not seem to indicate a purpose as that of projecting a ball or bullet.[4] If the "gonn" is regarded as a tube of wood or metal then different effects would have been possible. Filled with gunpowder, such a tube would be capable of ejecting a stream of sparks in much the same way as considered in **CHAPTER 2** in Bate's "Fire club" or Babington's "rockets for the ground". If the "gonn" was used in this way then a separate fire source would not have been necessary to create the effect; a piece of match would be sufficient to ignite the gunpowder. Alternatively, the "gonn" may have been filled with an incendiary mixture similar in effect to that used by the devil in *Il quaderno di segreti...*. Such a mixture is given in a Berlin MS circa 1425-50:

> Wilt du machen ain fliegends für das fert in die höchin vnd verbrennt was es begrifft, so nim ain tail colofonia das ist kriechisch hartz vnd ij. tail lebendigs schwebels vnd iij. tail salniter, das rib alles gar klein vnd rib es dann mit ainem linsatöl oder loröl das es darinn zergang vnd werd als ain confect vnd tu das in ain aichin ror das lang sy vnd zünd es an vnd blas in das ror, so fert es wohin du das ror kerst vnd verwüst vnd verbrennt alles das es ankumpt.[5]
> (If you will make a flying fire which rises above and burns what it encounters, take one part of colophonium, that is Greek resin [rosin], two parts of native sulphur and three parts of saltpeter. Rub all small and then rub it with one of linseed oil or laurel oil till it is taken up and becomes like a paste. And put this in a long bronze tube and kindle it and blow into the tube, when it goes to wherever you turn the tube and destroys and burns up everything it meets.).

This sort of incendiary mixture would need to have been "kindled" in the same way as the sulphur/aqua ardens mixture employed by the devil in *Il quaderno di segreti...* i.e. a separate fire source such as burning coal would need to be provided. In this event the phrase "& fyr" in the *Saint Meriasek* stage direction may refer to a coal fire in a brazier or fire pan. Although similar in materials and technique to that suggested earlier in *Il quaderno di segreti...*, the scale of the effect appears to be greater than that achieved by the devil using sulphur and aqua ardens. The size of the dragon and thus the scale of the effect required is indicated by a further stage direction at l.3949:

[sum of ye soudrys y sowlyd
(Some of the soldiers swallowed).[6]

The implication involved here is that the soldiers are swallowed through the open mouth of the dragon which is large enough to fulfil such a requirement.[7] The resultant flame or sparks need to be commensurate with that scale. A mouth of some four or five feet in height seems possible. If the mouth was larger than this then more than one "gonn" may have been necessary to achieve the effect, particularly if the "gonn" needed to be positioned far enough back in the mouth so as not to reveal to the audience the source of the effect or the method of its production. Given that the mouth of the dragon needs to be large enough to consume at least two soldiers, it is also possible that a person to produce the effects may have been positioned in the dragon. The ability to blow an incendiary mixture through a tube or tubes over coals in order to project flame seems possible and likely. Evidence of the development of this principle is to be found in nineteenth-century accounts where forge bellows blow lycopodium dust over fires contained in braziers.[8]

Stage directions concerning the "dragon" and the "gonn" in *The Life of Saint Meriasek* are of additional interest in that they refer to preparation of the effects. These directions clearly refer to theatrical artifice. Similar pretence is referred to by the direction concerning the "huge dragon", referred to in **CHAPTER 1**, in the Iranzo household in 1461. Not only did the dragon breathe "huge flames" but it ejected the boys who were soaked in "aquardiente" and "seemed that they were really being burned up in flames".[9]

The issue concerning the presence of an operator inside a dragon's head is referred to by the following account in the *Drapers' Repertory* for June 1541, concerning the *Midsummer Shows* in London:

3s.8d. for a gallon of 'aqua vitae' to burn in the dragon's mouth; 16d. to him that kept fire in the dragon's mouth:[10]

This illuminating account is important not only in its own right, but also in its corroborative value to the accounts of the Coventry Drapers in respect of maintenance of their hell mouth and its fire. Is the person "that kept fire" stationed inside the "dragon's mouth" or does he merely have access? If keeping the fire deals with maintenance, the function of "him that kept fire" is likely to have been concerned with replenishment of fuel and its effective use. In the event that fire is projected out of the "dragon's mouth" then "him that kept fire" is likely to have been the operator of the effect. There seems little point in having employed a person to keep the fire if he was not also concerned with the production of an effect. The relationship between the "'aqua vitae' to burn" and the "kept fire" is more difficult to determine. If the burning "aqua vitae" is synonymous with the "fire" in the "dragon's mouth" then the resultant flame would be almost colourless and invisible and once ignited would require little keeping or maintenance. The purpose of such burning "aqua vitae" is likely to have been theatrically ineffective unless its function was to create flame produced by the interaction of other elements, salts or powders. If this is the case then the business of keeping the fire would involve the production of flame other than that simply produced by "aqua vitae". In this event the technique of blowing a pyrotechnic mixture containing aqua vitae and some other element or salt, such as those described in *Il quaderno di segreti...* or the Berlin MS, over a flame produced by "aqua vitae" may have been involved. It is possible that the "aqua vitae" could be blown through a tube over a fire of aqua vitae but the resultant flame would be virtually invisible. One inference to be drawn from this information is that the "fire" may have been fuelled by something other than the "aqua vitae", such as coal or tow, and that the "aqua vitae" was used discretely or as part of a mixture with an element or salt to create a projected and visible flame effect.

References to dragons and other beasts casting out fire "continually", as indicated in **CHAPTER 1** for preparations of the Coronation of Henry VII's Queen Elizabeth of York in 1487, the coronation procession of Edward VI and the coronation celebrations for Anne Boleyn in 1533, suggest techniques that enable replenishment of fuel. The thirty or forty goose quills filled with sulphur and aqua ardens used by devils in *Il quaderno di segreti...* suggest a means of projecting fire over an extended time. Larger tubes containing incendiary mixtures and blown over fire may have been involved in these larger scale effects. The use of such technique implies the presence of an operator inside the heads of the beasts.

The business of keeping fire at the dragon's mouth is echoed and corroborated by reference to keeping fire at Hell mouth.[11] In the Bourges Parade of 1536 account is made of "a great serpent whistling and spitting fire from throat, nostrils, and eyes."[12] A similar effect is indicated in the Hell mouth of the Rouen *Nativity* play in 1474 when "flames of fire are thrown out from the nostrils, the eyes, and the ears".[13]

Between Hell's tower and limbo in the Paris *Resurrection* of 1419 was the pit of hell from which "shall come forth flaming sulphur,...".[14] In the *Anglo-Norman Adam* a stage direction informs: "et in eo facient fumum magnum ex[s]urgere," (and in Hell they shall make a great smoke arise,).[15] The sixteenth-century records at Coventry concerning the Cappers and their play of *The Resurrection and Descent into Hell* and the Drapers and their pageant of *Doomsday* refer to their respective Hell mouth properties.[16] Payments exist in the accounts of both guilds towards the building, refurbishment and maintenance of Hell mouth.[17]

However, there is one type of payment exclusive to the Drapers that concerns the keeping of fire at Hell mouth. A typical entry in the *Drapers' Accounts* records: "payd for kepyng of fyer at hell mothe iiijd.".[18] A separate function to keeping the fire is identified as that of "kepyng of hell movthe".[19] Sometimes such items refer to "kepyng of hell mowthe & the fyer".[20] One reference is made to "kepyng of the fyers". [21] Detailed information concerning the location, duration and number of performances given by the Drapers' guild is not extant. It is not clear whether references to "the fyer" indicate one or more than one performance. The single reference to "fyers" suggests more than one performance and different locations. Four pence seems to be the going-rate for "kepyng" whether this is determined by the singular or plural reference. A deduction made from the *Drapers' Accounts* is that three performances were held because of payments usually made to Robert Crow for making and setting on fire "iij worldes".[22]

These "worldes" are generally regarded as globes that represent the world.[23] If this is the case then an immediate assumption is that they consisted of lightweight material, such as paper, which was simply set on fire. Some of the later firework writers suggest methods and materials for constructing pyrotechnic globes. Norton gives details of a globe to be made along with two dragons on a line. He says: "These Draggons and Globes may be framed with Arches and Circles of thinn Latten [thin metal plate], fastened with small lynes, vntill the Body thereof bee framed to your minde" [**FIG.18**].[24] Babington also describes the construction of a sphere to signify the earth with the "Sunne" and the "Moone" represented in their respective positions [**FIG.19**].[25] In these examples the globes are fired by rockets, serpents or breakers placed around the globes in line with the equator or meridians. Jones describes two methods of making "Fire Globes", both of which are made of wood. Holes are drilled into the globes to take firework "cases" which are leadered [use of quickmatch] to adjacent ones to conduct the fire around the globes.[26] It is unclear whether the "worldes" of the Coventry Drapers were as developed as those in the recipes of firework writers.

The "worldes" appear to have been carried between performances and may possibly have operated as a conflagatory climax to the play of *Doomsday*. If three performances of the Drapers' pageant were held does this indicate the "kepyng" of three fires? The records do not refer to the transport of fire or Hell mouth between performances. It seems likely that Hell mouth was a separate structure to the pagent and carried independently between performances since payments in the respective *Drapers' Accounts* treat Hell mouth as a separate entity.[27] Some preparation of the fire at each performance would have been necessary, as at Mons,[28] if the fuel was coal, wood or tow. Should a fossil fuel have been used, the fire would need to have been contained in braziers or fire pans.

18. Norton's globe of "thin Latten, fastened with small lynes". He does
not refer to the reversed "E".
Norton, *The Gvnner*, before p.153.

The size of the Coventry Drapers' Hell mouth is not recorded, but it must have been large enough to take the fire, the person who kept Hell mouth, the person who kept the fire (if this was a different person to the one who kept Hell mouth), and the two devils referred to in the accounts.[29] The presence of a contained fire in Hell mouth is unlikely to have made much theatrical impact whether it was visible to or hidden from the audience.[30] Additions to the fire would have been necessary in order to create more spectacular light, flame or smoke. In the case of the Drapers' Hell mouth it seems that rosin might have been the appropriate material since payments for it occur in nearly all the relevant *Drapers' Accounts*.[31] The rosin in powdered form may have been simply sprinkled on to the fire by the two devils or "hym that kepte the

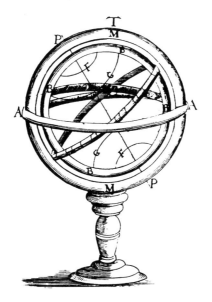

19. Babington's "sphere, with divers circles, some moveable, others fixed".
"M The fixed Meridian.
A A The Horizon.
E E The Equinoctiall.
E E [F F] The Eclipticke with the Sunne and Moone placed round.
P P The poles or axeltree about which all the inner circles move.".
Babington, *Pyrotechnia*, before p.45.

85

fyer".[32] In which case a cloud of flame and smoke would have been created instantly. It is also possible that projected flame might have been created by blowing the powdered rosin through a tube and over the fire. The technique is the same as that offered by Porta in **CHAPTER 3** and referred to here by Albertus Magnus:

> If thou shalt blow the herb called Colophonia, [or] Greek Pitch, beaten very small, upon the flame of the candle which a man holdeth in his hand, it augmenteth marvellously the fire, and lifteth up the flame unto the house roof. [33]

The presence of an operator to maintain or develop the fire source is possibly a common feature of the examples so far considered. However, smaller-scale dragons which created fire without the aid of an operator did so by different means. The stage direction, referred to in **CHAPTER 1**, in Robert Greene's *Friar Bacon and Friar Bungay* written between 1589 and 1592 indicates the following: "Heere Bungay coniures and the tree appeares with the dragon shooting fire.".[34] The content of the stage direction arises because Friar Bungay is challenged by Vandermast, a doctor, to determine which of the spirits of pyromancy or geomancy are most potent. The magical appearance of the tree and the dragon "That watcht the garden cald Hesperides, Subdued and wonne by conquering Hercules" is conjured to proove Bungay's assertion that geomancy is the stronger force.

If the dragon involved here is not large enough to conceal a pyrotechnic operator, and this seems likely given that the play was performed at the Rose and that the dragon may be positioned in or around the tree, then a seemingly independent means of "shooting fire" would need to be created. It may be inferred from the direction that both the "tree" and the "dragon" make an "appearance" and it has been suggested that they do so via a trap door on stage.[35] Whatever form of "appearance" occurs, operation of the "shooting fire" effect needs to be timed to take place on or just before the "appearance". This sort of effect points to the use of a firework of some kind; a "rocket for the ground" would be capable of producing the effect.

The record cited in **CHAPTER 1** from the *Revels Accounts* for 1552-3 indicates a different method of creating fire in a dragon's mouth. This account does not provide evidence of projected fire from the "dragon's mowthe" but it certainly does indicate fire in the mouth. The "dragon's head" is recorded separately from the "dragon's mowthe" which appears to be made out of metal plate. The function of the plate is presumably to protect the head from the fire created by the "stoppes". Tow (or oakum) is the fuel involved for "stoppes" appears to be the same kindling material as that encountered by Maximilla in the *Cornish Ordinalia*.[36] The burning "stoppes" seem to have been used in "ij fyer boxes", although all six of the plated boxes recorded may have been used to contain fire and strategically placed in the mouth, nostrils or eyes of the "dragon's head". Four of the boxes receive "trymmyng" and this may simply refer to the process of making good or alternatively to the act of decorating in order to disguise function. The "iiij[or] small cheines of yerne" may have been used to hang the "boxes with plate" inside the mouth or to create a moveable jaw. The "ynglish wier" seems to have been the means of tying constructional joints. Whether the "dragons head" was large enough to conceal an operator is unclear. If the fire was not projected but simply contained in the mouth, then an operator need not have been present; the effect may not have needed attention since the amount of plate involved would have provided adequate safety and protection. The fire effects so far considered appear to have been conducted at ground or stage level. However, attempts to simulate flying dragons are also recorded. It seems that one of the pyrotechnic techniques involved is that alluded to in respect of the dragon in *Friar Bacon and Friar Bungay*. Fireworks, referred to as "rockets for the ground" by Bate and Babington, are carefully implanted in the dragon's body and the whole construction is devised in such a way as to be propelled on a taut wire stretched between two strategic points.[37] This technique possibly explains the description of the fiery-flying dragon that purportedly flew over the meeting between Francis I of France and Henry VIII of England at the Field of the Cloth of Gold. Some doubt exists as to the validity of this explanation given the supposed height and distance of the journey. The progression of the dragon, albeit in translation, is described as that of "an undulating motion". This sort of movement would not be untypical of a weighted dragon being propelled or pulled over a taught wire/rope of some distance. The relative amount of "slack" in the wire/rope would increase with a greater distance between the anchor points, thus giving rise to a movement quality that may be described as "undulating". However, the graphic use of a dragon of this sort appears to be recorded in the eye-witness account, referred to in **CHAPTER 1**, concerning "a showe of fireworks" at Warwick during one of the Progresses of Elizabeth in 1572 **[APPENDIX 1A]**. The wire upon which the dragon seemingly travelled was fixed at one end "upon the fort" and the other end to some unspecified point. The dragon was both propelled and controlled upon the line. The technique of flying such representations is documented by

Norton, Bate [**FIG.20**] and Babington [**FIG.21**].[38] Instructions of the kind "How to make a Dragon, or any other creature to run on the line, by the help of fire," or "How to represent S.George fighting with a Dragon in fire on the Line," are typical of the ingenuity of these writers.[39] The two methods recorded by Babington and set out in **APPENDIX 4A** and **4B** refer to dragon representations of different scale. The second account informs us that the first dragon is "of a small size, of a foot in length, or thereabout;". Of the second, Babington is concerned with a dragon "of a greater magnitude, which cannot so easily bee forced with fire, in a straight line, without some artificiall help;" [**FIG.22**]. It is not obvious whether use of pasteboard in the first version would make for a heavier dragon than one employing withes covered with paper.[40] No doubt there is an optimum relationship between the size of the dragon and the propulsive force provided by the rockets. Larger rockets would not necessarily provide adequate thrust to a larger dragon – hence the need for Babington's second version. In the

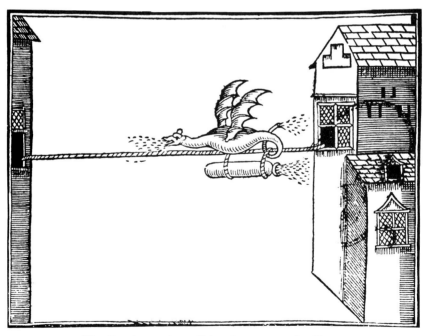

20. Bate's version of the dragon on the line.
Bate, *The Mysteryes of Natvre and Art*, p.79.

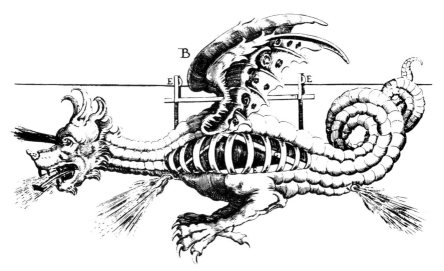

21. Babington's version of the dragon on the line.
Babington, *Pyrotechnia*, before p.37.
[APPENDIX 4A]

22. Babington's dragon of "a greater magnitude, which cannot so
easily bee forced with fire".
Babington, *Pyrotechnia*, before p.41.
[APPENDIX 4B]

first design, rockets are placed in the body of the dragon so as to propel the representation alternately forwards and backwards. The means of igniting the second rocket, for backward motion, is by installation of a small pipe "from the tayle of that rocket, to the mouth of the next, which commeth out at the belly". The pipe is both the conduit and protective casing to prevent accidental burning of the dragon.[41] Inside the tube is stouple or quickmatch to convey the fire.[42] Firing of the eyes and mouth of the dragon is made possible by creating sockets into which are placed slow mixtures, such as those used in Bate's fire clubs or stars and contained in paper tubes. These paper tubes or "coffins" are rolled upon wooden formers and glued. The composition of slow mixtures for stars varies according to the colours required.[43] Babinbgton does not suggest the same protection for the eyes and mouth of the dragon as he does the belly. Should such shielding have been necessary, a technique used elsewhere might have been applicable, namely, that of coating the eye-sockets and inside of the mouth with wet clay.[44] If, however, the purpose of the presumed dragon on the line at Warwick was to set fire to the canvas-covered fort, then no such protection would have been required, for additional firing of the head would have improved the chances of the fort being fired along with the dragon. Bate's recipe for flying dragons suggests that "the body must bee filled with divers petrars [petards], that may consume it,..."[45]

The Warwick dragon is likely to have been more the size of Babington's second dragon, given the scale of the mock battle and the fact that the dragon issued "huge flames and squibes". The means of projecting fire from the body of the dragon was through "divers hollow truncks of wood". Presumably these tubes contained gunpowder mixtures of the kind used in the rockets of the other version, although the combined effect does not seem to have been powerful enough to provide sufficient propulsive force to move the dragon along the line. The "divers small bals of fire" which are ejected "on a sudden" appear to be of the kind that are contained in roman candles of today. The principle involved in the construction of this effect is that contained in Babington's "trunck of fire" recipe [**APPENDIX 4C**]. Essentially the tube is packed with a slow mixture which in turn ignites the small canvas balls filled with star mixture.[46] At other times, "a great number of small fisgigs" are cast out. Babington acknowledges that fisgigs were sometimes called "serpents"[47] and it is known that the term was often loosely interchangeable with the word "squib". Some sources suggest differences between the "serpent" and the "squib".[48] Clearly the squibs referred to in the Warwick account were intended to create the same effect as the fisgigs indicated by Babington.

A development of the dragon-shooting-fire effect is described in an eye-witness account concerning a "playe of fyrwork" to celebrate the birthday of James I on the 19 June, 1617 [**APPENDIX 1G**]. The event took place in the outer close of the Palace of Holyroodhouse, Edinburgh. The eye-witness account is supplemented by evidence recorded in "The expenses maid upoun the fyirwarkis within the castell of Edinburgh and in the utter clois of the palace of Halyruidhous 19 June" which is contained in the *Accounts M.W.* [**APPENDIX 2B**]. Although the eye-witness account is further analysed in **CHAPTER 6**, it is the dragon device and the "playmeir" which here merit particular attention. It seems possible that the "playmeir" along with "so many fuilles with their belles, so many daunceres,..." was part of a preliminary "warm-up" activity to the main firework battle. The "playmeir casting fyr both behind and befor" was a play-mare, or hobby-horse.[49] *The Accounts M.W.* refer to the provision of the hobby-horse:

> For careing the hobby hors and the boy fra Bervick to
> Edinburgh   iiiilib. iiiis.
> ...
> For tackettis to the hobbie hors   iiis.
> ...
> To Ralf Dryden for his hobbie hors   iiiilib.[50]

Although it might be possible that these warm-up figures did not directly relate to the forthcoming battle, it is just as likely that they performed the function of a prologue. An indication of this is suggested by the hobby-horse "casting fyr both behind and befor", a mirroring, albeit in a different form, of the later behaviour of the dragon. The possibility also exists that the hobby-horse rider, "the boy fra Bervick" was dressed as St.George [Andrew] and that he too may have been a model.[51] The respective functions of these figures may be those found in dumbshows.

The presumed climax to the battle was the encounter between the dragon and St.George. The eye-witness account refers to St.Andrew as the opponent of the dragon although the *Accounts M.W.* refer to St.George in this role. Clearly, St.George as a figure is not represented and all references to him in the *Accounts M.W.* should be interpreted as ones to St.Anrew. This identification is confirmed by the eye-witness account which informs that "the Castle of Envy" possesses the badge of St.George as its emblem. The following references are taken from the *Accounts M.W.*:

For sex lynis to haill the dragoun and St.George
with   xlib. xvis.
...
To Ralf Ralinsone carver for making the dragon and
St.George   xiilib.
To him for making muldis to the plaisterers   xlib.
To a tailyeour and wrycht that wrocht with him 3 dayes
                                                   iiilib. xiis.
For a pair of gloves to St.George   viiis.
...
Item for making of St.George his speir at the fyir warkis to
him   xiis.[52]

Ralf Ralinsone was employed to create the device. The figures appear to be partially constructed from moulded plaster.[53] A tailor was engaged to costume St.Andrew and possibly work upon the dragon. Ralinsone was apparently helped by a "wrycht" to construct the respective frameworks. St.Andrew brandished his "speir" which was held in an expensive pair of gloves. In order to understand how the "sex lynis to haill the dragoun and St.George" might have been used, it

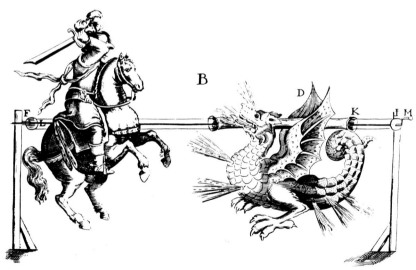

23. "S.George fighting with a Dragon in fire on the Line".
Babington, *Pyrotechnia*, before p.41.
[APPENDIX 4C]

may be helpful to refer to Babington's instructions on how to create this device [**APPENDIX 4C**]. Babington does not suggest the use of "sex lynis" to create the required action. In this design three lines are sufficient: one upon which the figures are to ride and two connected through the figures into a loop which travels over the pulleys [**FIG.23**]. If this sort of design was used at Edinburgh, the additional lines as suggested by the *Accounts M.W.* might have been used to secure retrieval by fixing a line to the back of each figure. Safety measures of this kind might be required given that the "fyrewarkmen" may not have been able to predict, with certainty, the eventual condition of the figures. The notion that St.Andrew and the dragon were conducted on this kind of line is supported by the observation that St.Andrew "met the dragon midway" and subsequently "cam home ryding". The latter action refers to St.Andrew being pulled backwards to the castle. In other respects, the dragon appears to behave as those already considered that use "rockets for the ground". In Babington's design, St.George wields a curtalaxe which is designed to contain fisgigs and lances.[54] These fireworks provide the pyrotechnic fight with the tubes of fire from the dragon. The eye-witness account informs us that St.Andrew and the dragon "foght aspace togither". It is possible, therefore, that the "speir of fyr" carried by St.Andrew was not merely in flame but it too contained fireworks in the end so that pyrotechnic battle could be engaged.[55]

Despite lavish preparation and execution of the pyrotechnic celebrations developed by the Earl of Leicester in honour of Elizabeth's visit to Kenilworth in 1575, the eye-witness accounts of Laneham and Gascoine do not contain references to dragons casting fire or being consumed by fire [**APPENDIX 1C**]. However, another document purportedly concerned with this visit needs to be considered as possible evidence. In an undated letter, attributed to the preparations of this celebration, Henry Killigrew wrote to the Earl of Leicester asking him to support a proposal from an Italian pyrotechnist for a programme of fireworks intended to be spread over three separate evenings.[56] Killigrew enclosed the Italian pyrotechnist's proposals in his letter to Leicester, indicating that two months work was envisaged and the total cost would be fifty pounds. Seven pounds had already been advanced to the pyrotechnist, by Killigrew, in order to construct a fountain which was to be presented to the Queen. The proposals are set out below:

La prima sera ne'l prato.
Si faranno certi artificij doue si vedranno discorrere a torno
certi serpenti di fuoco. Il che sara cosa molto piaceuole.

Item otto o dieci pignate con inuentioni di cose marauigliose & piaceuoli
Item de le aui uiue uolare atorno ne l'aria le quali getteranno fuoco da per tutto.
Item due cani & due gatti uiui li quali artificiosamente combattranno.

La seconda sera ne'l Cortile del palazzo.
Si uedrà un fonte dal quale scorrera vino acqua & fuoco sette o ott' hore continue. Qual fonte sara cosa degna di uedere per gli suoi marauigliosi artificij quali per essere tanti si lascia di scriuere.
Item tre ruote di fuoco mirabili & odorifere, & di diuersi colori.

La terza sera nel fiume.
Si uedra un dragone grande come un bue. quale volera due o tre uolte più alto che la torre di San Paolo, e stando si alto si consumera tutto di fuoco, & indi usciran subito da tutto'l corpo cani, e gatti & uccelli li quali uoleranno, & getteranno fuoco da per tutto che sarà cosa stupendissima.
Vi sono molte altre cose in questi artificij le quali per la lor difficultà non scriuo minutamente. Io le farò tutte benissimo secondo il danaro che per le spese mi sarà mandato.[57]

([The first evening in the meadow.
There will be constructed some works of art where serpents of fire will be seen spinning round, which will be very pleasant. Item eight or ten pots [of fire] with inventions of things marvellous and pleasing. Item some life-like birds to fly around in the air, who will throw out fire in all directions. Item two life-like dogs and two cats who will be skilfully made to fight.

The second evening in the courtyard of the palace.
A fountain will be seen from which wine, water, and fire will run for seven or eight hours continuously. This fountain will be a thing worth seeing for its marvellous effects, which are too numerous to describe. Item three wonderful wheels of fire, odoriferous and of diverse colours.

The third evening on the river.
A dragon as big as an ox will be seen, which will fly two or three times higher than the tower of St.Paul's, and staying

at that height it will be wholly consumed with fire, and then suddenly there will issue from the whole of its body dogs, cats, and birds which will fly about and throw out fire everywhere, which will be a most stupendous thing. There are many other things in these works of art which because of their complexity I do not describe in minute detail. I will make them all very well indeed in proportion to the money that will be sent me for expenses.])

It is unclear whether the planned pyrotechnics detailed above found their realisation during Elizabeth's visit to Kenilworth in 1575. Doubt exists because the outlined plans do not appear to accord with the principal eye-witness accounts of Laneham and Gascoine. Allowing for the notion that these proposals were intended to promote the work of the Italian pyrotechnist and appear as pretty and magical manifestations, there is no likeness to the "terror, and vehemencie" or "great peel of guns" described by Laneham. It is most likely that the artillery contribution to these effects was controlled by gunners and not the Italian pyrotechnist. Since Ambrose Dudley, Earl of Warwick and Master of the Ordnance was responsible for the pyrotechnic celebration for Elizabeth at Warwick in 1572, it seems feasible that he was also responsible for initiating and/or controlling the artillery at the 1575 celebration at Kenilworth. Given that the Italian pyrotechnist's firework entertainment was planned to occur on three separate evenings in "ne'l prato" (the meadow), "ne'l Cortile del palazzo" (the courtyard of the palace), and "nel fuime" (on the river), some correlation is suggested although not necessarily respecting the actual chronology of events as determined by the eye-witness accounts. Had the Italian proposals been implemented, might it have been reasonable to expect that such a spectacular effect as a "A dragon as big as an ox", consumed at a height of two or three times the height of St. Paul's tower would be included in the eye-witness accounts? Even if these proposals were not enacted before Elizabeth, appropriate pyrotechnic knowledge was available to give practical existence to the plan. The means by which the dragon was to "fly" in this proposal is not specified. The height at which the dragon was to "fly" however, does seem to be exaggerated. If the "tower of St.Paul's" refers to that of St.Paul's cathedral, then the height at which the dragon was intended to "fly", as suggested earlier, was between 978 feet and 1467 feet.[58] The operation and control of a dragon on the line at this overestimated height seems improbable. Even if the operating height of this device was lower than that outlined in the proposal, a different method of creating the dragon seems likely. Unlike Babington's dragons for the line, this dragon was required to "be wholly consumed" at the culmination of its "flying" sequence. At this point dogs, cats and birds "suddenly there will issue" from the spent body.If representations of the dragon, dogs, cats and birds were intended to be recogniseable by the spectator, then the depiction would need to have been formed on a static framework creating the illusion of movement according to order and rate of firing. Fireworks moving freely in the air would not have presented a consistent three-dimensional form necessary to the identity of the recorded animals. However, two-dimensional representation would have been possible. One appropriate technique was and still is known as lance work.[59] Babington refers to the technique as follows:

> HAving considered of what largenesse you will have your letters or figures, make them of pastboard, leaving a hollow to put in small quils, (which shall be filled with a cleare and strong mixture) then put in your quils, and glue them fast in;[60]

The "quils" which are from $2^1/_2$ inches to 4 inches in length and filled with a slow mixture[61] are placed and glued around the periphery of the shaped pastboard.[62] Quickmatch is used to link and ignite the "quils" and used as leaders[63] to ignite "quils" in different parts of the depicted shape, so that it takes fire rather more quickly than if it is fired from just one place. Bate suggests that "fiends, or fearfull apparitions" are made in another manner:

> THese must bee made of the compositions for Starres, wrought upon cotton weeke dipped in *aqua vitae*, wherein camphire hath beene dissolved, and after what fashions your fancy doth most affect.[64]

Effectively this recipe is for quickmatch that needs to be shaped into the appropriate configuration and ignited to give the required image. Either of these techniques could have been used in the Italian design. Similarly, the requirement of "de le aui uiue uolare atorno ne l'aria le quali getteranno fuoco da per tutto" (some life-like birds to fly around in the air, who will throw out fire in all directions) may have consisted of one or other of these techniques. Several outlines of birds placed closely together on a frame would be ignited in rapid succession, simulating flight and igniting other fireworks, such as "golden rain"[65] to scatter fire.[66]

Extensive accounts exist of the firework celebrations to mark the marriage of Frederick and Elizabeth (*Heaven's Blessing and Earth's Joy*) in

1613.[67] The various accounts of this event, as indicated in the **INTRODUCTION**, consist of a mixture of eye-witness accounts and descriptions of intended narrative. Separation of the two forms of information in order to evaluate evidence is both important and difficult. Some lengthy "True Descriptions" are recorded by "John Taylor, the Water Poet". These accounts do indeed have a poetic quality about them which brings into question their authenticity as eye-witness accounts. An example of this kind of writing is offered by John Taylor in "A true Description" of the contribution made to the celebration by "Mr.Thomas Butler, Gunner and Servant to the King's Royall Majestie" [**CHAPTER 1**]. Saint George armed with a "burning launce", a "fiery sword" and a "burning flaming feather" in his helmet confronts the dragon:

> where, in conclusion, after a terrible and long-endured combat, with his launce he gores the hell-hound under the wing, that he presently, after most hideous roring and belching of fire, is vanquished and slaine.[68]

Although the description relates the narrative of the event, it is doubtful that the account describes what happened. The anonymous contemporary report contained in *MS B.L.Additional 70518* [**APPENDIX 1F**] refers to the same narrative: "the aforesaid knight, approchinge toward the said Castle, who shalbe first encountred, by a dragon, whome he shall sley,...". Brock suggests that "contemporary reports of this event are so lengthy and detailed, and agree so closely, as to suggest that they were based on a 'hand-out' circulated by the fire-workers responsible...".[69] Indeed, had Brock gained access to the proposal contained in *MS B.L.Additional 70518* he may have considered that his suggested "hand-out" had been found. This account deals precisely with the content found in John Taylor's descriptions but refers to it as a proposal, not as an event that has happened. The descriptions offered on behalf of the gunners John Nodes, Thomas Butler, William Bettis, John Tindall and William Fishenden seem to represent statements of intent. The possible discrepancy between such accounts and events as they happened is referred to in a letter by Mr.Chamberlain to Sir Dudley Carleton shortly after the 11th of February:

> On Thursday night [the 11th] the Fire-workes were reasonably well performed, all save the last Castle of fire, which bred most expectation, and had most devices; but, when it came to execution, had worst success.[70]

Any shortcomings in the firing of John Nodes' "pavilion", Thomas Butler's "Castle or Tower of Brummond", William Bettis' "Castle" or John Tindall's "Castle of Envie" are not mentioned in the accounts by John Taylor. An anonymous description of the firework events "upon the Thursday before the Wedding" is of a different quality to the previous ones and does seem to possess the authority of an eye-witness account:

> After this, in a most curious manner, an artificiall Fire-worke with great wonder was seene flying in the ayre, like unto a Dragon, against which another fierie vision appeared, flaming like to St.George on horsebacke, brought in by a burning Inchanter, betweene which was there fought a most strange battell continuing a quarter of an hower or more; the Dragon being vanquished, seemed to rore like thunder, and withall burst in peeces and so vanished; but the Champion, with his flaming horse, for a little time made shew of a tryumphant conquest, and so ceased.[71]

Not only does this account refer to the firework event as having happened, it also records some apparently naïve, yet telling, responses. Another "fierie vision" appeared flaming "like to St.George" and was involved in a "strange battell". These expressions of strangeness and wonder do not appear to be those of someone on the "inside" with knowledge of the event. Nor are they particularly helpful in their precision as to the various mechanisms of the effects. It does not seem that the device of St.George and the dragon is like that suggested by Babington, for the dragon "seene flying in the ayre" is an "artificiall Fire-worke". Likewise, " St. George on horsebacke" is seen as a "fierie vision...flaming". The encounter between St.George and the dragon is seen as "a most strange batell". The climax to this battle occured when the dragon "burst in peeces and so vanished;". Clearly, the figures are realised and defined in flame and the observations point towards lancework or figures depicted in quickmatch or impregnated rope. The notion that the dragon "burst in peeces and so vanished" also indicates the end of a fired sequence in lancework, impregnated rope or perhaps less likely, quickmatch. If the dragon was a three-dimensional figure fired by "rockets for the ground" then it is unlikely to have disintegrated or vanished at the end of the firing sequence.

CHAPTER 6

Royal Firework Theatre: A Postlude

IN THE second half of the sixteenth century imported pyrotechnic skill became available that enabled fire effects to form dramatic statements in their own right.[1] Such pyrotechnic and theatrical understanding found its most complete expression in the development of a form of mock battle centred on a castle which was sometimes referred to as the "fort holding". The sieging of a castle or fort is an emblematic device often found in medieval and Tudor tournaments, art and literature.[2] The representation or enactment of battles between vice and virtue often provided the symbolic, dramatic and pyrotechnic content of "fort holdings". Although earlier examples of castle sieges occur in *The Castle of Perseverance*, *Mary Magdalene* and other entertainments,[3] the form evolved by "fort holdings" depends upon the development of artillery and pyrotechnic expertise.

An account for 1556-7 from Trinity College, Cambridge indicates the basic nature and scope of the "fort holding":

> Item a shew in trinite college in ther courte of the wynninge of an holde & takinge of prisoners, with waytes trumpettes gonnes & squybbes.[4]

In the event that good triumphs over evil, the assumption involved here is that the "wynninge" was carried out by the virtuous and defence of the "holde" was conducted by the eventual "prisoners". A narrative, albeit a simple one, is likely to have provided justification and order of firing of "gonnes & squybbes". Similarly, the contribution of the "waytes" and "trumpettes" is also likely to have indicated punctuation of

99

the attack upon and defence of the "holde". Given the limited space in which the event took place the "gonnes" are likely to have provided sound but not projectiles. The "squybbes", however, are likely to have been thrown at and from the "holde".

A similar arrangement is recorded at York in the 1554-5 accounts as "A sham fight on Shrove Tuesday" and was conducted by "the honest yong men of this Citie".[5] The show consisted of "one sorte in defendyng a fort and thother in makyng thassaults" and was watched by "my Lord Mayour and Aldermen and wholle Comonaltye of this Citie...". The "yong men of this Citie" were seemingly paid "tenne shillyngs" for "dyvisyng and preparyng the same".

One of the most interestingly documented pyrotechnic battles is that employed at the baptism celebrations of James I in 1566. Only a meagre amount of eye-witness evidence exists for this event; the bulk of information consists of payments recorded in *The Accounts*[6] [**APPENDIX 2A**]. The content of these accounts comprises details of payments concerning people involved in the preparation and execution of the celebration together with aspects of organisation and ingredients for the firework drama.

The baptism of James I and the accompanying celebrations took place in Stirling between 17th and 19th December, 1566:

> Vpoun the nyntene day, the quenis majestie maid ane bankett to the saidis ambassatouris and lordis, in ane verry diligate fassoune at evin; thair wes masry and playing in all sortis, befoir supper; than ane fort haldin in Striueling besyid the kirk-yaird, quhairin wes artailzerie, schote fyre ballis, fyre speris, and all vtheris thingis plesand for the sicht of man;[7]

The description contained in this account provides little information concerning the nature of the "fort holding". Reference to "artailzerie, schote fyre ballis, fyre speris, and all vtheris thingis plesand for the sicht of man" affords only a hint of what took place. [**FIG.24**].[8] However, *The Accounts* are of considerable assistance in helping to illuminate the eye-witness account and further clarify and confirm features of the action.

The siege and defence of the fort was carried out by soldiers dressed in appropriate costume as "lansknychtis" (lance knights), "morres" (mores), "contrefait devillis" (counterfeit devils) and "hieland wyld men" (highland wild men). Johnne Chisholme, "comptrollar of the artailyerye" was the principal organiser of the event. Seven soldiers or

100

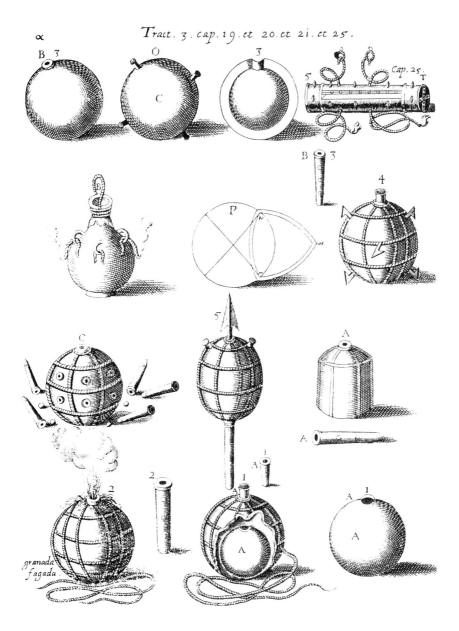

24. Some forms of fire ball showing the means of binding the ball and shape of templates to cut the required canvas. Norton, *The Gvnner*, before p.155.

"ordinars" under the leadership of James Hector and Charles Bourdeous, "principall ordinaris", comprised the team who were responsible for the "executioun of the forth asseigeing and handilling of fyrework". These men, along with others, were engaged for several weeks in Leith in the preparation and manufacture of fireworks and combustible items.[9] In all, nineteen costumed men conducted the battle. It is not clear from *The Accounts* whether the nine men previously mentioned existed in addition or were subsumed under the nineteen costumed men.

Combustible items other than fireworks were made in Leith and included "cransis", "tourteantis" and "flambeantis". Of these objects, perhaps the "cransis" are the least difficult to identify. *The Accounts* inform us that a tailor from Leith was paid for "making and sewing of the fyre cransis...". The several payments for canvas in *The Accounts* suggest the material worked upon by the tailor. The purpose of the "cransis" was to show "lycht in the forth" when hung from "gibettis" of "double fir spars". If these objects were to burn for sometime in order to give light, packing of some sort would seem to have been necessary under the outer canvas wrapping. Such material is suggested by reference in *The Accounts* to "twa men for fetching furth of the castell of sum auld towis..." together with the record that Johnne Lamy and Henry Scherar, "marinellis", were engaged from the 10th December to the 13th December "in heitting pik (pitch) and tar, oppinning out towis (rope) and dipping of nummer of toureantis and cransis...". The dipping of the "cransis" took place in "ane borrowit tar trough quhairin was tarrit the cransis". The "cransis" were garlands or wreaths presumably formed by wreathing the strands of the opened-out rope around a former, covered in canvas and dipped in tar.

The identity of the "tourteantis" is less clear. Anna J.Mill transcribes "tourteantis" as "tourtrantis".[10] Neither of the forms of this word exists in the appropriate dictionaries, although "tour" is included as "turf, sod, peat"[11] and "trant" as "to act as a carrier".[12] The possibility exists that this is another type of wreath or torch consisting of turf-like material, possibly moss and dipped in pitch. The *O.E.D.* offers "tortis" as "A twisted chain; a wreath.".[13] Although the final identity of the "tourteantis" is unclear, it seems that they were smaller than the "cransis" since payment is made "for the len (loan) of ane pik pot xv dayis quhairin was made the tourteantis ijs.". Additionally, they were small enough to be packed along with the fireworks into "thre tuyme (empty) puncheouns quhairin was pakkit the maist pairt of the small fyreworkis and tourteantis send out of Leyth to Stirviling.".

Payment for "flambeantis" is recorded in *The Accounts* as follows:

> Item for xvij plaittis of quhit yron quhairof was maid fyve
> flambeantis   xix s. x d.

A separate payment of xvj s. is made for "making of the saidis fyve
flambeantis of quhit yron". Mill transcribes "flambeantis" as
"flambrantis". Like the "cransis" and "tourteantis" neither of these
words are recorded in the appropriate dictionaries. It seems that the
"flambeantis" are required to be in flame yet not consumed since they
are made of white iron. An account concerning the fifteenth-century
Whitsuntide Paris *Resurrection* play may point to an explanation:

> Here shall descend a fiery brand (**brandon de feu**) from
> Paradise that shall be round like a circle and shall be all
> soaked in burning spirit (**eaue vive**), and in the middle of
> this blazing circle should be a pigeon of white metal (**fer
> blanc**) surrounded by fire which does not burn it. And all
> round the circle should be tongues of fire (**langues
> ardentes**) which should fall on Our Lady, on the women,
> on the apostles and disciples.[14]

Given the nature and purpose of the baptismal celebrations for James
I it seems possible that some emblematic device, such as a coat of arms,
was created out of the plates of iron leaving the rest of the device to
burn as suggested above.[15]

The particular order or sequence of incident in the presentation is
not known, although the style of the piece is indicated by a mixture of
animate and inanimate representations. Whether these portrayals were
symbolic or allegorical is similarly not clear, although inferences may be
made from the choice of costumed dramatis personae recorded in *The
Accounts*:

> *Item* for twenty aucht gaitt skynnis quhairof was maid four
> hieland wyld mens cleithingis from heid to fute, price of
> the peice iijs., summa v li. xij s.
> ...
> All this bougrem abone writtin maid in fyftein cleithingis,
> to wit four lansknychtis, four for morres, four for horsmen
> and thre for contrefait devillis, quhilkis cleithingis war
> distributit to fyftein soldiouris of the companyes quha
> combattit within and without the forth togidder with the
> foirsaidis hieland men having the executioun of the
> fyreworkis in thair handis

103

squibbes and balles of fyre" may not have been in uniform/costume. The "balles of fyre" appear to have been thrown by hand and also fired by chambers. At least two kinds of "balles of fyre" appear to have been employed: one consisting of a basic gunpowder mixture capable of being projected "over the Castell, and into the myds of the Towne" and no doubt responsible for the kind of damage which "made a hole as big as a man's head"; and secondly one which "falling into the ryver Aven, wold for a tyme lye still, and than agayn rise and flye abrode, casting furth many flashes and flambes". The second of these fire balls may well have contained "rockets for the ground" [**FIG.25**].

The description given in the Warwick account concerning the fire ball that remained still upon the water and suddenly rose into action again is similar to the description given by Gascoine in his *Princely Pleasures at Kenelworth Castle, 1575*.[21] Although there is no evidence of the Kenilworth firework entertainments consisting of narrative or symbolic content, some of the pyrotechnic effects and techniques were similar.[22] [**APPENDIX 1C**]. The essential difference to note here is that the fireworks at Kenilworth operated under water rather than on the water,

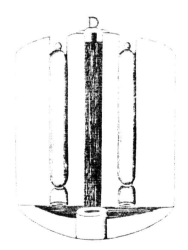

25. A cylindrical fire ball containing stickless rockets.
"This ball may bee made somewhat cillindricall, in regard of the length of the rockets to be placed in it, as you have made this for to cast forth once, so you may make another to cast forth twise, as I have formerly shewed you for the water ball. The forme is represented in the 16 Figure, by the letter D.".
Babington, *Pyrotechnia*, before p.63.

as at Warwick. Fire balls required to operate on the water were made of wood or canvas that was sealed using rosin, pitch and tallow. Underwater fire balls, as indicated earlier, were usually made of canvas and ballasted with lead. Bate requires the operator to "fire it well and cast it into the water, and it will fume and boyle up slowly".[23] Of itself, this Bate recipe does not entirely account for Gascoine's description, but canvas balls containing stickless rockets, star balls or petards may account for this observation. Gascoine may have seen the components in the form of star balls or petards being released and not the immediate release of the fire ball itself. If rockets were placed inside the ball they may have driven the ball erratically through the water and the observed stillness may have occurred due to the length of time taken to burn any connecting stouple.

Descriptions of events relating to Elizabeth's Progress to Kenilworth in 1575 are well known. Four eye-witness accounts concerning the firework celebrations are extant. Other than Gascoine's account of the Sunday celebrations there are three descriptions by Laneham variously describing the events of Saturday, Sunday and Thursday evenings of the first week.[24] Whether Elizabeth saw the fireworks on Saturday evening, shortly after her arrival and having been "conveied up to chamber"[25] is not clear, although she was obviously intended to hear this reception, for Laneham records that "the noiz and flame were heard and scene a twenty myle of.". What the Queen would have heard, according to Laneham, was "so great a peal of gunz, and such lightning by fyrwork a long space toogither,...". Laneham's account of the Sunday evening display complements that of Gascoine but is less factual and more poetic in description [**APPENDIX 1C**]. Laneham's account of the Thursday evening celebration is described in more simple terms and introduces two notions different from the Saturday and Sunday descriptions. The first observation is that the fireworks were "compeld by cunning to fly too and fro" which implies the use of "runners". Secondly, the fireworks were "too mount very hye intoo the ayr upward,..." which implies rockets of the conventional kind, balanced by sticks. Alternatively, the reference may be to the use of "flying saucissons".[26]

Evidence concerning the "fort holdings" at Cambridge, Stirling and Warwick does not specifically refer to symbolic or allegorical content. However, other celebrations like the one to welcome Elizabeth to Bristol in 1574 were clearly dependant on such material. Robert Ricart "The Maire of Bristowe" writes in his "Kalendar":

> And duringe her abode here (amonge other thinges
> devised for plesure) there weare iiij c. soldiers in one sute
> of apparell, whereof iij c. weare harquebussiers and j c.

pikemen in corselettes. Also there was made a greate large forte standinge in Trenemill meade over againste Gibtaylor, which was assaulted by land and water iij. daies. And there was also another litle forte called the base fortt, standinge upon the hill beyond, which was wonne the first night that the assault was given. And the Queene was there at euerie assault duringe the saide iij. daies, for whose standinge there was builded a large scaffolde of tymber in the Marshe. Whiche martiall experiment beinge verie costlie and chargeable (especially in gonnepowder), the Queene and Nobilitie liked verie well of, and gaue Mr.Maior and his brethren greate thankes for theire doinges.[27]

The scene was set on the first day; a large fort referred to as "the Citie" and representing "Peace" was built. Nearby, another smaller fort described as a "littell Bastillion, builded on a hil," was also constructed. This fort was called "Feeble Pollecie". A personification known as "Dissension" gave speeches which in turn moved to arms both "War" (the attackers) and "Peace" (the defenders). The speech given by "Dissension" to "War" was not permitted to be heard by the Queen but was presented to her in a book. However, the speeches delivered by "Dissension" were "don in action".

On the second day further speeches were delivered "for the better understanding of the devised Triumphe" and "Dissension" again spoke to "War" and "Peace":

On thoes words was warres in sutch a stoer that you might see the feeld all over spred with soldiers, and so they marched down a hill, and maed a goodly shoe full against the littel Fort (called Feble Pollecie); and repolsing in all the soldiours of the same, wan it with great fury, and so rased it, and overthrow hit down to earth.[28]

Soldiers from the main fort tried to offer support to "Feeble Pollecie" but were in turn driven back and their fort was beseiged. The attack continued without resolution until "by tortch light the Prince from her skaffold went to her lodgyng, and in the mean season som fierworks wear seen...".

The following day the main fort received support in the form of "divers Gentilmen of good callynge from the Court, which maed the shoe very gallant,...". With an incoming tide "up the water from Kyng-road cam three brave galleys, chasing a ship that cam with vittayls to the Fort.". After a "Gentilman" offered a speech to the Queen" (which hazarded the Gentilman's lief)" battle continued "with a shoe of fight on land and sea, till the very night approtched, at which time the Prince partted,...". By this time "neither the Fort, nor the wickednes of the World (which warres represented), was desirous of further trobuls," and so a personification, "Perswasion", spoke of the folly of war and "what quietnesse coms by a mutual love and agrement.". However, "Perswasion" was dismissed and "the battry was planted befoer the Fort,". When the Queen was in position on her scaffold "so went the Battry of, and the assaut was given in as mutch order as might be; the Enemie was three times repolsed, and beholdyng nue suckors commyng from the Courte to the Forts great comfort, the Enemye agreed on a parley,...". After the conditions of the peace agreement were drawn up "both the sides shot of their artillery, in sien of a triumphe, and so crying "God save the Queen", these triumphes and warlik pastimes finished.".

The three day entertainment was devised and organised by Thomas Churchyard, who also wrote the various speeches.[29] For his "travayle bothe in the Fortes and concernyng oracions" he was paid "vjli. xiijs. iiijd.". The proceedings were witnessed by the Queen from a "gallery in the marsh" for which "xixli. iiijs. iijd." was paid. The considerable sum of "lxxxjli. viijs. iiijd." was paid to "Mr.Domynyck Chester for charges of the ij fortes with other busynes". Presumably, Chester was responsible for building the forts, which were constructed of timber covered with canvas. Thomas Symons was paid "ivli ivs. vid." for the provision of "bords" that seemingly formed the framework of the forts. Both forts were covered in retrieved canvas which was previously used to cover the "highe crosse when it was in gilting and payntyng". Some "clix ells" of canvas "covered the ii Forts". Payment to Mr.Richard Cole for "lockeram (bockeram) and canvas 230 yardes & 13 ells for souldiors dublettes" is recorded, but it is not clear whether any of this canvas was used in the construction of the forts. The "generall of all the armye" was Captain Shute and payment made to him for "his travaile" appears to include overall responsibility for the army during Elizabeth's visit; he was paid "xvjli. xiijs. iiijd.". During the visit some "iiijc. soldiers in one sute of apparell, whereof iijc. weare harquebussiers and jc. pikemen in corselettes" are recorded as being on duty. Not all these soldiers appear to take part in the "fort holding" for payment is only made to "lxxxv pyoners who wrought at the Fortes". William Saltern and Thomas Dewnson are paid "ixli. xvs. vjd." for "charges of the grete ordnance". Both corn(ed) powder and serpentyn [mealed] powder is recorded in substantial quantities. A total of ccxili. viis. iid. was paid for gunpowder that was used in ordinance and "som fierworks"[30] [**CHAPTER 1**].Further pulverisation of powder mixtures is indicated by payment for "the nete charges of casting of 7 morters of Brasse & making of pestells iijli. iijs. iijd.".[31]

Another entertainment for Elizabeth was that hosted by the Earl of Hertford at Elvetham, Hampshire in 1591. This event seems to be considerably more imaginative in its intention than previous celebrations. The occasion was not a "fort holding", as so far described, but a poetic conception that drew upon classical and Elizabethan mythology, nature and politics. The setting for this four-day diversion was created by the Earl in the grounds of his house:

> Betweene the Earl's house and the foresayd hill, where these roomes were raised, there had been made in the bottom, by handy labour, a goodly Pond, cut to the perfect figure of a half moon. In this Pond were three notable grounds, where hence to present her Majestie with sports and pastimes. The first was a Ship Ile, of a hundred foot in length, and four-score foote broad, bearing three trees orderly set for three masts. The second was a Fort twenty foot square every way, and overgrown with willows. The third and last was a Snayl Mount, rising to foure circles of greene privie hedges, the whole on height twentie foot, and fortie foote broad at the bottom. These three places were equally distant from the sides of the ponde, and everie one, by a just measured proportion, distant from the other.[32]

Although the principal firework contribution to this entertainment took place on the third day, an effect not unlike those produced by dragons in the previous chapter occurred during the second day in the Snayle Mount which "nowe resembleth a monster, having hornes full of wild-fire, continually burning.".[33]

The use of artillery in the form of "a peale of a hundred chambers" discharged from the "Snayl Mount" and "a like peale" fired from the "Ship Ile" seems similar to the use of ordinance so far considered. However, evidence concerning the nature and disposition of fireworks at Elvetham presents some different features. The precise identity of "a globe of all manner of fire-works, as big as a barrel" is unclear. The simile is useful in attempting to determine the scale of the effect, but use of the word "globe" is ambiguous. The "globe" does not appear to be of the kind considered in **CHAPTER 5** concerning the "worldes" of the Coventry Drapers. If the term "globe" refers to a sphere whose identity and purpose is simply to act as a decorative sphere, then its function in containing "all manner of fire-works" may simply have been a practical one. Alternatively, the term "globe" may refer to an attempt to portray "the world" as a planet. Babington presents a recipe with the title "How to represent the sphere, with diverse circles, some moveable, others fixed.".[34] The "spheare" is to be made "either of wood or mettall, the outward circles representing the meridian circle with the horizon".[35] The "meridian" and "horizon" are thus fixed circles while the "eclipticke shall bee excentricke to the equinoctiall" and allowed to rotate around pivots through the north and south poles. The movement of these inner circles is created by "fastening rockets about the equinoctials". The science upon which the design is based is that "according to the rules of *Ticho Brahe*".[36]

Reference to "many running rockets uppon lines" offers strong evidence of "runners" or "swevels". The nature of the produced spectacle would clearly have depended upon the number of lines used and the frequency of firing. Presumably, the "runners" were threaded on to the line before it was tightened, which would limit the number of "runners" on any given line. Additional visual value may have been achieved if Bate's technique of binding "two Rockets together, with the breech of one towards the mouth of the other" was used.[37]

Jean Wilson suggests that the "many fire-wheeles, pikes of pleasure, and balls [balles-Nichols] of wilde fire" may be the precursors to "our modern Catherine-wheels, golden rain, and roman candles.".[38] The suggestion that "fire-wheels" were "Catherine-wheels" depends upon definitions. If, by "Catherine-wheels", Wilson refers to a firework that consists of "a long, thin case wound in a spiral round a central, circular block, which is pierced by a hole to receive the pin on which the firework revolves",[39] then the historical comparison is improbable. However, if by "Catherine-wheels" she refers to larger wheels mounted horizontally or vertically and fired by linked rockets around the periphery of the wheel, then Wilson's interpretation may be correct.[**FIG.26**].[40] This sort of wheel is more generally referred to as a "girandole".[41] The scale of such wheels seems more appropriate to a firework event of this dimension. Norton suggests:

> The Worckes may be framed both for verticall, and also for Horizontall Mouers, either vpon great woollen spinning Wheeles, Coach Wheeles, or other Wheeles, made of purpose easie to runne round, and the greater the better shew... [**FIG.27**][42]

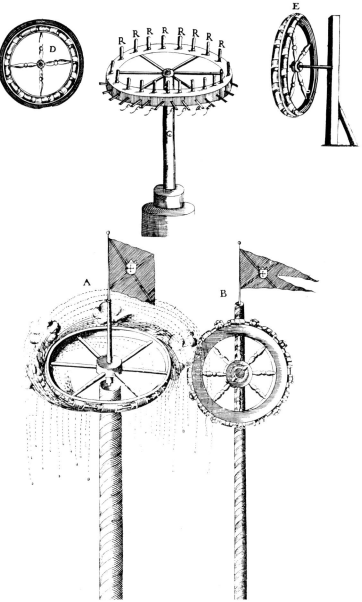

26. Varieties of vertical and horizontal fire wheels.
Babington, *Pyrotechnia* before p.19 and p.25;
Norton, *The Gvnner*, before p.153;
Bate, *The Mysteryes of Natvre and Art*, p.78.

Because of the momentum gained by the firing of successive rockets when placed around the wheel, Norton further suggests that "Tyres of coloured Fires, Serpents, breakers, or shewers of Gold," may be placed between the rockets "as you shal think with time between them fitted, that the Wheele may moue from the ending of euery Rocket, vntill the beginning of the next, with a Sulpher Match betweene them.".

The term "pikes of pleasure" may refer to a wide range of fireworks placed on the ends of poles or pikes. The term does not exist in sixteenth and seventeenth-century firework books. However, "ball[e]s of wilde fire, which burned in the water" are those previously referred to at Warwick and Kenilworth, of which a number of recipes exist.[43]

Perhaps the pinnacle of achievement concerning the development of the "fort holding" is that represented by the one in Edinburgh in 1617 for James I. The principal evidence, as detailed in **CHAPTER 5**,

27. A hand-held rotating firewheel.
Isacchi, *Inventioni*, p.115.
BL 5894 Inventioni Isacchi 1579.
By permission of The British Library.

concerning this "fort holding" exists in two forms: one is a detailed eye-witness account offered by "John Crowe, the younger" to "Mr.Alden" in a letter dated, 1July, 1617[44] and the other is to be found in the *Accounts M.W.* John Crowe's letter to Mr.Alden informs us:

> Then went his Majestie into his pallace and sate in ane window with his nobilles, and beheld a playe of fyrwork; their was many thousands beholders of it; I myselff was one. The play breifflie was thus. It was actet in the nicht. Their was 2 castles erected in the utter court, one castle at the one end off the court and another castle at the uther end, the one called the pallace of St.Androis, the other the Castle of Envy. It was acted and played by the yong men of Edenborrow.

The basic type of battle structure so far encountered at Stirling, Warwick and Bristol is to be witnessed in the "playe of fyrwork" devised for James. Before battle commenced, as indicated in **CHAPTER 5**, there appear to have been some preliminary warm-up activities. The battle lines were clearly drawn up between the respective castles, "the Castle of Envy" and "the pallace of St.Androis". On one level the proceedings may be seen to have represented a battle between St.Andrew and St.George. However suggestive or symbolic was the presence of St.George, a statement of intent was presumably communicated to the "many thousands beholders of it" through the symbolic representations of the castles. St.Andrew's ultimate victory also indicates the purpose of the piece. Beyond the designation of the two castles and the symbolic representation of the protagonists there is no further evidence of any discernable narrative. The collective effects are the only extant indicators of the nature of this theatre.

Whether the event was as exciting as John Crowe indicates or whether the account merely gives emphasis to his own excitment is not clear. Certainly, more action is described than in previous eye-witness accounts of such battles and the impression is given that the action is continuous. To represent some evenness of military strength it might be conjectured that "the Castle of Envy" possessed the fire-balls since "the pallace of St.Androis" retained St.Andrew to finally slay the dragon. The phrase "the one castle schuityng fyrballes at the other,", is unclear as to whether one or both castles shot the fire-balls. Both castles were stoutly defended and the respective armies evenly matched, for John Crowe informs us that there were "so many twix the Castles fychting, so many keiping every Castle, sumtymes the one syd winning, then agane

114

retyring bak and flying.". No doubt this made for engaging theatrical tension and spectacle. The armies consisted of "so many hagbuttes, so many muscetters, thair ensignes, thair horsmen, thair footmen runing with speires off fyr,..." [**FIG.28**]. If the fire spears required targets, then it may be presumed that their function was to set alight whatever was hit. As considered in the Stirling "fort holding", one or other of the castles seems to have been the target. This notion is further supported by the information that "four hieland men, dressed up so of purpos,... came out of the pallace of St.Androis with their boues and arrowes of fyr," and "did win the Castle of Envy..." [**FIG.29**]. As a result of this action by the "hieland men", the "castle was throuen down, the men taken prisoners, and the captain sould have bein, as it wer, hanged.". Although the "speires off fyr" and the "arrowes of fyr" were no doubt

28. A knight on horseback. The horse is covered with crystal and reflective mirrors. Careful timing is given to the ignition of the tubes of powder that produce streams of fire. Isacchi, *Inventioni*, p.125.
BL 5894 Inventioni Isacchi 1579
By permission of the British Library.

targeted upon the castles, there is no evidence that the latter were burned to the ground. The phrase "throuen down" used to refer to the sacking of "the Castle of Envy" is too vague to indicate precise meaning. Were the action of this event to have been limited to that which is "acted and played by the yong men of Edenborrow", it would of itself be dramatic.[45] Yet Crowe's account indicates use of further inanimate devices. It is not clear whether these pyrotechnic contrivances were employed simultaneously with the action, or sandwiched between the respective skirmishes. In some instances timed use of pyrotechnic "set-

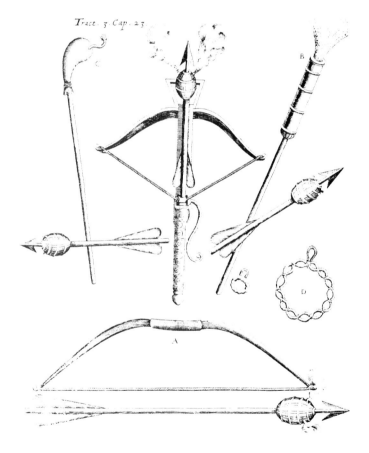

29. Bows and arrows fitted with small canvas fire balls.
Norton, *The Gvnner*, before p.157.

pieces" may have enhanced the battle spectacle; in others, relative effectiveness of small-scale devices may have been eclipsed by larger battle sequences.

The first of these devices consisted of "quheilles runing round about of fyr and so many schotes into it,...". These "quheilles" are recorded in *The Accounts M.W.* as "tua great reames quheilles xls." and "tua litle reames quheillis xxxvis.".[46] It is not clear where these four wheel rims were located in relation to the castles or whether they were mounted horizontally or vertically. Their purpose was to hold "rockets for the ground" around the outside edge, which when ignited created the necessary propulsion. These wheels may be the same or similar devices to the ones ascribed to Elvetham. The reference to "so many schotes into it...", presumably refers to the use of breakers or reports, located round the face of the wheel rim. Usually these consisted of quills filled with a basic gunpowder mixture and ignited by the use of slow mixture or quickmatch.[47]

The eye-witness account informs that between the two castles "was a devys set up that schot so many schotes...". This appears to be a "fire-pump" [**FIG.30**] [**APPENDIX 4 D**]. The account continues to describe "a thing going about with horsmen and footmen;...". Presumably this "thing" operated in a horizontal mode in order to show off the horsemen and footmen to their best visual advantage. This "thing" may have been a simple machine powered by rockets. Babington demonstrates several devices and explains their methods of operation.[48] The example that most resembles John Crowe's description is one that consists of 10 parallel belts upon which are fastened miniature soldier figures [**FIG.31**]. These belts are held by and allowed to rotate upon two separated parallel rollers, so that the soldier figures constantly appear and disappear, rather in the manner of the moving targets in a shooting gallery. One of the rollers contains gear wheels on either end which in turn are driven by screw-threaded rods attached to fire wheels, driven by rockets.[49] Reference to the "quheill [that] wald about agane" indicates a fire wheel that was placed in close proximity to the parrallel belt device and when both mechanisms were in operation it appears as if the wheel pursued the soldiers. Alternatively, the "quheill [that] wald about agane" could have been the same wheel that was used to drive the screw-threaded rods. Further reference to "so many schottes" again indicates reports or breakers. The "man maid of timber in the mids of the quheill" seems to have rotated on a tight horizontal axis as the wheel turned, allowing his ensign to follow and flutter. It is possible that this miniature representation was intended to symbolise the larger battle in which St.Andrew was to succeed.

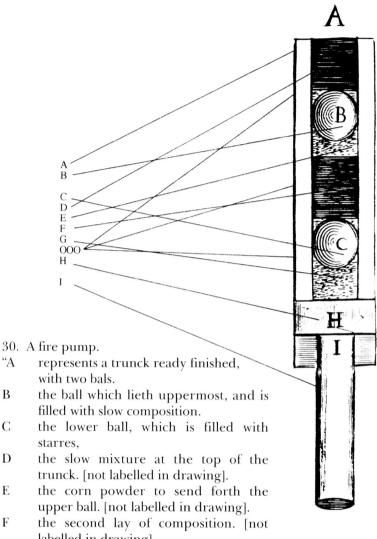

30. A fire pump.
"A   represents a trunck ready finished,
      with two bals.
B   the ball which lieth uppermost, and is
      filled with slow composition.
C   the lower ball, which is filled with
      starres,
D   the slow mixture at the top of the
      trunck. [not labelled in drawing].
E   the corn powder to send forth the
      upper ball. [not labelled in drawing].
F   the second lay of composition. [not
      labelled in drawing].
G   the powder for sending forth the lower ball. [not labelled in
      drawing].
OOO three places left for arming the said trunck. [not labelled in
      drawing].
H   the bottom of the trunck, which must be two inches thick.
I   a place left to put in a post of wood for it to stand on."
                    Babington, *Pyrotechnia*, p.42 and before p.45.
                         [**APPENDIX 4 D**].

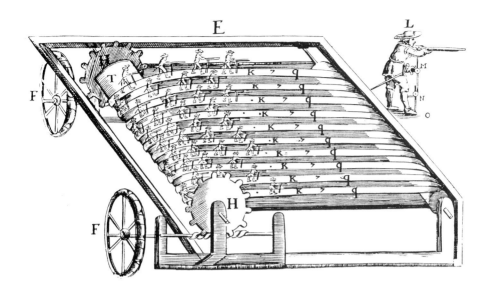

31. A devise powered by fire wheels.

"E   represents the whole frame, with all the parts therof.

F F   are the two fire wheeles, being placed one at each end of the rowler.

G G the screwes, being fastned to each fire wheele, which move the two wheeles placed on the rowler. [not labelled in drawing].

H H the two wheeles being placed at each end of the rowler.

I I   two rowlers, about which the girts do passe, which carry the whole body of men. [not labelled in drawing].

K K the girts on which the figures are placed, each girt having upon it ten, so that in the whole there will be an hundred.

L   represents the figure of a man standing in that posture as hee ought to bee made.

M   Is the detent which is fastened to the right arme, and is to slide on a joynt, being fastened to the thigh; so that it may move the arme.

N   another detent which moveth the former, as it passeth by the pin.

O   the pin which putteth by the said detent as it commeth to it.

qq   the said pins in their right places."

Babington, *Pyrotechnia*, before p.34 and p.35.

119

Although the "fort holdings" at Warwick and Bristol made use of the River Avon (two different rivers with the same name that flow into the Bristol Channel), the respective battles were conducted essentially on land.[50] The entertainments at Kenilworth and Elvetham were different in that they took place in landscapes in which water was an integral design feature. However, aquatic versions of the "fort holding" genre, if it may be so considered, are recorded on the Thames in London.[51]

In June 1550 Edward VI witnessed a "fort holding" on the Thames in which the action or plot may have been realised only in such aquatic conditions. The assault on the fort was a naval one. The "forty or fifty other souldiours", captained by "mr. Winter",[52] defended the fort and were finally vanquished. The attack upon the fort was launched by "4 pinessis with their men in wight ansomely dressed". The "yelow piness" employed to defend the fort was driven off and the assault upon the fort took place "with cloddes, scuibes, canes of fire, dartes made for the nonce, and bombardes,...". The "cloddes" involved here seemingly possessed no pyrotechnic value for they were simply clods of earth used as thrown objects. The "scuibes" seem straightforward but the "canes of fire" imply hollowed out sticks capable of projecting fire. In principle this device operated in the manner of Bate's fire club. Norton also describes a version of "canes of fire":

> Also it will be a pleasant spectacle to behold, to see two men issue forth at co[n]trary places, armed with small Trunks or Staues,...[who] shall Combat together in Fire...And the Trunkes and Staues furnished with Cane Armed,...[53]

The "canes of fire" presumably contained slow mixtures which were ignited at the top [**FIG.32**]. The canes were bound or "armed" with cord to prevent splitting under pressure of the gunpowder reaction. The "dartes made for the nonce" may have been light-weight fire spears, fire arrows or other pointed and fired implements. The "bombardes" could indicate fire balls or the means of firing them.[54] According to the eye-witness account the attackers "at lenght came with their pices, and burst the utter walles of the castill". The word "pices" may refer to weapons or the means of conveyance from the "4 pinessis" to the fort. The bursting of the outer walls of the castle presumably refers to a staged manipulation of this effect rather than the actual destruction of the edifice. One method of achieving such an effect is suggested by payment for a "Castell with y^e falling sydes" in the *Revels Accounts* for 1581.[55] At this point the defenders were driven back into the "second ward" [56] from which they rallied in order to sink one of the

32. Combat with "Cane armed". Norton, *The Gunner*, before p.155.

"pinessis". The climax of the battle seems to have been achieved when "th' admiral of the navy with three other pinesses" finally won the fort and took "the yellow ship".

The eye-witness account that describes the mock naval battle for Edward VI makes no reference to the imaginative identity or narrative purpose of any of the protagonists. The battle, as described in this account, may have existed as spectacle in its own right. Identified individuals such as "mr.Winter" and "th' admiral of the navy" exist in the account by virtue of their professional roles as sailors.

A similar aquatic "fort holding" took place, again on the Thames, in 1610 as part of the celebrations to mark the Creation of Henry Prince of Wales (*London's Love to Prince Henry*). In this instance the identity of the castle is known to have been Turkish and the attendant vessel whose purpose was to defend the castle was also Turkish.[57] The vessels which attacked the castle were "the merchants" and "the men of warre":

> In conclusion, the merchants and men of warre, after a
> long and well-fought skirmish, prooved too strong for the
> pirate [Turkish vessel], they spoylde bothe him and blewe
> up the castle, ending the whole batterie with verie rare and
> admirable fire-workes, as also a worthie peale of chambers.

Despite the probability that some personnel on board "the merchants" and the "men of warre" were well practised in the manipulation of gunpowder, it is unlikely that the castle was actually blown apart. The fate of this castle is likely to be a staged one as considered in relation to the mock battle for Edward VI.

Perhaps the most remarkable synthesis of pyrotechnic mock conflict and imaginative narrative occurred in the presentation devised by John Taylor, "the Water Poet", in 1613 to celebrate the marriage of Frederick and Elizabeth (*Heaven's Blessing and Earth's Joy*). An indication of the "Preparations For The Fire-Works On The Thames, 1612-13" is suggested by the following account:

> The preparations for Fire-works and Fights upon the water
> are very great, and have already consumed above £.6000,...
> besides four Floating-castles with Fire-works, and the
> representation of the town, fort, and haven of Argier upon
> the land.[58]

The "Fire-works and Fights" were two separate events: the "Fire-works" were performed on the night of Thursday, 11 February and the

"Fights" [sea fight] on the following Saturday. Although John Taylor was responsible for the dramatic device, the pyrotechnics were controlled by "the Maister-gunner of England" who:

> on the shore did performe many skilfull and ingenious exploits with great bumbards, shooting up many artificiall balls of fire into the ayre, which flew up in one whole fierie ball, and in their falling dispersed into divers streams like rainebowes in many innumerable fires. After all which was discharged a great peale of chambers, to the contentment of the Royall Spectators, and the great credit of the performers.

Although the "Maister-gunner of England" retained charge of the artillery and pyrotechnics, further sub-division of labour and responsibility, as indicated in **CHAPTER 5**, seems to have been devolved to Mr.John Nodes, Gunner; Mr.Thomas Butler, Gunner; William Bettis; Mr.John Tindall, Gunner and Mr.William Fishenden, Gunner. The first four of these men each had responsibility for the pyrotechnic effects emanating from and surrounding one of the four castles. John Nodes was responsible for the "strong impregnable pavilion, in the which he immures and encloses this beautiful Amazonian Queene [Lucida] with her attendant Ladies". Thomas Butler's charge was the "inchanted Castle or Tower of Brumond". William Bettis' castle was unnamed but his pyrotechnic preparations "had contrived in such sort, that if the weather had bin rainy or windy, yet his dessignments should have beene accomplished". The castle for which John Tindall was responsible "called the Castle of Envie" was situated on a rock "called the Rock of Ruine" surrounded by "a troblous sea, called the Sea of Disquiet". William Fishenden was responsible for the set-piece pyramid. The description of the "fierie ball" above is quite complete and needs to be considered when contemplating records of fire balls elsewhere.

Each of the named gunners has a "True Description" of his contribution to the "Fire-workes" ascribed to him. It is unlikely that the gunners wrote these descriptions, not necessarily because they were incapable of doing so, but because the language used is that of the narrative which applies a poetic value to the so-called observations. It is likely that John Taylor was the author. Detailed accounts exist of the plot of this entertainment although the previously unpublished document *MS BL Additional 70518* is quite economical in its description of intention:

> A laday beinge distressed by an Enchanter take a tower for
> her refuge <u>and</u> is releeued by a knight.

St.George, the knight in question, promises his allegiance to the "laday" [Lucida] and declares that he will kill the dragon and the giant in the Enchanter's castle. In order "to passe away the time" Lucida "delights him with these pastimes following, being all Fire-workes". After the display of fireworks, St.George journeys to the Enchanter's castle and kills both dragon and giant. Similarly, the Enchanter is killed "with a septer in his hand, bound vnto a piller, <u>and</u> burnt to death." The castle or "Tower of Brummond" is itself finally fired. This seems to complete the story, for the fireworks surrounding William Bettis' castle did not depend on the delivery of a narrative. The fireworks that emanated from John Tindall's castle, "the Castle of Envie", were related to a self-contained narrative which seems to have had no bearing upon the St.George episode. Simply, "the Castle of Envie" built upon the "Rock of Ruine" in the "Sea of Disquiet" was attacked by three ships known as "Good-will", "True-love" and "Assurance":

> These three shippes and Captaines [Loyalty, Trust and Circumspection] with their valarous and confident associates assault this Castle of Envie, where, after halfe an houres fight or thereabouts, by the invincible prowesse of the assaylants the hell-borne defendants were vanquished, their Castle utterly razed, demolished, and subverted, with rackets, breakers, blowes, and reports innumerable.

These, then, were the principal narrative components of the firework entertainment and it needs to be remembered that the narrative was communicated through fireworks or firework devices; the protagonists were communicated through inanimate means. Consideration has already been given in **CHAPTER 5** to the composition of "St.George" and the "dragon" and the same type of construction may be suggested for the "giant" and the "enchanter" in Thomas Butler's "Castle or Tower of Brummond".

The firework display, ostensibly for St.George, in John Nodes' "pavilion" was intended to consist of "sundry fires in circuler motions, truncks burninge castinge foorth balls, <u>and</u> buttons of fire, <u>and</u> the rails round about yeildinge fire of diuers sort<u>es</u>". Catherine-wheels, fire pumps, pin-wheels and rockets tied to the rails all seem to be involved here. A second device is described as "2 bucks chased w<u>i</u>th hound<u>es</u>, <u>and</u> huntsmen followinge the game yeilding many sort<u>es</u> of fires to flie diuers wayes.". This sequence of the display is referred to by an eye-witness account as follows:

> Out of the same mount or hill of earth ["made upon the water"] flew another strange peece of artificiall Fire-worke, which was in the likenes of an hunted hart, running upon the waters so swiftly, as it had bene chaced by many huntsmen. After the same issued out of the mount a number of hunting-hounds made all of fire burning, pursuing the aforesaid harte up and downe the waters, making many rebounds and turnes with much strangenes, skipping in the ayre as if it had bene a usuall hunting upon land.

The "hunted hart" and "hunting-hounds" that consisted of "fire burning" may have been required to run on the line across the water, seemingly between castles. Although these manifestations may have been pulled backwards and forwards along the line, it does not seem that they were solid creatures like previous St.George and the dragon examples. The animal shapes probably existed in outline as lance work or more probably as impregnated rope or tow. Rope dipped in tallow and/or coated with pitch, shaped into the appropriate form may have burned for an extended period and been capable of travelling along a line.[59] The "skipping in the ayre" of the "hart" may have derived from alternate slackening and tightening of a line caused by the weight of a frame that held the images or the movement of the barges or lighters upon which stood the castles. A third sequence was composed by John Nodes so that "there doth march round about the pavilion artificiall men, which shall cast out fires, as before, as it were in skirmish". Babington offers a number of recipes involving "artificiall men" but the scale appears to be too small for this event.[60] His versions are effectively pyrotechnic automata. Since the Royal party observed the event "being placed in the galleries and windows about his Highnes' Court of Whithall", it seems unlikely that the small-scale effects offered by Babington would have been observeable over such distance. The "artificiall men" are thus likely to have existed as outlined figures formed in the manner suggested for the "hart" and "hunting-hounds" and intended to run on the line. It seems possible that these representations were at least life size.[61] Rockets to simulate their weapons were seemingly part of the design. The fourth sequence involves the "laday" [Lucidia, or the Queene of Amazonia] who "with all hir Traine of virgin Ladyes, with fires marcheth round as the men did before, with the fire flying dispearsedly divers ways". These figures were probably made in the same way as the "artificiall men" and required to travel the same circuit round the castle. The final feature of John Nodes' contribution:

> aloft within the turret shall runne, whirling round, a fyerie globe, with the turret and all on fire, with many more greater blowes then before had bin heard.

Unlike the Elvetham "globe", the "globe" here appears to be consumed by fire. After this device "St.George" is seen to leave the "Amazonian Queene, Lucida" and ride to the "inchanted Towre of Brummond".

At this point, Thomas Butler took over responsibility for the continuation and development of the pyrotechnic narrative. The encounter between "St.George" and the "dragon" has already been considered and is accounted for in three separate descriptions: the proposals of *MS BL Additional 70518*, a description of the pyrotechnic narrative and an eye-witness account. The latter reference, however, does not deal with the killing of the "giant" or the "Enchanter". The pyrotechnic narrative accounts refer to the "inchanted Towre of Brummond" as being "in hight forty foote and thirty square, betweene which and the Pavilion of the Amazonian Queene is a long bridge". It is doubtful that an actual bridge existed, given the movement of the barges or lighters that supported the castles. The narrative does not make a bridge essential to the battle between "St.George" and the "dragon" providing rope or wire was suspended for their encounter. The castle consisted of "foure squares of the Tower" or "foure turrets" that "are fyred with fire and innumerable lights, with abundance of rackets flying to and fro in the ayre, giving divers reports as before." When the main castle was fired "upon two of the corner turrets are two globes fyered, betwixt each globe, at two other corner turrets, are two men, catching as it were at the globes which still turn from them, and they chasing and following the globes, still burning and turning till all be extinguished with fire; always rackets flying, and reports thwacking, and lights burning". If the castle was as big as previously indicated then it is unlikely that the "two men, catching as it were" literally interfered with the revolving globes. The effect of ejected fire from the "two men" seemingly driven towards the globes may account for this description.

William Bettis' castle and its fireworks was not concerned with the development of narrative. A great variety of fireworks "representing and assuming divers variable shapes and imaginary formes" were involved and continued for "the space of an houre or thereabouts". Apart from rockets, reports and flashes of all kinds a "set-piece" effect, similar perhaps to the one devised by John Nodes, concerned "a stagge or hart, hunted and chased with dogges, all their bodies being artificially made and proportioned in one flame of fire; where the following hounds were plainely seene to pull downe and vanquish the stagge which they before had chased". The significance of this description concerns the design being "in one flame of fire". This account clearly refers to an outline in tow or rope, fired perhaps in more than one stage in order to realise the image of the final kill. According to one pyrotechnic account "divers other rackets" were seen "flying aloft into the ayre, which rackets did assimilate the shapes or proportions of men, women, fowles, beastes, fishes, and other formes and figures". If this effect took place then it is not likely to have been effected by rockets. The capacity for rockets to carry the necessary number of stars to achieve such designs is limited. Most of the space in a rocket is taken up by the mixture to propel it into the sky. Today, such aerial designs are possible, but are usually conducted by shells fired from mortars:

> Pattern shells, by the exact placing of stars within the globe of the shell itself, make recognizable designs in the night sky when the shell is detonated. The stars are thrown out into the shapes of crosses, circles, cherry blossoms, butterflies, bouquets, even letters.[62]

If the sequence of events as outlined in John Taylor's account indicates the actual order of firing then John Tindall's contribution through his "Castle of Envie" was the one which the eye-witness account suggests as having "most expectation, and had most devices; but, when it came to execution, had worst success". Clearly, the narrative outlined earlier is imaginative. If, however, the order of firing was that contained in *MS BL Additional 70518* then it seems that William Bettis' offering is that which "had worst successs".

A further contribution was offered by William Fishenden in the form of:

> Piramides of 20 foote square <u>and</u> 18 foote high with a globe in the topye turninge round, only by the force of the fire, the whole body beinge fixed at the bases immediately turnes all into flames of fire, and as a pillar or fountaine of fire, from the topp to the bottome, shall streame foorth into

sundry light<u>es</u>, rockett<u>es</u>, <u>and</u> breakers, givinge reportes,
<u>and</u> castinge fireballs, into the aier streaminge in theire
discent.[63]

   The "globe" in this instance appears to have been turned by rockets
fixed to a meridian at 90° to the pivoting axis [cf.Babington's device].
The pyramid was seemingly set alight from the base and the rising
flames ignited the other fireworks placed higher up in order to produce
the effects described.

   The mixture of eye-witness material and fire-worker's accounts for
Heaven's Blessing and Earth's Joy provides colourful and detailed
information concerning the intention and results of this theatrical event.
Presumably the detail contained in the narrative accounts exceeds that
which might be communicable to an audience. The wonder expressed
in one of the eye-witness accounts dwells on the spectacle rather than
the narrative. Perhaps this should not be too surprising if the creation of
pyrotechnic magic of this kind and on this scale happened only on rare
public occasions.

Conclusion

WHEN I started this work I little thought that I would become involved in the discoveries presented here, for my initial intention was to investigate the use of sound and light in the medieval and Tudor theatre. Such revelatory material opens up an area of study that may affect and modify what is already known about medieval and Tudor theatre. Some surprising insights emerge in connection with the knowledge and skill required to implement the techniques and effects referred to in this work. The investigation goes beyond previous works into the development of fireworks in England and Scotland and tackles for the first time the relevance of pyrotechny to the medieval and Tudor theatre.

One of the ways in which this work extends beyond previous work of others is in the identification and analysis of accounts. Such writers have not recognised or utilised any of the Scottish records contained in *The Accounts* or *The Accounts M.W.* Although Anna J.Mill has included (as Appendices) some items in *The Accounts* and *The Accounts M.W.* in her *Mediaeval Plays in Scotland*, she does not address their theatrical relevance. Similarly, the accounts in England have not been acknowledged or assessed in any historical studies of early pyrotechny.

Of principal significance in the findings presented here is the understanding gained from application of firework writers' work to explain the value and purpose of ingredients and processes recorded in the accounts. The considerably detailed records contained in *The Accounts* and *The Accounts M.W.* may be explained or illuminated by recipes in both early and later firework books. For example, analysis of the records in *The Accounts* concerning the *Baptismal Celebrations* provides opportunity to reconstruct a large part of this pyrotechnic event and indicate its form. Although fewer Scottish records exist, the ones that are available give more detail than their English counterparts.

Even so, the same process may be used to explain the value and purpose of apparently simple and seemingly inconsequential items in the accounts. For instance, the significance of such materials as canes, paper, packthread and cord in the records at Maidstone, Kent, has been made apparent through the ability to relate individual items to others in terms of pyrotechnic function and purpose. The significance of such items as rosin, starch and aqua-vitae as recorded at Coventry, Newcastle, New Romney and at Court has been established in this way. It has been possible to move towards clearer understanding of pyrotechnic entertainments through comprehension of individual ingredients and their purpose.

Similar importance may be attached to the information given by the "explicit" stage direction. Such directions are frequently "explicit" in both form and function. In stating practical requirements they identify and acknowledge conditions to be realised. Again, firework writers' recipes offer considerable insight into the means by which particular effects or techniques may be achieved. For instance, the requirement contained in the direction concerning Belyal in *The Castle of Perseverance* is apparently quite clear. Yet the practical realisation of this instruction becomes clearer when pyrotechnic understanding derived from firework writers' recipes is applied to it. The use of goose quills and "slow mixture" would have satisfied the requirement.

Eye-witness accounts are often valuable in their own right; they explain themselves. However, in this work the content of eye-witness accounts has been further illuminated by reference to the processes described by firework writers. Just as the requirement expressed in the direction in *The Castle of Perseverance* may be illuminated by firework writers' recipes, the eye-witness account at Seurre concerning Satan's accident may be similarly explained.

I hope I have taken the necessary caution in my examination of some evidence which purports to be eye-witness material and separated it from other eye-witness observations. The so-called "true descriptions" offered by John Taylor appear to be fictional even though they may relate to and indicate intention. Nichols appears to be aware of such discrepancy when he writes: "Notwithstanding all these eulogies of honest John Taylor, these very sumptuous Fire-works do not appear on the whole to have succeeded; see Mr.Chamberlaine's Letter hereafter. N.".[1] Interestingly, it might be possible to attach greater importance to the acknowledged second-hand account of the Warwick entertainment in 1572 than to the "true descriptions" by John Taylor.

It is clear that the content of early firework writers' books effectively offers new evidence in the understanding of medieval and Tudor theatre. Some further caution must be exercised here for firework writers' books have been known for some time to other pyrotechnists. However, careful analysis of these works has not previously occurred. Similarly, the use of these books to explain conditions in the medieval and Tudor theatre has also not taken place. The necessary know-how to create special effects is evident, even if appropriate scientific understanding is not developed and perhaps this notion requires some further consideration.

The bulk of twentieth-century writers on pyrotechnics have relied heavily on Brock's *Pyrotechnics: the Art and History of Firework-making* and his *A History of Fireworks* for their understanding. Because Brock's two books have been influential in establishing what is thought to be known about earlier developments in pyrotechny, some erroneous assumptions may have been perpetrated. Although Brock was able to consult the writings of early firework writers and make use of eye-witness accounts, he did not utilise emergent records or stage directions in plays. Had he consulted the latter forms of evidence, he may not have been able to make some apparently firm assertions as to the relative understanding of early pyrotechnists. A number of ingredients are recorded in accounts and lists of firework materials long before Brock considered them to be known by pyrotechnists. If such items possess value in later recorded pyrotechnic processes why must it be assumed that their use was not known of in the sixteenth century? The fact that twentieth-century understanding may be better advanced than that practised in the sixteenth century does not preclude the notion that such early pyrotechnists did not know what effects were caused by given ingredients. It is possible to know what effect would be created by the incorporation of a given ingredient in a firework mixture without possessing a twentieth-century chemical understanding of its interaction. To assume otherwise ignores appropriate evidence and may lead to an arrogant or patronising disregard of earlier knowledge.

Since Brock wrote his books (one being the re-writing of the other), a considerable amount of additional information has emerged in the form of accounts and records. The diligence and assiduity with which such documentation has and is being retrieved through the publication of records is not only to be commended, but such work is creating a climate of critical respect for the unearthed detail. *REED* editors do not tend to be bamboozled by the significance of their discoveries. It is for others to attempt to establish new understanding of earlier conditions through the careful use of such records. Brock, like earlier twentieth-century writers and scholars of medieval theatre, is coming under close scrutiny concerning the assumptions upon which his knowledge was

131

based. It is the wider and more accessible availability of records that is modifying or changing existing or presumed knowledge. Brock, like all of us, was a product of his age.

Records concerning the aquisition of pyrotechnic materials in the fourteenth and fifteenth centuries point to the principal agents in the trading process as espicers or spicers and apothecaries.[2] Ingredients such as aqua-vitae, bees wax, gums, gum resins, camphor and many different oils were acquired in this way. Many of these items are to be found in John Hestor's late sixteenth-century list of "Oiles, vvaters, Extractions, or Essence Saltes, and other Compositions" [**APPENDIX 3A**]. In the fifteenth and sixteenth centuries the provision of pyrotechnic materials was largely conducted through guilds of grocers or merchants. Sometimes, members of other guilds are recorded as taking part in the transactional chain e.g. Drapers. Examples of this sort of involvement occur most frequently among guild members who operated on behalf of the guild in preparation of a celebratory event, such as that recorded in the example of the *Ironmongers' Registers* for 1567 [**CHAPTER 1**], in respect of the guild's contribution to the *Lord Mayors' Show*. In such cases, the normal craft or trade practice of the guild was not that associated with the pyrotechnic requirement of the celebration. The named person who was paid to obtain the ingredient was thus a middleman.

Grocers or merchants were accordingly the principal suppliers of gunpowder in the sixteenth century. Initially, it may seem odd that grocers were concerned with the provision of gunpowder until recognition is made of the guilds' earlier trade in saltpetre [**APPENDIX 3B**]. Grocers were also responsible for trade in sulphur, alum, verdigris, vermillion, wax, rosin, flax, turpentine, oils, gums and gum resins [**CHAPTER 1** and **APPENDIX 3B**]. The establishment of this trade is corroborated by the "Privilege of Garbling..." bestowed upon the Grocers' Company in London by Henry VI in 1447 [**CHAPTER 1**].

Evidence concerning operators of pyrotechnics for Royal and public shows in the sixteenth century exists in records and accounts and overwhelmingly points to the available expertise as that belonging to His Majesties Gunners. The two centres of expertise were London and Edinburgh and it appears that the initial skill developed in these centres came from other European countries. His Majesties Gunners operated from the Tower of London and Edinburgh Castle, with some appropriate skill residing among the military at Berwick. The Master of the Ordinance could always command such skill when needed in various parts of the country. Other military personnel, who were not necessarily gunners, also made contributions to firework events. Early writers on pyrotechnics were or had been gunners. The principal late sixteenth and early seventeenth-century books that deal with pyrotechny do so in the shadow of imparted knowledge about gunnery.

His Majesties Gunners were employed at the "fort holdings" of Stirling, Warwick, Bristol and Edinburgh as well as the celebrations at Kenilworth and Elvetham. Gunners were also contracted into the delivery of respective guild pageants for the *Lord Mayors' Show* in London. Although the role and function of His Majesties Gunners is clear in some public shows and Royal celebrations, the pyrotechnic operators in the production of plays is less clear. Even if military personnel were not involved in play production, it is most likely that the acquired skill of those responsible for such effects was passed on by or learned from the military.

Of further importance in the presentation of plays is the notion that the production of light in the medieval and Tudor theatre was frequently concerned with functions other than illumination of action. Some stage directions clearly point to the symbolic use of light in order, perhaps in the first instance, to maintain fidelity to the biblical narrative or additionally to create atmosphere. The atmospheric possibility, however, may be more of a by-product. The use of light to illuminate action did take place but does not seem to have been a general or primary concern.

Examples of lighting instruments and the principles by which they operated, as provided by Hugh Platte, do not appear to have been examined since they were written in the sixteenth century. Although other writers have referred to the principles of reflection and focus in early forms of lighting, none of them have specifically used examples provided by Platte. Instances of such lighting sources have been made usually with reference to continental examples. Modern writers often refer to these sort of lamps and lanterns as having existed in the sixteenth century yet do not provide appropriate evidence.[3] Platte's descriptions are therefore important in that they reveal understanding and practice of such lighting principles in late sixteenth-century England.

As indicated in relation to the direction in *The Castle of Perseverance* some specific techniques have been advanced in respect of devils who carry or project fire. Knowledge of these techniques has remained dormant. Similarly, the particular techniques of projecting fire out of hell mouth and dragons have not been previously recognised or identified.

Another significant discovery in this work is one of form. Identification of the pyrotechnic mock-battle, or "fort holding" and its theatrical form has not previously been acknowledged. The simplest version of this entertainment requires a body of men to defend a fort while another group attacks it. The weapons used to conduct the battle include artillery, harquebuses, fire balls, fire spears, fire arrows, rockets and squibs. Other pyrotechnic set-pieces such as fire wheels, fire pumps and animals and objects shaped in fire may create diversionary yet integral aspects of the form. Much of the available evidence concerning "fort holdings" occurs in the form of eye-witness accounts that identify the combatants. The point at which such identification takes place indicates the beginnings of narrative. The extent to which narrative is employed in these pyrotechnic mock-battles varies with the available evidence. However, the theatrical climax to the battle occurs when one side wins possession of the fort. Victory may result through one side storming the fort or by inanimate means such as a fired, flying dragon landing on the fort.

The "fort holding" clearly exists as theatre. Its content, shape, form and conscious purpose enable it to be defined as such. Antecedants of the form appear to lie in the thirteenth and fourteenth centuries in the *Pas d'Armes* of chivalric romance and heraldic enactment. This form of entertainment is paralleled by the Courtly *Jousts at Barriers*. Seemingly, both remained popular by being up-dated; the former with the latest pyrotechnic innovation and the latter with the scenic accoutrements of Court Masques.[1] The development of the "fort holding" as a theatrical event represents a synthesis of content, form and function in the use of fireworks. Although pyrotechnic processes were clearly involved in a supportive capacity as special effects in plays, the extension of the effects to become theatre in their own right is demonstrated by the "fort holding". In this form the fireworks are both the medium and the message: they make the statement and provide the theatrical justification for that statement.

The mock battle to celebrate the birthday of James I in Edinburgh may well have been the last of its kind in England or Scotland. Although unrecorded after the event, this example of the "fort holding" seems to have marked a climax in the development of this kind of theatre in England and Scotland. The relationship between inanimate pyrotechnic devices and the narrative figures played by "the yong men of Edenborrow" appears to have been fused in such a way as to consolidate the distinctive identity of the "fort holding". Although this form of theatre does not seem to have continued or developed in England or Scotland, there is evidence to suggest that it took strong root in Spain and Mexico.

Between 1625 and 1627 Thomas Gage observed and recorded a "fort holding" in Chiapa de los Indios in Mexico in his *The English-American his Travail by Sea and Land: or, A New Svrvey of the West-Indias,...*:

> This Towne lyeth upon a great river, [Grijalva], whereunto
> belong many boats and Canoas, wherein those *Indians* have
> been taught to act sea-fights, with great dexterity,.... They
> will arme with their boats a siege against the Town, fighting
> against it with such courage til they make it yeeld, as if they
> had been trained up all their life to sea-fights.... They will
> erect Towers and Castles made of wood and painted cloth,
> & from them fight either with the boats or one against
> another, with squibs, darts, and many strange fire-works, so
> manfully, that if in earnest they could perform it as well as
> they do it in sport and pastime, the *Spaniards* and Fryers
> might soon repent to have taught them what they have.[5]

It should be noted that a number of remarkable examples of the
form still exist in Spain and Mexico where they are generally referred to
as *fiestas de moros y cristianos*.[6] Like the sixteenth and early seventeenth-
century English and Scottish examples, these Spanish "fort holdings"
are conducted on foot, horseback or as naval battles. Sometimes as
many as 2500 participants make up the respective armies of "Moors"
and "Christians" and it is the latter who usually defeat the former. The
practical purpose of the battle remains the same; to win possession of
the castle.

When Chris Philip wrote to me in January 1993, he said, "I must say
I cannot recall much that was written in any of the books that I possess
(about 300) or any of those that I examined in various Libraries that
mentioned your particular theatrical interest.".[7] Such a statement from
a bibliographer of firework books may provide an explanation as to why
little has been known about pyrotechny in the medieval and Tudor
theatre. At the same time the statement indicates that the use of
fireworks in the theatre or as theatre has not been considered. Although
fireworks and their effects may not necessarily qualify as theatre, they
may be considered as such depending on purpose and organisation.
The development of the "fort holding" exemplifies this phenomenon.

Material has been presented in this work which suggests that the role
of fire and flame as special effects in the medieval and Tudor theatre
was not a constant one. In some instances the pyrotechnic special effect
was used to simulate a real moment or condition that was intended to
convince the audience of its authenticity. Some effects clearly operated
in this way. However, the resultant verisimilitude does not automatically
imply a theatrical desire for realism. Although the special effect may
simulate a reality, its purpose may not be concerned with achieving a
realistic effect. The effect may be used as an end in itself and recognised

as such. The automatic assumption that all special effects in fire and flame were used to support the illusion of reality must be considered cautiously. William Donald Young argued the existence of such a relationship without offering sufficient caution concerning assumptions based on theatre practice of his own time. Clearly, special effects were used to support the intention of the play or event. Whether the audience was conditioned into the belief that the special effect was the real thing, simulated it or represented it varies with the available evidence. It might be conjectured that the illusion of reality was sought by those "explicit" stage directions that contain the notion "as if...", where the agreed pretence is communicated to an audience.[8] Simulation of reality is clearly less important to effects whose purpose is to communicate narrative. In this case, the nature, purpose and context of fireworks and their timed execution determine communication of the theatrical statement.

Use of flame as special effect in the creation of fire, light and heat was much more manipulable than might be presumed. The danger and risks involved with the foregoing effects did not prevent them from being required or executed. The late twentieth-century "mind-set" that pulls us towards negating evidence because of our own preoccupation with issues of safety must not be allowed to interfere with the evidence and what it tells us.

Notes

Introduction

1. 'Submission to the Department of Trade & Industry Regarding Firework Controls', *British Safety Council* (1997), 7; 'Consultation on Draft Fireworks (Safety) Regulations 1997', *Department of Trade and Industry* (1997), 1-5. For recent sociological insights into preoccupation with safety, see Frank Furedi, *Culture of Fear:Risk-Taking and the Morality of Low Expectation* (London: 1997).
2. Gustave Cohen, *Histoire De La Mise En Scène Dans Le Théâtre Religieux Francais Du Moyen Age* (Paris: 1926); Gustave Cohen, *Le Livre De Conduite Du Régisseur et Le Compte Des Dépenses pour le Mystère De La Passion joué à Mons en 1501* (Paris: 1925); William Donald Young, *Devices and Feintes of the Medieval Religious Theatre in England and France*, unpublished Ph.D. dissertation (Stanford: 1959).
3. Manfred Pfister, *The Theory and Analysis of Drama* (Cambridge: 1988), pp.15-16; Gary Lynn Chancellor, *Stage Directions in Western Drama: Studies in Form and Function*, unpublished Ph.D. dissertation (Madison,Wisconsin: 1980); Robert Karl Johnson, 'Stage Directions in the Tudor Interlude', *Theatre Notebook* XXVI (Autumn 1971), 36-42; Richard Hosley, 'The Gallery over the Stage in the Public Playhouse of Shakespeare's Time', *Shakespeare Quarterly* VIII (1957), 16-17.
4. R.M.Lumiansky and David Mills (eds.), *The Chester Mystery Cycle*, Early English Text Society, SS3 (London: 1974), I, p.49.
5. Lumiansky and Mills (eds.), *The Chester Mystery Cycle*, I, p.48.
6. Thomas Sharp, *A Dissertation on the Pageants or Dramatic Mysteries anciently performed at Coventry* (Coventry: 1825; rpt. Wakefield: 1973).
7. Sharp, *A Dissertation on the Pageants*, vii.
8. Despite the importance of these records, they are, technically, secondary sources.
9. The exposure of Collier is well considered in S.Schoenbaum, *Shakespeare's Lives* (Oxford: 1970), pp.332-61; E.K.Chambers, *The Elizabethan Stage* (Oxford: 1923; rpt. 1974), I, xv; F.P.Wilson, *The English Drama 1485-1585* (Oxford: 1969), p.204.
10. John Wasson, 'Types and Analysis of Records', in Joanna Dutka (ed.), *Records of Early English Drama: Proceedings of the First Colloquium* (Toronto: 1979), p.128.

11. S.Schoenbaum, *Shakespeare's Lives* pp.396-432; Alexandra F.Johnston, 'What if No Texts Survived ?', in Marianne G.Briscoe and John C.Coldewey (eds.), *Contexts for Early English Drama* (Bloomington: 1989), p.1; Alexandra F.Johnston, '"All the world was a stage": Records of Early English Drama', in Eckehard Simon (ed.), *The Theatre of Medieval Europe: New Research in Early Drama* (Cambridge: 1991), p.117.

12. Examples include Robert Davies, *Extracts from the Municipal Records of the City of York during the Reigns of Edward IV. Edward V. and Richard III.* (London: 1843); G.A.Carthew, 'Extracts from Papers in the Church Chest of Wymondham', *Norfolk Archaeology* IX (1884), 121-152; Karl Pearson, *The Chances of Death and Other Studies in Evolution* (London: 1897), II, pp.413-23; A.Clark, 'Maldon Records and the Drama', *Notes and Queries* Tenth Series, VII (1907), 181-3: 342-3: 422-3; also Tenth Series, VIII (1907), 43-44; Andrew Clark, 'Great Dunmow Revels, 1526-1543', *Essex Review* IXX (1910), 189-98; Charles J.Cox, *Churchwardens' Accounts* [Chelmsford] (London: 1913).

13. John Nicholl (ed.), *Some Account of the Worshipful Company of Ironmongers* (London: 1851; second ed., London: 1866). Subsequently referred to as Nicholl...*Ironmongers*.

14. E.K.Chambers,*The Mediaeval Stage* (London: 1903; rpt.1967), 2 vols.

15. James Balfour-Paul (ed.), *Accounts of the Lord High Treasurer of Scotland* (Edinburgh: 1902-8), III, 1506-7; IV, 1507-13; V, 1515-31; VI, 1531-38; VII, 1538-41; VIII, 1541-46; Charles T.McInnes (ed.), *Accounts of the Treasurer of Scotland* (Edinburgh: 1970), XII, 1566-74. These sources will henceforth be referred to as *The Accounts* and a list of firework ingredients found in volume VII, 1538-41 will be referred to as *Maister Wolf and Cristopheir*.

16. Albert Feuillerat (ed.), *Documents Relating to the Office of the Revels in the time of Queen Elizabeth* (Louvain: 1908; rpt. New York: 1963); Albert Feuillerat (ed), *Documents relating to the Revels at Court in the time of King Edward VI and Queen Mary* (Louvain: 1914; rpt. New York: 1963).

17. W.W.Greg (ed.), *Malone Society Collections* (Oxford: 1911), I. The latest volume in the series is edited by Nigel Bawcutt (ed.), *Malone Society Collections* (Oxford: 1993), XV.

18. Anna Jean Mill, *Mediaeval Plays in Scotland* (St.Andrews: 1924; rpt. New York: 1969).

19. R.T.D.Sayle (ed.), *Lord Mayors' Pageants of the Merchant Taylors' Company in the 15th, 16th & 17th Centuries* (London: 1931).

20. John James Lambert (ed.), *Records of the Skinners of London - Edward I to James I* (London: 1933).

21. F.M.Salter, *Mediaeval Drama in Chester* (Toronto: 1955; rpt. New York: 1968).

22. Alexandra F. Johnston and Margaret Rogerson (eds.), *Records of Early English Drama: York* (Toronto: 1979), 2 vols. Subsequently referred to as *REED:York*.

23. *REED:York*, I, vi.

24. *REED:York* embraced those dramatic records previously printed in J.S.Purvis, *From Minster to Market Place* (York: 1969); Angelo Raine (ed.), *York Civic Records* (Wakefield/York/London: 1939-1953), Record Series, I -

VIII; Maud Sellers (ed.) *York Memorandum Book* (London: 1912 [for 1911], 1915 [for 1914]), 2 vols., CXX, CXXV; Maud Sellers, *The York Mercers and Merchant Adventurers 1356-1917* (London: 1918), CXXIX; Robert Davies, *Extracts from the Municipal Records of the City of York....*

25. See n.15. References to the firework celebrations at the baptism of James I in 1566 at Stirling are subsequently referred to as the *Baptismal Celebrations*.

26. Henry M.Paton (ed.), *Accounts of the Masters of Works for Building and Repairing Royal Palaces and Castles 1529-1615* (Edinburgh: 1957), I; John Imrie and John G.Dunbar (eds.), *Accounts of the Masters of Works for Building and Repairing Royal Palaces and Castles 1616-1649* (Edinburgh: 1982), II. Further references to these two volumes will be to *The Accounts M.W.* A list of firework ingredients contained in I concerning the second wife of James V and her entry into Edinburgh in July 1538, will be referred to as *Entry of Marie of Lorraine*. Expenses incurred at the celebration to mark the birthday of James I of England in Edinburgh, 1617 and contained in II are referred to as the *Birthday Celebrations*.

27. Peter Meredith and John E.Tailby (eds.), *The Staging of Religious Drama in Europe in the Later Middle Ages:Texts and Documents in English Translation* (Kalamazoo: 1983).

28. Ian Lancashire (ed.), *Dramatic Texts and Records of Britain: A Chronological Topography to 1558* (Cambridge: 1984).

29. Wasson, 'Types and Analysis of Records' in Joanna Dutka (ed.), *Proceedings...*, xi, pp.118-25.

30. Joanna Dutka, Helen Ostovich (eds.), *REED Newsletter* (1976-); Meg Twycross, Peter Meredith, Sarah Carpenter (eds.), *Medieval English Theatre* (1979-); Clifford Davidson (ed.),*The Early Drama, Art, and Music Review* [formerly *The EDAM Newsletter*] (1978-).

31. Johnston, 'All the world was a stage' in Eckehard Simon (ed.), *The Theatre of Medieval Europe*, pp.124-5.

32. Glynne Wickham, *Early English Stages 1300 to 1660* (London: 1963; rpt.1971), II, pt.1, pp.186-96.

33. For exceptions see Johnston, 'All the world was a stage' in Eckehard Simon (ed.), *The Theatre of Medieval Europe*, p.125.

34. Audrey Douglas and Peter Greenfield (eds.), *Records of Early English Drama: Cumberland Westmorland Gloucestershire* (Toronto: 1986), pp.317-9. Subsequently referred to as *REED: CWG*.

35. *REED:CWG*, pp.421-2, n.290.

36. *REED:CWG*, pp.253, 423, n.298.

37. Chris Philip, *A Bibliography of Firework Books* (Winchester: 1985).

38. Vannoccio Biringuccio, *De La Pirotechnia* (Venetia: 1540); translation by Cyril Stanley Smith and Martha Teach Gnudi, *The Pirotechnia of Vannoccio Biringuccio* (New York: 1942; rpt.1959), p.403; Philip, *A Bibliography of Firework Books*, pp.21-3; Maurice J.D.Cockle, *A Bibliography of Military Books up to 1642* (London: 1957; rpt. 1978), p.240.

39. Peter Whitehorne, *Certaine wayes for the ordering of Soldiours in battleray, and setting of battayles, after diuers fashions, with their maner of marching: And also Fugures of certayne newe plattes for fortification of Townes: And more ouer howe to*

make Saltpeter, Gunpouder, and diuers sortes of Fireworkes or wilde Fyre, with other thinges appertayning to the warres. (London: 1573). This edition is a reprint of the one published in 1562. Philip, *A Bibliography of Firework Books*, pp.165-6; Cockle, *A Bibliography of Military Books up to 1642*, pp.11-12; J.B.Partington, *A History of Greek Fire and Gunpowder* (Cambridge: 1960), p.336.

40. Philip, *A Bibliography of Firework Books*, p.166; Cockle, *A Bibliography of Military Books up to 1642*, p.12.

41. Cyprian Lucar, *Three Bookes of Colloqvies concerning the Arte of Shooting in great and small pieces of Artillerie...written in Italian, and dedicated tby Nicholas Tartaglia...And now translated into English by CYPRIAN LVCAR...Also the said CYPRIAN LVCAR hath annexed vnto the same three bookes of Colloqvies a Treatise named LUCARAPPENDIX collected by him out of diuers Authors in diuers languages to show vnto the Reader the properties, office, and dutie of a Gunner, and to teach him to make and refine artificial saltpeeter, to sublime brimstone for gunpowder to make coles for gunpowder, to make gunpowder of diuers soretes and of diuers colours, to make gunmatches,...to make and vse diuers Trunkes, and many sortes of fireworkes...* (London: 1588); Philip, *A Bibliography of Firework Books*, p.87; Cockle, *A Bibliography of Military Books up to 1642*, pp.32-6.

42. Robert Norton, *The Gvnner Shewing The Whole Practise Of Artillerie: With all the Appurtenances therevnto belonging. Together with the making of Extraordinary Artificiall Fireworkes, as well for Pleasure and Triumphes, as for Warre and Seruice.* (London: 1628); Philip, *A Bibliography of Firework Books*, pp. 106-7; Cockle, *A Bibliography of Military Books up to 1642*, p.90.

43. Francois de Malthe, *A Treatise of Artificial Fire-vvorks both for VVarres and Recreation...Newly written in FRENCH, and Englished by the Authour THO:MALTHVS.* (London: 1629); Philip, *A Bibliography of Firework Books*, pp.91-2; Cockle, *A Bibliography of Military Books up to 1642*, pp.93-4.

44. John Bate, *The Mysteryes of Natvre and Art: The Second Booke, Teaching most plainly, and withall most exactly, the composing of all manner of Fire-works for Triumph and Recreation.* (London: 1634; facs. rpt. Amsterdam: 1977); Philip, *A Bibliography of Firework Books*, pp.17-9; Raymond Toole Stott, *A Bibliography of English Conjuring 1581-1876* (Derby: 1976), 2 vols., I, pp.42-3.

45. John Babington, *Pyrotechnia Or, A Discovrse Of Artificiall Fire-works...* (London: 1635; facs. rpt. Amsterdam: 1971); Philip, *A Bibliography of Firework Books*, pp.14-6; Cockle, *A Bibliography of Military Books up to 1642*, p.102. The frontispiece contained in the facsimile is not in the BL copy.

46. Casimir Simienowicz, *The Great Art Of Artillery Of Casimir Simienowicz, Formerly Lieutenant-General of the Ordnance to the King of Poland. Translated from the French, By George Shelvocke, Jun.Gent.* (London: 1729); Philip, *A Bibliography of Fireworks*, pp.134-7.

47. According to Smith and Gnudi, "the chapters in the *Waies* [Whitehorn's book] describing mines, bombs, military fireworks, saltpeter, and gunpowder are practically nothing more than translations of Biringuccio's chapters on these topics...", *The Pirotechnia of Vannoccio Biringiccio*, xxiii. Bate copies, without acknowledgement, the description of a lighting device from Platte; Bate,*The Mysteryes of Natvre and Art*, p.157; Hugh Platte,*The Jewell House of Art and Natvre* (London: 1594), pp.31-2.

140

48. See Alan St.Hill Brock, *Pyrotechnics: The History and Art of Firework Making* (London: 1922); George Washington Weingart, *Dictionary and Manual of Pyrotechny* (New Orleans: 1937); Tenney Lombard Davis, *The Chemistry of Powder and Explosives* (New York: 1943; rpt. Hollywood: 1970); George Weingart, *Pyrotechnics* (New York: 1947); Alan St.Hill Brock, *A History of Fireworks* (London: 1949); Herbert Ellern, *Modern Pyrotechnics: Fundamentals of Applied Physical Pyrochemistry* (New York: 1961); Reverend Ronald Lancaster, *Fireworks: Principles and Practice* (New York: 1972); Takeo Shimizu, *Fireworks: The Art, Science and Technique* (Tokyo: 1981).

49. Albertus Magnus, *The Secrets of Albertus Magnus. Of the Vertues of Hearbs, Stones, and certaine BEASTS* (London: 1617). See also Michael R.Best and Frank H.Brightman (eds.), *The Book of Secrets of Albertus Magnus...* (Oxford: 1973). This volume is compiled from different early editions.

50. Thomas Hyll, *A Briefe and pleasant Treatise, Intituled: Naturall and Artificiall Conclusions* (London: 1586); Toole Stott, *A Bibliography of English Conjuring*, pp.120-4; Trevor Hall, *A Bibliography of Books on Conjuring in English from 1580 to 1850* (Lepton: 1957), p.48. The earliest available edition of Hyll's work is 1581, although Toole Stott claims that "Hill's *Conclusions* first appeared in 1566 and continued to be reprinted after his death round about 1599, and often anonymously.".

51. Platte, *The Jewell House of Art and Natvre*; Toole Stott, *A Bibliography of English Conjuring*, p.189; Hall, *A Bibliography of Books on Conjuring*, p.70. Hall refers to the 1653 edition of Platte's *The Jewell House of Art and Natvre* but not the one of 1594.

52. John White, *A Rich Cabinet, with Variety of Inventions* (London: 1651).

53. John Stow, *The Annales of England...* (London: 1601); Edmund Howes,*The Annales or Generall Chronicle of England...* (London: 1615).

54. Raphael Holinshed, *Holinshed's Chronicles of England, Scotland, and Ireland.* (London: 1586; rpt. London: 1807-8), 6 vols.

55. H.Ellis (ed.), *Hall's Chronicle...* (London: 1548; rpt.1809).

56. *Grafton's Chronicle* [A Chronicle at Large] (London: 1569; rpt. 1809), 2 vols.

57. John Nichols, *The Progresses and Public Processions of Queen Elizabeth* (London: 1823), 3 vols. Hereafter referred to as *Progresses...Elizabeth.*

58. John Nichols, *The Progresses, Processions, and Magnificent Festivities of King James the First* (London: 1828), 4 vols. Subsequently referred to as *Progresses...James.*

59. J S.Brewer, J.Gairdner, and R.H.Brodie (eds.), *Letters and Papers, Foreign and Domestic, of the Reign of Henry VIII* (London: 1864-1920), 21 vols. Addenda (1929-32), 2 vols.

60. *Calendar of State Papers, Domestic Series, Edward VI, Mary, Elizabeth* (London: 1856-71), 7 vols.

61. *Calendar of State Papers and Manuscripts, Relating to English Affairs, existing in the archives and collections of Venice and in the other libraries of Northern Italy* (London: 1864-1947 [for 1940]), 38 vols.

62. John Gough Nichols (ed.), *The Diary of Henry Machyn, Citizen and Merchant - Taylor of London, From A.D. 1550 to A.D. 1563.* (London: 1848).

63. Nichols, *Progresses...James*, II, pp.527, 530-538. See **APPENDIX 1F**. The existence of the description is referred to in Richard Ward (ed.), *The Manuscripts of His Grace the Duke of Portland preserved at Welbeck Abbey, Thirteenth Report, Appendix, Part II* (London: 1893), vol. II, p.22.
64. Nichols, *Progresses...James*, II, p.530.
65. Nichols, *Progresses...James*, II, pp.530-1.
66. Nichols, *Progresses...James*, II, pp.532-5.
67. Nichols, *Progresses...James*, II, pp.534-5.
68. Brock suggests that the descriptions may have been "based on a 'hand-out' circulated by the fire-workers responsible...", *A History of Fireworks*, p.35.
69. Nichols, *Progresses...James*, II, p.533.
70. Implicit stage directions may be written in the margin, amongst the text or within the line pattern of the text; also they may be rubricated or part rubricated.
71. Martin Stevens and A.C.Cawley (eds.), *The Towneley Plays*, Early English Text Society, SS13 (Oxford: 1994), p.61, l.58. Translation by Peter Meredith. For a discussion of this and other stage directions in the Towneley play of *Jacob* see Philip Butterworth, 'Stage Directions in the Towneley Play of Jacob', *The National Arts Education Archive Occasional Papers in the Arts and Education*, 6 (1996), 1-8.
72. Stevens and Cawley (eds.), *The Towneley Plays* p.214, l.333.
73. A thorough analysis of the possible relationship between stage directions and staging conventions in the Elizabethan theatre occurs in Alan C.Dessen, *Elizabethan Stage Conventions and Modern Interpreters* (Cambridge: 1984).

Chapter 1

1. References to "squibs" in play texts occur in the following: Percy Simpson (ed.), *Ben Jonson's Everyman In His Humour* (Oxford: 1919), pp.5-6; James Shirley, *The Doubtful Heir* in *The Dramatic Works and Poems of James Shirley* (notes by Gifford and later Dyce), IV (London: 1833), prologue; John S.Farmer (ed.),*The Two Merry Milkmaids* in *Old English Drama* (London: 1914), prologue; C.H.Herford, Percy and Evelyn Simpson (eds.), *Ben Jonson* (Oxford: 1947), VIII, p.208; John Melton, *Astrologaster or the Figure-Caster* (London: 1620; rpt. 1975), p.31. See also *O.E.D.* sb.1 SQUIB; Thomas Kentish, *The Pyrotechnist's Treasury: The Complete Art of Firework-Making* (Boulder, Colorado: c.1976), pp.91-7; Bate, *The Mysteryes of Natvre and Art*, pp.72-3; Babington, *Pyrotechnia*, p.14; Lancaster, *Fireworks: Principles and Practice*, p.163; Lucar, *Appendix*, p.83. The process of making "rockets for the ground" and "squibs" was much the same; they differed in size. De Malthe, *A Treatise of Artificial Fire-vvorks*, pp.78-80; Weingart, *Pyrotechnics*, pp.112-3.
2. William Smythe, "citezen and haberdasher of London 1575," offers "A breffe description of the Royall Citie of London" and writes: "And to

make waye in the streetes, there are certayne men apparelled lyke devells, and wylde men, with skybbs,...", Sayle (ed.), *Lord Mayors' Pageants*, p.2. A vivid description of spectator involvement is offered by the account of Horatio Busino [Orazio Busino], chaplain to Piero Contarini, Venetian Ambassador, concerning the Lord Mayors' procession in London. He writes: "From the windows an incessant shower of squibs and crackers were thrown into the mass beneath, for which the boys scrambled when they were cold.", *Calendar of State Papers (Venice)*, XV, p.59.

3.   Jean Robertson and D.J.Gordon (eds.), 'A Calendar of Dramatic Records in the Books of the Livery Companies of London 1485-1640', *Malone Society Collections* (Oxford: 1954), III, pp.38,39,41,45; Lambert (ed.), *Records of the Skinners*, p.208; Sayle (ed.), *Lord Mayors' Pageants*, pp.22, 26, 36, 48; Nicholl...*Ironmongers*, pp. 84-5; Alan H. Nelson (ed.), *Records of Early English Drama: Cambridge* (Toronto: 1989), 2 vols., I, p.199. Subsequently referred to as *REED: Cambridge*.

4.   John S.Farmer (ed.), *A Play of Love* in *The Tudor Facsimile Texts* (London: 1909).

5.   Mark Eccles (ed.), *The Macro Plays*, Early English Text Society, OS 262 (London: 1969), p.1.

6.   Geoffrey Bullough (ed.), *Promos and Cassandra* in *Narrative and Dramatic Sources of Shakespeare* (London: 1958), II, p.484.

7.   Allessandro Vitale-Brovarone (ed.), *Il quaderno di segreti d'un regista provenzale del Medioevo: Note per la messa in scena d'una Passione* (Alessandria: 1984), pp.50-3.

8.   Herford, Percy and Simpson (eds.), *Ben Jonson*, VI, p.254.

9.   Whitley Stokes (ed.), *Gwreans An Bys: The Creation of the World* (Berlin: 1863), p.28, l.325.

10. Edwin Norris (ed.), *The Ancient Cornish Drama* (Oxford: 1859; rpt.New York/London: 1968), 2 vols., I, pp.200-1.

11. Lumiansky and Mills (eds.), *The Chester Mystery Cycle*, I, p.36.

12. Whitley Stokes (ed.), *The Life of Saint Meriasek, Bishop and Confessor* (London: 1872), pp.120-1, l.2091.

13. W.W.Greg (ed.), *The Old Wives Tale* in *Malone Society Reprints* (Oxford: 1908), l.670.

14. W.W.Greg (ed.), *Alphonsus King of Aragon* in *Malone Society Reprints* (Oxford: 1926), l.1246; George Chapman, *Caesar and Pompey* in *The Comedies and Tragedies of George Chapman Now First Collected with Illustrative Notes and A Memoir of the Author in Three Volumes* (London: 1873), III, p.140; Fredson Bowers (ed.), *The Virgin Martyr* in *The Dramatic Works of Thomas Dekker* (Cambridge: 1958), III, p.453, l.122; A.R.Walker (ed.), *Four Plays Or Moral Representations In One* in *The Works of Beaumont & Fletcher* (Cambridge: 1912), X, p.362.

15. John S.Farmer (ed.), *A Looking Glass for London, etc.* in *Old English Drama* (London: 1914).

16. Peter Meredith and John E.Tailby (eds.), *The Staging of Religious Drama in Europe in the Later Middle Ages: Texts and Documents in English Translation*, Early Drama, Art, and Music Monograph Series, 4, Medieval Institute

Publications (Kalamazoo: 1983), p.101; G.G.Coulton, *Life in the Middle Ages* (Cambridge: 1929), 4 vols.,II, pp.138-40.

17. John Hampden (ed.), *Three Plays* (London: 1940), p.285.

18. John S.Farmer (ed.), *Friar Bacon and Friar Bungay* in *Old English Drama* (London: 1914).

19. Frank Sidgwick and W.W.Greg (eds.), *The Battle of Alcazar* in *Malone Society Reprints* (Oxford: 1907), ll. 1262, 1275, 1279.

20. John S.Farmer (ed.), *Grim the Collier of Croyden* in *Five Anonymous Plays* (London: 1908; facs.rpt.1966), pp.105, 108, 177, 180.

21. Donald C.Baker, John L.Murphy and Louis B.Hall Jr. (eds.), *The Late Medieval Religious Plays of Bodleian MSS Digby 133 and E Museo 160*, Early English Text Society, OS 283 (Oxford: 1982), p.7, l.182.

22. Meredith and Tailby (eds.), *The Staging of Religious Drama*, p.245; Gösta M.Bergman, *Lighting in the Theatre* (Stockholm: 1977), p.36; William Donald Young, *Devices and Feintes*, pp.75,76.

23. Baker, Murphy and Hall (eds.),*The Late Medieval Religious Plays*, p.47, l.691; Mary Loubris Jones, 'Sunlight and Sleight-Of-Hand in Medieval Drama', *Theatre Notebook* XXXII, 3 (1978), 119-21.

24. Meredith and Tailby (eds.), *The Staging of Religious Drama*, p.95.

25. Greg (ed.), *The Old Wives Tale*, ll.500, 796.

26. Richard Simpson (ed.), *The Famous History of the Life and Death of Captain Thomas Stukeley* in *The School of Shakespeare* (London: 1878), I, pp.248-9, l.2272.

27. Sidgwick and Greg (eds.), *The Battle of Alcazar*, ll.1262, 1275, 1279.

28. Farmer (ed.), *Grim the Collier of Croyden*, pp.105, 108, 177, 180.

29. Meredith and Tailby (eds.), *The Staging of Religious Drama*, pp.231, 232, 234, 236, 238.

30. Meredith and Tailby (eds.), *The Staging of Religious Drama*, p.97.

31. John S.Farmer (ed.), *The Cobbler's Prophecy* in *Old English Drama* (London: 1911).

32. Norman Davis (ed.), *Non-Cycle Plays and Fragments*, Early English Text Society, SS1 (London: 1970), p.79, l.672, p.80, l.712.

33. Lucy Toulmin Smith (ed.), *York Plays* (London: 1885; rpt.New York: 1963), pp.372-395. See also Richard Beadle (ed.) *The York Plays* (London: 1982), pp.333-43.

34. Richard Beadle and Peter Meredith (eds.), *The York Play: A facsimile of British Library MS Additional 35290* (Leeds: 1983), ff.207^V-213^V.

35. Stevens and Cawley (eds.), *The Towneley Plays*, pp.323-35.

36. Lumiansky and Mills (eds.), *The Chester Mystery Cycle*, I, pp.346-7.

37. Norris (ed.), *The Ancient Cornish Drama*, I, p.459, l.2988.

38. Stokes (ed.), *The Life of Saint Meriasek*, pp.104-5.

39. Meredith and Tailby (eds.), *The Staging of Religious Drama*, p.102.

40. Meredith and Tailby (eds.), *The Staging of Religious Drama*, p.114. See also p.113.

41. W.W.Greg (ed.), *The Second Maiden's Tragedy* in *Malone Society Reprints* (Oxford: 1910 [for 1909]), p.61.

42. Lumiansky and Mills (eds.), *The Chester Mystery Cycle*, I, p.325. This translation by Peter Meredith. See also the translation by David Mills in

The Chester Mystery Cycle (East Lansing: 1992). Mills translates the requirement as "physical light".

43. Stokes (ed.), *The Life of Saint Meriasek*, p.228, ll.3941, 3947.

44. Thomas Hearne (ed.), *Antiquarii de Rebvs Britannicis Collectanea* (London: 1774), 6 vols., IV, p.218.

45. *Hall's Chronicle*, p.638; *Grafton's Chronicle*, II, p.322.

46. John G.Nichols (ed.), *Literary Remains of King Edward the Sixth* (London: 1857), 2 vols., I, p.287.

47. H.Ellis (ed.), *Hall's Chronicle*, p.799; Brewer, Gairdner and Brodie (eds.), *Letters and Papers, Foreign and Domestic*, VI, pp.276-8.

48. *Holinshed's Chronicles*, IV, p.645; Edmund Howes, *The Annales or Generall Chronicle of England*, p.714.

49. John S.Farmer (ed.), *Friar Bacon and Friar Bungay* in *Old English Drama* (London: 1914) [no scene divisions]; see edition by J.A.Lavin (London: 1969), p.56; Feuillerat (ed.), *Documents Relating to the Office of the Revels*, p.345.

50. Feuillerat (ed.), *Documents relating to the Revels at Court*, p.108; Lancashire (ed.), *Dramatic Texts and Records of Britain*, p.146; Feuillerat, *Documents Relating to the Office of the Revels*, p.140; Chambers, *The Mediaeval Stage*, II, p.346.

51. John Eliot Hodgkin, *Rariora* (London: 1902), 3 vols., III, *Halinitropyrobolia*, iii; Sir Joseph Ayloffe, 'An historical description of an ancient picture in Windsor-castle, representing the interview between king Henry VIII. and the French king Francis I. between Guînes and Ardres, in the year 1520', *Archaelogia* III (1786), 185-229; Sydney Anglo, 'Le Camp du drap d'or et les Entrevues d'Henri VIII et de Charles Quint', in J.Jacquot (ed.), *Les fêtes de la renaissance* (Paris: 1960), II, pp.8-134; Sydney Anglo, 'The Hampton Court painting of the Field of the Cloth of Gold considered as an historical document', *The Antiquaries Journal* XLVI, part II (1966), 287-307; Joycelyne G. Russell, *The Field of the Cloth of Gold: Men and Manners in 1520* (London: 1969), p.176.

52. Nichols, *Progresses...Elizabeth*, I, p.320.

53. Hardy, W.J. (ed.), *The Manuscripts of Lord Kenyon [A Calendar]*, Historical Manuscripts Commission, 14th Report, Appendix, pt.4 (London: 1894), pp.22-3.

54. C.E.McGee, 'Fireworks for Queen Elizabeth', in N.W.Bawcutt (ed.), *Malone Society Collections* (Oxford: 1993) XV, pp.204-5; E.K.Purnell, *Report on the Pepys Manuscripts preserved at Magdalene College, Cambridge*, Historical Manuscripts Commission (London: 1911), pp.178-9; C.E.McGee and John Meagher, 'Preliminary Checklist of Tudor and Stuart Entertainments: 1588-1603', *Research Opportunities in Renaissance Drama* XXIV (1981), 77. They suggest a date of 1565 not 1575 as suggested by Purnell. See also R.J.P.Kuin, *Robert Langham: A Letter* (Leiden: 1983), pp.6-7, 124.

55. Nikolaus Pevsner, *The Buildings of England: London* (London: 1973), I, p.44. The only church in Kenilworth at that time was that of St.Nicholas. See Nikolaus Pevsner and Alexandra Wedgewood, *The Buildings of England: Warwickshire* (London: 1966), p.317.

56. Nichols, *Progresses...James*, II, p.532.

57. Meredith and Tailby (eds.), *The Staging of Religious Drama*, pp.91, 103.
58. Meredith and Tailby (eds.), *The Staging of Religious Drama*, p.157.
59. Meredith and Tailby (eds.), *The Staging of Religious Drama*, p.90.
60. Paul Studer (ed.), *Le Mystère D'Adam* (Manchester: 1918; rpt. 1928), p.29; Richard Axton and John Stevens (eds.), *Medieval French Plays* (Oxford: 1971), pp.35-6; Allardyce Nicoll, *The Development of the Theatre* (London: 1927; rpt.1966), p.53. Translation from Nicoll.
61. R.W.Ingram (ed.), *Records of Early English Drama: Coventry* (Toronto: 1981), pp.167, 242, 245, 256, 469, 472. Subsequently referred to as *REED: Coventry.*
62. Raine (ed.), *York Civic Records*, VIII, p.161.
63. *REED:York*, I, p.410; Francis Collins (ed.), *Register of the Freemen of the City of York from the Civic Records* (Durham: 1897), 2 vols, II, pp.6,13,14,15,19,31,46; Raine (ed.), *York Civic Records*, VIII, p.155.
64. *REED:York*, I, p.410; Francis Collins (ed.), *Register of the Freemen of the City of York*, II, p.21.
65. *REED: York*, I, pp.389, 419; Francis Collins (ed.), *Register of the Freemen of the City of York*, II, pp.12,13.
66. David Galloway (ed.), *Records of Early English Drama: Norwich 1540-1642* (Toronto: 1984), p.80. Subsequently referred to as *REED: Norwich*. Percy Millican (ed.), *The Register of the Freemen of Norwich 1548-1713: A Transcript with an Introduction. An Appendix to those Freemen whose apprenticeship Indentures are enrolled in the City Records, and Indexes of Names and Places* (Norwich: 1934), pp.71, 231.
67. Joseph Bettey (ed.), 'Two Tudor Visits to Bristol' in *A Bristol Miscellany* 37 (1985), pp.10,11.
68. *REED:York*, I, p.434.
69. Nicholl...*Ironmongers*, p.88; Robertson and Gordon (eds.), *Malone Society Collections*, III, p.46.
70. Nicholl...*Iromongers*, p.91.
71. Charles Welch (ed.), *Register of Freemen of the City of London In the Reigns of Henry VIII and Edward VI* (London: 1908), p.99.
72. Giles E.Dawson (ed.), 'Records of Plays and Players in Kent 1450-1642', *Malone Society Collections* (Oxford: 1965), VII, p.191.
73. Lawrence M.Clopper (ed.), *Records of Early English Drama: Chester* (Toronto: 1979), pp.70, 505. Subsequently referred to as *REED: Chester.*
74. Dawson (ed.), *Malone Society Collections*, VII, p.201.
75. Dawson (ed.), *Malone Society Collections*, VII, p.210.
76. Dawson (ed.), *Malone Society Collections*, VII, p.201.
77. David Galloway and John Wasson (eds.), 'Records of Plays and Players in Norfolk and Suffolk 1330-1642', *Malone Society Collections* (Oxford: 1980), XI, p.129.
78. Raine (ed.), *York Civic Records*, VIII, p.167.
79. Robertson and Gordon (eds.), *Malone Society Collections*, III, p.34.
80. Feuillerat (ed.), *Documents relating to the Revels at Court*, pp.108,110.
81. J.Payne Collier (ed.), *Household Books of John Duke of Norfolk, and Thomas Earl of Surrey; Temp 1481-1490* (London: 1844), pp.339, 340. Despite Collier's dubious reputation, the account is corroborated in Anne

Crawford, *The Household Books of John Howard, Duke of Norfolk, 1462-1471, 1481-1483* (Stroud: 1992), II, pp.337-340.

82. Paton (ed.), *The Accounts M.W.*, I, p.233.
83. Balfour-Paul (ed.), *The Accounts*, VII, p.357.
84. Balfour-Paul (ed.), *The Accounts*, VI, p.454.
85. E.A.Brayley Hodgetts (ed.), *The Rise and Progress of the British Explosives Industry* (London: 1909), p.212.
86. Hodgetts (ed.), *The Rise and Progress*, p.211.
87. Hodgetts (ed.), *The Rise and Progress*, p.212; Sayle (ed.), *Lord Mayors' Pageants of the Merchant Taylors*, p.52; Robertson and Gordon (eds.), *Malone Society Collections*, III, p.47.
88. Lambert (ed.), *Records of the Skinners of London*, p.208.
89. McInnes (ed.), *The Accounts*, XII, pp.403-409.
90. Imrie and Dunbar (eds.), *The Accounts M.W.*, II, pp.89-93.
91. Baron Heath, *Some Account of the Worshipful Company of Grocers of the City of London* (London: 1869), p.412.
92. John Hestor, *These Oiles, vvaters, Extractions, or Essence Saltes, and other Compositions; are at Paules wharfe ready made to be solde, by IOHN HESTER, practitioner in the arte of Distillation; who will also be ready for reasonable stipend, to instruct any that are desirous to learne the secrets of the same in few days, etc.* (London: 1588). BL C.60.o.6.
93. Nelson (ed.), *REED: Cambridge*, I, pp.179-80, II, p.1126. The translation offered here is an ammended one by Peter Meredith.
94. Nelson (ed.), *REED: Cambridge*, I, p.181, II, p.1127.
95. Feuillerat (ed.), *Documents Relating to the Office of the Revels*, p.142.

Chapter 2

1. Robertson and Gordon (eds.), *Malone Society Collections*, III, p.5; Robert Withington, *English Pageantry* (Cambridge: 1918), 2 vols., I, p.40.
2. Robertson and Gordon (eds.), *Malone Society Collections*, III, p.6.
3. *O.E.D.* II. 6. a. REED "A reed used as a dart or arrow; hence poet. an arrow.". The following direction in Thomas Dekker's *London Triumphing* of 1612 records "their arrowes, which they shoote vp into the aire, breake there out in fire-workes,", Sayle (ed.), *Lord Mayors' Pageants*, p.105; The *Ironmongers Registers* for 1534-5 record payment for " 3s. for rockets and reeds to shoot about the Castle,"; Robertson and Gordon (eds.), *Malone Society Collections*, III, p.26; Nicholl...*Ironmongers*, Appendix, xvi; Withington, *English Pageantry*, I, p.41.
4. *O.E.D.* sb.1 REED.
5. Bate, *The Mysteryes of Natvre and Art*, p.92.
6. Bate, *The Mysteryes of Natvre and Art*, p.60.
7. Feuillerat (ed.), *Documents relating to the Revels at Court*, p.67.
8. Bate, *The Mysteryes of Natvre and Art*, p.92.

9. Bate, *The Mysteryes of Natvre and Art*, p.72. See **CHAPTER 1**, n.1.
10. Hampden (ed.), *Three Plays*, p.285; Baker, Murphy and Hall (eds.), *The Late Medieval Religious Plays*, p.7, l.182.
11. Lambert (ed.), *Records of the Skinners of London*, p.208.
12. Robertson and Gordon (eds.), *Malone Society Collections*, III, p.39; Sayle (ed.), *Lord Mayors' Pageants*, pp.22, 26.
13. Robertson and Gordon (eds.), *Malone Society Collections*, III, p.41; Sayle (ed.), *Lord Mayors' Pageants*, p.36.
14. Robertson and Gordon (eds.), *Malone Society Collections*, III, p.45; Nicholl...*Ironmongers*, p.85.
15. Sayle (ed.), *Lord Mayors' Pageants*, pp.48, 78, 83, 90, 102.
16. Nicholl...*Ironmongers*, p.98.
17. Nichols (ed.), *The Diary of Henry Machyn*, p.125; Sayle (ed.), *Lord Mayors' Pageants*, p.2; *REED: Chester*, pp.258-9. For examples of devils "casting fire" in early seventeenth-century plays, see R.Warwick Bond (ed.), *The Bugbears* in *Early Plays From The Italian* (Oxford: 1911), Act IV, Sc.1, Act IV, Sc. III; Thomas Heywood, *The Brazen Age* in *The Dramatic Works of Thomas Heywood, Now First Collected with Illustrative Notes and a Memoir of the Author in Six Volumes* (London: 1874; rpt. New York: 1964), III, p.175; Thomas Heywood, *The Silver Age* in *The Dramatic Works of Thomas Heywood, Now First Collected with Illustrative Notes and a Memoir of the Author in Six Volumes* (London: 1874; rpt. New York: 1964), III, pp.159, 160; Robert Davenport, *A New Tricke to Cheat the Diuell*, (London: 1639), Act V, Sc.I; James Shirley, *The Doubtful Heir*, prologue; John Melton, *Astrologaster or the Figure-Caster*, p.31.
18. J.J. Anderson (ed.), *Records of Early English Drama: Newcastle upon Tyne* (Toronto: 1982), p.55. Subsequently referred to as *REED: Newcastle*.
19. David George (ed.), *Records of Early English Drama: Lancashire* (Toronto: 1991), p.43. Subsequently referred to as *REED: Lancashire*.
20. Nichols (ed.), *The Diary of Henry Machyn*, p.196. See also pp.13, 18, 47, 72-3, 96, 240, 261, 203-4.
21. Eccles (ed.), *The Macro Plays*, p.1; Bate, *The Mysteryes of Natvre and Art*, p.73; de Malthe, *A Treatise of Artificial Fire-vvorks*, p.81. The technique appears to have been known in Italy; see Giovanni Battista Isacchi, *Inventioni...nelle quali si manifestano varij Secreti, & vtili auisi a persone de gverra, e per i tempi di piacere* (Parma: 1579), pp. 123-5; Hodgkin, *Rariora*, III, p. 8; E. and G. S. Battisti, *Le macchine cifrate di Giovanni Fontana* (Milano: 1984); C.Walter Hodges,*The Globe Restored* (London: 1953), pp.116-7, fig.54.
22. Meredith and Tailby (eds.),*The Staging of Religious Drama*, p.266; William Donald Young, *Devices and Feintes*, pp.83-4.
23. Eccles (ed.), *The Macro Plays*, p.61.
24. Philip Butterworth, ' Gunnepowdyr, Fyre and Thondyr ', *Medieval English Theatre* 7:2 (1985), 68-76.
25. Meredith and Tailby (eds.), *The Staging of Religious Drama*, p.261.
26. W.W.Greg (ed.),*The Prodigal Son* in *Malone Society Collections*, I, pt. I, p.27; John S.Farmer (ed.), *The Two Merry Milkmaids*, prologue; J.R.Mulryne (ed.),*Women BewareWomen* in *The Revels Plays* (London: 1975), Act V, Sc.I, l.7.
27. Vitale-Brovarone (ed.), *Il quaderno di segreti,* p.36.

28. The "d'aigo arden" also acts as a combustion agent.
29. For appropriate methods see Best and Brightman (eds.), *The Book of Secrets of Albertus Magnus*, pp.109-10; Partington, *A History of Greek Fire and Gunpowder*, p.53; Protective clothing seems to have been provided for those helping to create the hell effects at Mons; see Cohen, *Le Livre De Conduite Du Régisseur*, p.516.
30. Meredith and Tailby (eds.), *The Staging of Religious Drama*, p.121; N.D.Shergold, *A History of the Spanish Stage from Medieval Times until the end of the Seventeenth Century* (Oxford: 1987), p.125, n.1; William Tydeman, *The Theatre in the Middle Ages* (Cambridge: 1978), p.77.
31. Levinus Lemmius, *The Sectret* [sic] *Miracles of Nature: In Four Books* (London: 1658), The Second Book, p.146.
32. Sir John Bourchier (Lord Berners), *The Chronicle of Froissart* (London: 1903), VI, pp.96-100.
33. Glynne Wickham, *Early English Stages 1300 to 1660* (London: 1959; rev.rpt. London and Henley, 1980), I, p.397, Plate 32.
34. Hyll, *A Briefe and pleasaunt Treatise*, D[V.], D1[r.] See Trevor Hall, *Old Conjuring Books* (London: 1972), pp.31-46.
35. This may be the source of Hyll's recipe since *The Book of Secrets* is considered to have been widely available. See Best and Brightman (eds.), *The Book of Secrets of Albertus Magnus*, Introduction.
36. Best and Brightman (eds.), *The Book of Secrets of Albertus Magnus*, p.105.
37. Platte, *The Jewell House of Art and Natvre*, p.31; Albert A.Hopkins, *Magic, Stage Illusions, Special Effects and Trick Photography* (New York: 1898; rpt. New York: 1976), p.150; J.C.Cannell, *The Secrets of Houdini* (London: 1931; rpt. New York: 1973), p.118; Ricky Jay, *Learned Pigs & Fireproof Women* (London: 1987), pp.261-5.
38. Norris (ed.), *The Ancient Cornish Drama*, I, p.200-1.
39. For a similar requirement see Heywood, *The Silver Age*, p.155.
40. Stokes (ed.), *Gwreans An Bys:The Creation of the World*, p.28, l.325.
41. See Loubris Jones, ' Sunlight and Sleight-of-Hand', 118-9; Philip Butterworth, ' Book-Carriers: Medieval and Tudor Staging Conventions', *Theatre Notebook* XLVI, 1 (1992), 15-30; Philip Butterworth, ' Comings and Goings: English Medieval Staging Conventions', *The Early Drama, Art, and Music Review* 18, 1 (Fall 1995), 25-34.
42. T. Hughes, *The Misfortunes of Arthur* in *Dodsley's Old English Plays* (London: 1874), IV, p.261.
43. Anon., *Hocus Pocus Junior:The Anatomy of Legerdemain* (London: 1654), E[V.]; Nathaniel Wanley,*The Wonders of the Little World: Or a General History of Man* (London: 1678), Book 1, Ch.8; Anon., *Demonologia, or Natural Knowledge Revealed* (London: 1827), pp.382-3; Edwin Sachs, *Sleight of Hand: A Practical Manual of Legerdemain For Amateurs and Others* (London: 1885), pp.72-3; Hopkins, *Magic, Stage Illusions, Special Effects and Trick Photography*, pp.150-1.
44. Hyll, *A Briefe and pleasaunt Treatise*, C8[r.] and D 1[V.]
45. See H.Dean, *The Whole Art of Legerdemain, or Hocus Pocus In Perfection* (London: 1722), pp.66-7; Letter dated Ashbourn, Derb. Jan 20 in *The Gentleman's Magazine and Historical Chronicle* (London: 1755), XXV, 59.

46. *O.E.D.* sb. TOUCHWOOD.
47. Sachs, *Sleight of Hand*, p.73; Hopkins, *Magic, Stage Illusions, Special Effects and Trick Photography*, p.151.
48. Hyll, *A Briefe and pleasaunt Treatise*, C 8^r.
49. William Hone, *The Everyday Book*, (London: 1866), 2 vols., II, pp.386-90.
50. Vitale-Brovarone (ed.), *Il quaderno di segreti*, pp.50-3.
51. The sort of protection I am thinking of is a hood of the kind worn by racing drivers today.
52. Cohen, *Le Livre De Conduite Du Régisseur,* pp.498-9.

Chapter 3

1. Chambers, *The Mediaeval Stage*, II, pp.23, n.5, 393; Karl Young, *The Drama of the Medieval Church* (Oxford: 1933), 2 vols, I, p.408; Cox, *Churchwardens' Accounts*, p.270; Pamela Sheingorn, *The Easter Sepulchre in England* (Kalamazoo: 1987), p.90. The incident is recorded in Mathew Ch.28, 2-4 and is also to be found in the later thirteenth-century *Ordo Paschalis* at Klosterneuburg. A later thirteenth-century version is recorded in a *Ludus Paschalis* from the *Carmina Burana* collections found at the Bavarian Monastry of Benidiktbeuern. Both accounts are contained in Young, *The Drama of the Medieval Church*, I, p.423, l.60 and p.435, l.69.
2. John Baptista Porta, *Magia Naturalis* (Naples: 1558); English translation, *Natural Magick* (London: 1658); facs.rpt. of English translation Derek J.Price (ed.), *Natural Magick* (New York: 1957), p.301. The technique is also recorded by Albertus Magnus in *The Secrets of Albertus Magnus*. He substitutes the rosin, colophone for the sulphur: "If thou wilt blowe the hearbe called Colophonia.Greeke pitch beaten very small, upon the flame of the candle, which a man holdeth in his hand, it augmenteth marvellously the fire, and lifted up the flame unto the house rough.". See also Best and Brightman (eds.), *The Book of Secrets of Albertus Magnus*, p.110; Partington (p.54) translates as follows: "Take colophonium and pitch, grind to a very fine powder and project this by a tube [blowpipe] into a fire or into a candle flame. This reading...gives a method of producing a cloud of fire...and is produced in theatres by lycopodium dust.". The translation should not read "colophonium and pitch" but "colophonium or pitch". Best and Brightman correctly translate "pitch" as "Greek pitch".
3. Sebastian Serlio, *The Five Books of Architecture: An Unabridged Reprint of the English Edition of 1611* (New York: 1982), f.26^v.
4. *REED: Coventry*, pp.221, 242, 465, 469, 472.
5. See Nicoll, *The Development of the Theatre*, p.62; William Donald Young, *Devices and Feintes*, p.82.
6. *REED: Newcastle*, p.55.
7. Dawson (ed.), *Malone Society Collections*, VII, p.209.

8. R.Warwick Bond (ed.), *The Bugbears*, Act V, Sc.I, p.123; *O.E.D.* v.1 POUND.

9. Richard Simpson (ed.), *A Warning For Faire Women* in *The School of Shakespeare* (London: 1878), II, p.243, ll.51-2. See also Thomas Heywood, *The Silver Age* in *The Dramatic Works of Thomas Heywood Now First Collected with Illustrative Notes and A Memoir of the Author in Six Volumes* (London: 1874; rpt. New York: 1964), III, p.159.

10. Isacchi, *Inventioni*, pp.109-10.

11. Claude Fortuné Ruggieri, *Élémens de Pyrotechnie, divisés en cinq parties;... Suivis d'un Vocabulaire et de la Description des principaux Feux d'artifice qui ont été tirés à Paris depuis 30 ans, etc.* (Paris: 1821); English translation, Stuart Carlton (ed.), *Principles of Pyrotechnics* (Buena Vista, California: 1994), p.228.

12. Best and Brightman (eds.), *The Book of Secrets of Albertus Magnus*, pp.89, 109, 110; Derek J.Price (ed.), *Natural Magick*, p.299; Platte, *The Jewell House of Art and Natvre*, p.31; J.C.Cannell, *The Secrets of Houdini*, p.118.

13. F.J.Furnivall (ed.),*The Digby Plays* (London: 1896; rpt.1967), p.34.

14. Darryll Grantley, 'Producing Miracles' in Paula Neuss (ed.), *Aspects of Early English Drama* (Cambridge: 1983), p.87.

15. Baker, Murphy and Hall (eds.),*The Late Medieval Religious Plays*, xxx, p.18; cf. stage direction.

16. *O.E.D.* sb.1 TEMPEST.

17. *O.E.D.* a. FERVENT.

18. Examples occur in Dekker, Webster, Middleton, Marston and Kirke. In Act V, Sc.I, of *The Roaring Girl* by Dekker, Moll describes a rogue to be "like a fire-worke to run vpon a line betwixt him and me."; Fredson Bowers (ed.), *The Roaring Girl* in *The Dramatic Works of Thomas Dekker* (Cambridge: 1958), III, p.82, ll.11-12. Dekker also refers to the practice in *The Honest Whore, Part 2* in Act II, Sc.I when Orlando Friscobaldo declares: "troth Mistris, to tell you true, the fireworkes that ran from me vpon lines against my good old Master, your father, were but to try how my young Master, your Husband loued such squibs:"; Fredson Bowers (ed.), *The Honest Whore, Part 2* in *The Dramatic Works of Thomas Dekker* (Cambridge: 1955), II, p.159, ll.211-14. In Dekker's *The Whore of Babylon* the Empresse says: "Let vs behold these fire-workes, that must run Vpon short lines of life:"; Fredson Bowers (ed.), *The Whore of Babylon* in *The Dramatic Works of Thomas Dekker* (Cambridge: 1955), II, p.537, ll.89-90. In Act IV, Sc.III, of *Northward Ho* by Thomas Dekker and John Webster the practice is alluded to as follows:

> Bell. But what say you to such young Gentlemen as these are.
> Baud. Foh, they as soone as they come to their lands get vp to London, and like squibs that run vpon lynes, they keepe a spitting of fire, and cracking till they ha spent all, and when my squib is out, what sayes his punke, foh, he stinckes.

Fredson Bowers (ed.), *Northwood Ho* in *The Dramatic Works of Thomas Dekker* (Cambridge: 1955), II, p.459. In Act I, Sc.II, of *The Fawn* by John Marston the following description occurs in response to a question about the nature of the birthday celebrations for Prince[ss] Dulcimel:

> Page. There be squibs, sir; which squibs, running upon lines, like some of our gaudy gallants, sir, keep a smother, sir, with flishing and flashing, and, in the end, sir, they do, sir——
>
> Nym. What, sir?
>
> Page. Stink, sir.

A.H.Bullen (ed.),*The Fawn* in *The Works of John Marston* (London: 1887), II, p.121. An explicit stage direction in Act II, Sc.I, of *If this be not a Good Play, the Devil is in it* by Thomas Dekker requires "Fire-workes on lines" in Fredson Bowers (ed.), *The Dramatic Works of Thomas Dekker* (Cambridge: 1958), III, p.150, l.193. The process is further acknowleged in Kirke's *The Seven Champions of Christendome*:

> Clow.[ne] I would you had 'em, they'd give much content; Oh I doe love those things a life i' faith. Have you any squibs in your Country? any Green-men in your shows, and Whizers upon lines, Iacke Pudding upon Rope, or Sis in fireworkes?

J.K[irke], *The Seven Champions of Christendome* (London: 1638), Actus Tertius, H^V-H2.

19. Bate, *The Mysteryes of Natvre and Art*, pp.76,77.
20. Babington, *Pyrotechnia*, pp.16,17; Norton, *The Gvnner*, p.152.
21. Babington, *Pyrotechnia*, p.17.
22. Nichols, *Progresses...Elizabeth*, III, p.118.
23. Meredith and Tailby (eds.), *The Staging of Religious Drama*, p.105.
24. Serlio, *The Five Books of Architecture*, f.26^V; see *Ben Jonson's Everyman In His Humour*, prologue.
25. Nicolo Sabbatini, *Pratica di Fabricar Scene E machine Ne' Teatri* (Ravenna: 1638; facs. rpt. Roma: 1955), p.126; Barnard Hewitt (ed.), *The Renaissance Stage: Documents of Serlio, Sabbattini and Furtenbach* (Coral Gables, Florida: 1958; rpt.1969), p.172; Lily B.Campbell, *Scenes and Machines on the English Stage during the Renaissance. A Classical Revival* (Cambridge: 1923), p.157; Richard Southern, 'the stage groove and the thunder run', *Architectural Review* LXXXXV (May 1944), 135-6; Richard Southern, *Changeable Scenery* (London: 1952), p.230; Frances Ann Shirley, *Shakespeare's Use of Off-Stage Sounds* (Lincoln, Nebraska: 1963), p.7.
26. Hopkins, *Magic, Stage Illusions, Special Effects and Trick Photography*, pp.303-4; Nicoll, *The Development of the Theatre*, p.61; Shergold, *A History of the Spanish Stage*, p.281.
27. A thunder barrell was stored in the "Buttre" at St.John's College, Cambridge; *REED: Cambridge*, I, p.128. Payment is recorded for "a thondre barrell" at Westminster School in 1565-6; Chambers, *The Elizabethan Stage*, II, p.73. The drapers at Coventry record payment for their barrell to make the "yerthe

quake"; *REED: Coventry*, pp.230, 474; J.C.L.Simonde de Sismondi, *Historical View of the Literature of the South of Europe* (London: 1872-7), 2 vols., II, p.240; Shergold, *A History of the Spanish Stage*, pp.189-90; Meredith and Tailby (eds.), *The Staging of Religious Drama*, pp.105, 157-8, 197; William Dunlap, *The Life of George Fred. Cooke* (London: 1815), 2 vols., I, pp.10-13.

28. Baker, Murphy and Hall (eds.),*The Late Medieval Religious Plays*, p.15.
29. Lucar, *Appendix*, p.83; Bate, *The Mysteryes of Natvre and Art*, pp.72-3; Babington, *Pyrotechnia*, p.14; Kentish, *The Pyrotechnist's Treasury* (c.1976), p.96; Lancaster, *Fireworks: Principles and Practice,* p.163.
30. Hampden (ed.), *Three Plays*, p.257.
31. *REED: Coventry*, p.308.
32. W.J.Lawrence, *Pre-Restoration Stage Studies* (Cambridge, Mass.: 1927), p.230.
33. Shimizu, *Fireworks: The Art, Science and Technique*, pp.125, 130; Lancaster, *Fireworks: Principles and Practice*, pp.48-49.
34. *REED: Coventry*, p.308.
35. Meredith and Tailby (eds.), *The Staging of Religious Drama*, p.199.
36. Meredith and Tailby (eds.), *The Staging of Religious Drama*, p.244. See also p.247.
37. Meredith and Tailby (eds.), *The Staging of Religious Drama*, pp.231, 232, 234, 236, 238.
38. Meredith and Tailby (eds.), *The Staging of Religious Drama*, p.197.
39. Meredith and Tailby (eds.), *The Staging of Religious Drama*, p.149.
40. Meredith and Tailby (eds.), *The Staging of Religious Drama*, p.149.
41. Shimizu, *Fireworks: The Art, Science and Technique*, p.78; Lancaster, *Fireworks: Principles and Practice*, pp.188, 237.
42. Lancaster, *Fireworks: Principles and Practice*, p.188.
43. Lancaster, *Fireworks: Principles and Practice*, p.188.
44. Shimizu, *Fireworks: The Art, Science and Technique*, p.78; Lancaster, *Fireworks: Principles and Practice*, p.188.
45. Shimizu, *Fireworks: The Art, Science and Technique*, p.78; Lancaster, *Fireworks: Principles and Practice*, p.188; Davis, *The Chemistry of Powder and Explosives*, p.122.
46. Davis (ed.), *Non-Cycle Plays and Fragments*, pp.58-89; Celia Cutts, 'The Croxton Play: An Anti-Lollard Piece', *Modern Language Quarterly* V (1944), 60.
47. Alfred W.Pollard (ed.), *English Miracle Plays, Moralities and Interludes* (Oxford: 1890; rpt.1973), xlv; Chambers, *The Mediaeval Stage*, II, p.427; Hardin Craig, *English Religious Drama of the Middle Ages* (Oxford: 1955; rpt.1968), pp.326-7; Arnold Williams, 'The Comic in the Cycles', in Neville Denny (ed.), *Medieval Drama* (London: 1973), p.123; David Bevington (ed.), *Medieval Drama*, (Boston: 1975), pp.754-56. Some writers have recognised merit in the play. See E.K.Chambers, *English Literature at the Close of the Middle Ages* (Oxford: 1945; rpt.1971), p.46; A.P.Rossiter, *English Drama From Early Times To The Elizabethans: Its Background, Origins and Developments* (London: 1950; rpt.1962), p.73; Charles Mills Gayley, *Representative English Comedies* (New York: 1903), 4 vols., I, xxxviii - xxxix; Mary del Villar, 'Some Approaches to the Medieval English Saint's Play', *Research Opportunities in Renaissance Drama* XV-XVI (1972-73), 88.

48. Davis (ed.), *Non-Cycle Plays and Fragments*, p.73, l.480, p.74, l.515, p.82, l.777, p.83, l.825. See Meredith and Tailby (eds.), *The Staging of Religious Drama*, pp.102-3, 105, 110-13.

49. Davis (ed.), *Non-Cycle Plays and Fragments*, p.78, l.660; Craig, *English Religious Drama*, pp.324-7; Chambers, *English Literature*, pp.45-6.

50. Davis (ed.), *Non-Cycle Plays and Fragments*, p.79, l.672.

51. Other examples include Hardin Craig (ed.), *Two Coventry Corpus Christi Plays*, Early English Text Society, ES87 (London: 1957; rpt. 1967), p.42, l.292; Hermann Deimling and Dr.Matthews (eds.), *The Chester Plays*, Early English Text Society, ES62, ES115 (London: 1892; rpt.1968 and 1916 rpt.1968), 2vols, I, p.23, l.80, p.81, l.420, p.92, l.168; Norris(ed.), *The Ancient Cornish Drama*, I, p.201, l.2628.

52. Meredith and Tailby (eds.), *The Staging of Religious Drama*, passim.

53. Davis (ed.), *Non-Cycle Plays and Fragments*, p.79, l.674.

54. Grantley, 'Producing Miracles', p.85.

55. William Tydeman, *English Medieval Theatre 1400-1500* (Cambridge: 1978), p.59.

56. Daniel V.Thompson,*The Materials of Medieval Painting* (London: 1936), pp.103-8; A.H.Church, *The Chemistry of Paints and Painting* (London: 1890), pp.146-51.

57. Balfour-Paul (ed.), *The Accounts*, VII, p.357.

58. Davis, *The Chemistry of Powder and Explosives*, p.122.

59. Meredith and Tailby (eds.), *The Staging of Religious Drama*, p.107; Shergold, *A History of the Spanish Stage*, pp.63-4.

60. Meredith and Tailby (eds.), *The Staging of Religious Drama*, p.106.

61. Potassium chlorate ($KClO_3$) and potassium perchlorate ($KClO_4$) are two additional oxidising agents used today. See Lancaster, *Fireworks: Principles and Practice*, pp.46-7.

62. Bate, *The Mysteryes of Natvre and Art*, p.63; Babington, *Pyrotechnia*, pp.55-8; Lucar, *Appendix*, pp.80,81; Simienowicz, *The Great Art of Artillery*, pp.174-85.

63. Bate, *The Mysteryes of Natvre and Art*, p.63; Simienowicz, *The Great Art of Artillery*, pp.174-6.

64. Davis, *Non-Cycle Plays and Fragments*, p.80, l.712.

65. Meredith and Tailby (eds.), *The Staging of Religious Drama*, p.112.

66. Grantley, 'Producing Miracles', pp.84-5.

67. Meredith and Tailby (eds.), *The Staging of Religious Drama*, pp.268-9.

68. Young, *The Drama of the Medieval Church*, II, pp.154, 164.

Chapter 4

1. Michael Faraday, *A Course of Six Lectures on the Chemical History of a Candle* (London: 1861; rpt. c.1960); Oliver C. De C.Ellis, *A History of Fire and Flame* (London: 1932).

2. Babington, *Pyrotechnia,* pp.60, 41, 56-7; Lucar, *Appendix,* p.84; Hyll, *A Briefe and pleasaunt Treatise*, A5^{r}, A5^{v}.
3. William T.O'Dea, *The Social History of Lighting* (London: 1958), p.213.
4. David J.Eveleigh,*Candle Lighting* (Aylesbury: 1985), pp. 7, 13.
5. Gilbert White, *The Natural History of Selborne* (London: 1788-9; rpt. London: 1977), pp.180-3; William Cobbett, *Cottage Economy* (London: 1822; rpt. Oxford: 1979), pp.144-5; Leroy Thwing, *Flickering Flames: A History of Domestic Lighting through the Ages* (Vermont: 1958), pp.97-9; Gertrude Jekyll, *Old West Surrey* (London: 1904; facs.rpt.Dorking: 1978), pp.101-7; Ellis, *A History of Fire and Flame*, p.279.
6. Examples are to be found in the small museum at Haddon Hall, Derbyshire. See also Platte, *The Jewell House of Art and Natvre*, p.48.
7. Thomas Wright (ed.), *Churchwardens' Accounts of the Town of Ludlow in Shropshire, from 1540 to the end of the Reign of Queen Elizabeth* (London: 1869), p.3.
8. *REED: Coventry*, p.110.
9. For concern about the damage created by smoke from torches see Gerald Eades Bentley, *The Jacobean and Caroline Stage* (Oxford: 1941-68), 7 vols., VI, pp.265,285.
10. Brock, *A History of Fireworks*, p.196; Lancaster, *Fireworks: Principles and Practice*, pp.37,39,184; Kentish, *The Pyrotechnist's Treasury* (c.1976), p.10; Lieutenant Robert Jones, *A New Treatise on Artificial Fireworks* (London: 1765), pp.62-3; Bate, *The Mysteryes of Natvre and Art*, pp.62,63,71.
11. Sayle (ed.), *Lord Mayors' Pageants*, pp.30,36,41; Robertson and Gordon (eds.), *Malone Society Collections*, III, pp.24,29; *REED: Cambridge*, I, p.234; *Progresses...Elizabeth*, I, p.167; David W.Blewitt, 'Records of Drama at Winchester and Eton, 1397-1576', *Theatre Notebook* XXXVIII, 3 (1984), 139; *REED: CWG*, p.303; David N.Klausner (ed.), *Records of Early English Drama: Herefordshire Worcestershire* (Toronto: 1990), pp.430, 433. Subsequently referred to as *REED: HW*.
12. Glynn Wickham, *Early English Stages 1300 to1660*, I, plates 32, 33; R.C.Strong and J.A.van Dorsten, *Leicester's Triumph* (Leiden and London: 1964), pp.41-7.
13. Nicholl...*Ironmongers*, p.84; Lucar, *Appendix*, p.84.
14. O'Dea, *The Social History of Lighting*, p.68; Thwing, *Flickering Flames*, p.100; *REED: Cambridge*, I, p.167; *REED: CWG*, p.303.
15. For illustrations of cressets see Sharp, *A Dissertation on the Pageants*, Plate 9, opp. p.51; William Hone,*The Every-Day Book* (London: 1825; rpt.London: 1866), I, pp.416-7; Francis Douce, *Illustrations of Shakespeare, and of Ancient Manners* (London: 1839), pp.264-5; Nicholl...*Ironmongers*, p.62; J.R.Green, *A Short History of the English People* (London: 1893), III, p.992; John Caspall, *Fire and Light in the home pre-1820* (Woodbridge, Suffolk: 1987), p.257.
16. An exception occurs in the *Cappers' Records* at Coventry for 1544; *REED: Coventry*, p.168.
17. *REED: Coventry*, p.168.
18. Apart from the illustrations contained in n.15, see Chambers, *The Elizabethan Stage*, II, p.543, n.3; W.J.Lawrence, *The Elizabethan Playhouse and Other Studies* (Stratford-upon-Avon: 1913), Second Series, p.13.

19. Nicholl... *Ironmongers*, p.64; *REED: Coventry*, pp.115,157,184; John Wasson (ed.), *Records of Early English Drama: Devon* (Toronto: 1986), pp.94,370. Subsequently referred to as *REED: Devon*.
20. Robertson and Gordon (eds.), *Malone Society Collections*, III, xvi.
21. *REED: Coventry*, pp.118,129; Sharp, *A Dissertation on the Pageants*, p.187.
22. *O.E.D.* sb.2 BEAT; *O.E.D.* vbl. sb. obs. BEETING.
23. *REED: Coventry*, pp.115,127,157.
24. *REED: Devon*, pp.94,370; 90,366. Translation by Peter Meredith.
25. The rolled-up balls of oakum may have been bound with thread. See *REED: Devon*, pp.91,367.
26. Lucar, *Appendix*, p.84.
27. Hyll, *A Briefe and pleasaunt Treatise*, A5ᵛ, A5ʳ.
28. Robertson and Gordon (eds.), *Malone Society Collections*, III, xvi; *REED: Norwich*, p.101.
29. W.Y.Durand, 'Palaemon and Arcyte, Progne, Marcus Geminus, and the theatre in which they were acted, as described by John Bereblock (1566).', *Publications of the Modern Language Association of America* XX, New Series, XIII (1905; rpt.1961), 504-5; *REED: Cambridge*, II, p.1145.
30. Partington, *A History of Greek Fire and Gunpowder*, pp.51-3, 85-6; S.Harrison Thomson, 'The Texts of Michael Scot's Ars Alchemie', *Osiris* V (1938), 523-59; R.J.Forbes, *A Short History of the Art of Distillation* (Leiden: 1948), pp.60-9; Lu Gwei-Djen, Joseph Needham and Dorothy Needham, 'The Coming of Ardent Water', *Ambix* XIX (1972), pp.69-112; C.Anne Wilson, 'Philosophers, *Iosis* and Water of Life', *Proceedings of the Leeds Philosophical and Literary Society* XIX, part V (1984), pp.45-93.
31. Gwei-Djen, Needham and Needham, 'The Coming of Ardent Water', 70; Wilson, 'Philosophers, *Iosis* and Water of Life', 61; *Calendar of State Papers (Venice)*, VIII, p.535, Item 1034.
32. Wilson, 'Philosophers, *Iosis* and Water of Life', 61.
33. Gwei-Djen, Needham and Needham, 'The Coming of Ardent Water', 70, n.9; Forbes, *A Short History*, p.66; Payment is made in *The Accounts M.W.*, II, p.92 for "a pynt of double aquavitae iiiilib.". This expensive spirit may have been distilled more than once in order to be described as such.
34. Don Alessio Ruscelli, *The second part of the Secretes of Maister Alexis of Piemont, by hym collected out of diuers excellent aucthours* [sic] (London: 1563), f.1; Forbes, *A Short History*, pp.60-9.
35. Bate, *The Mysteryes of Natvre and Art* p.66; Best and Brightman (eds.), *The Book of Secrets of Albertus Magnus*, p.110; Partington, *A History of Greek Fire and Gunpowder*, pp.51,52,86.
36. Serlio,*The Five Books of Architecture*, f.26ᵛ; Derek J.Price (ed.), *Natural Magick*, p.257. This simple technique may be tried by soaking a cotton handkerchief in brandy and setting it alight. The flame produced is virtually colourless and does not burn the material. Even ragged strands of cotton are not consumed.
37. Brock, *A History of Fireworks*, pp.195-6.
38. H.Dussauce, *A Practical Treatise on the Fabrication of Matches, Gun Cotton, Colored Fires and Fulminating Powders* (Philadelphia: 1864), pp.189-213; V.E.Johnson, *Chemical Magic* (London: 1920), pp.53-4.

39. Feuillerat (ed.), *Documents Relating to the Office of the Revels*, p.308; Chambers, *The Elizabethan Stage*, I, p.232.

40. *REED: Cambridge*, I, p.185; II, p.966.

41. Serlio, *The Five Books of Architecture*, f.26^V.

42. J.Alan B.Somerset (ed.), *Records of Early English Drama: Shropshire* (Toronto: 1994), 2 vols., I, p.184. Subsequently referred to as *REED: Shropshire*.

43. McInnes (ed.), *The Accounts*, XII, p.404.

44. Bate, *The Mysteryes of Natvre and Art*, p.66; Brock, *A History of Fireworks*, p.153.

45. Hyll, *A Briefe and pleasaunt Treatise*, C5^r, C6^V.

46. McInnes (ed.), *The Accounts*, XII, p.404.

47. Lucar, *Appendix*, p.81.

48. Brock, *A History of Fireworks*, p.155.

49. Balfour-Paul (ed.), *The Accounts*, VII, p.357.

50. Lucar, *The third booke of Nicholas Tartaglia his Colloquies*, p.72.

51. Serlio, *The Five Books of Architecture*, f.26^V.

52. Brock, *A History of Fireworks*, p.155.

53. Dawson (ed.), *Malone Society Collections*, VII, p.209.

54. Hyll, *A Briefe and pleasaunt Treatise*, B4^r.

55. Balfour-Paul (ed.), *The Accounts*, VII, p.357.

56. A.C.Crombie, *Robert Grosseteste and the Origins of Experimental Science* (Oxford: 1953), pp.218-9; Smith and Gnudi (eds.), *The Pyrotechnia of Vannoccio Biringuccio*, pp.385-7; Lynn White Jr., *Medieval Technology and Social Change* (London: 1962), pp.89-90; Lynn White Jr., *Medieval Religion and Technology* (Berkley, Los Angeles, London: 1978), p.127.

57. Smith and Gnudi (eds.),*The Pyrotechnia of Vannoccio Biringuccio*, p.385.

58. Meredith and Tailby (eds.), *The Staging of Religious Drama*, p.114.

59. Smith and Gnudi (eds.),*The Pyrotechnia of Vannoccio Biringuccio*, pp.385-90.

60. Biringuccio recounts the following anecdote concerning the convergence of light: "One day, when for amusement he [a German friend of Biringuccio] was standing in a window to watch a review of armed men in the city of Ulm, he bore with the sphere of his mirror for a quarter of an hour on the back of shoulder armor of one of those soldiers. This not only caused so much heat that it became almost unbearable to the soldier, but it inflamed so that it kindled his jacket underneath and burned it for him, cooking his flesh to his very great torment. Since he did not understand who caused this, he said that God had miraculously sent that fire on him for his great sins."; Smith and Gnudi (eds.), *The Pyrotechnia of Vannoccio Biringuccio*, p.387.

61. *Holinshed's Chronicles*, IV, p.645; Strong and van Dorsten, *Leicester's Triumph*, p.42.

62. Strong and van Dorsten, *Leicester's Triumph*, p.42.

63. Bergman, *Lighting in the Theatre*, p.47.

64. *Holinshed's Chronicles*, IV, p.644; This particular feature is absent from the engraving contained in Strong and van Dorsten, *Leicester's Triumph*, p.49,n.1.

65. Nicoll, *The Development of the Theatre*, p.274.

66. W.R.Streitberger (ed.), *Malone Society Collections*, (Oxford: 1986), XIII, p.58; Morton Paterson, "The Stagecraft of the Revels Office during the

Reign of Elizabeth', in Charles T.Prouty (ed.), *Studies in the Elizabethan Theatre* (1961), pp.45-8. Clearly, Paterson was not aware of this reference since he declares: "No mention is made in the accounts of either footlights, mirrors or reflectors. If mirrors, in particular, were used to any extent, the accounts would surely have included them.".

67. R.B.Graves, 'Stage Lighting at the Elizabethan and Early Stuart Courts', *Theatre Notebook* XXXVIII, I (1984), 27; Graves points out that the seasonal nature of the Revels accounts makes it difficult to identify particular productions and their locations.

68. Platte, *The Jewell House of Art and Natvre*, p.32.

69. Derek J.Price (ed.), *Natural Magick*, p.359.

70. Derek J.Price (ed.), *Natural Magick*, pp.359-60.

71. White, *Medieval Religion and Technology*, pp.87-8,127.

72. Platte, *The Jewell House of Art and Natvre*, p.31; John Bate, *The Mysteryes of Natvre and Art: The Third Booke Of Drawing, Limming, Colouring, Painting, and Graving* (London: 1634; facs.rpt. Amsterdam: 1977), p.157.

73. Hewitt (ed.), *The Renaissance Stage*, pp.224-7; Bergman, *Lighting in the Theatre*, p.85.

74. Hewitt (ed.), *The Renaissance Stage*, p.226.

75. Hewitt (ed.), *The Renaissance Stage*, pp.224-5.

76. Platte, *The Jewell House of Art and Natvre*, p.32.

77. Serlio, *The Five Books of Architecture*, f.26[v].; Hewitt (ed.), *The Renaissance Stage*,p.34; C.F.Bell, 'The Artificial Lighting of the Court Scene', in Herford, Percy and Simpson (eds.), *Ben Jonson* (London: 1950), p.412.

78. *O.E.D.* II, 7 CONDENSER.

79. John White, *A Rich Cabinet,with Variety of Inventions*, B1[v].

80. John Rovenzon, *A Treatise of Metallica*, (London: 1613), C2[v], C2[r]; A.Sauzay, *Marvels of Glass-Making in All Ages* (London: 1870), p.214.

81. See E.S.de Beer, 'The Early History of London Street-Lighting', *History* XXV (1941), 311-24; Lettie S.Multhauf, 'The Light of Lamp-Lanterns: Street Lighting in 17th-Century Amsterdam', *Technology and Culture* XXVI, 2 (1985), 236-52.

82. Eveleigh, *Candle Lighting*, p.3.

83. If the light source did not receive protection, then the following recipe offered by Don Alessio Rusceli might be applicable: "To make a Candell that can not be put out. Take Virgyne Waxe, and Brimstone well purged, asmuche of the one as of the other, and melte it togyther and make thereof a Candel, the which will neuer be put oute vntill it be burned and consumed to the ende."; Don Alessio Rusceli,*The second part of the Secretes of Maister Alexis of Piemont*, f.8[v]. Other similar recipes are given by Hyll, *A Briefe and pleasaunt Treatise*, A7[r]; Derek J.Price (ed.), *Natural Magick*, p.300.

84. Gaetano Milanesi (ed.), *Le Vite De' Più Eccellenti Pittori Scultori Ed Architettori scritte da Giorgio Vasari* (Firenze: 1881), VI, p.442; A.M.Nagler, *Theatre Festivals of the Medici 1539-1637* (New Haven/London: 1964), p.15; Bergman, *Lighting in the Theatre*, p.56.

85. Bergman, *Lighting in the Theatre*, p.61; Nagler, *Theatre Festivals of the Medici*, p.10.

86. Stanley J.Kahrl (ed.), *Malone Society Collections* (Oxford: 1972), VIII, Appendix A, p.96; Meredith and Tailby (eds.), *The Staging of Religious Drama*, p.114.
87. H.Ellis (ed.), *Hall's Chronicle*, p.596.
88. Nicoll, *The Development of the Theatre*, p.277.
89. Serlio, *The Five Books of Architecture*, f.26^V.
90. Platte, *The Jewell House of Art and Natvre*, p.31.
91. Hewitt (ed.), *The Renaissance Stage*, p.226.
92. Platte, *The Jewell House of Art and Natvre*, p.31.
93. White, *A Rich Cabinet, with Variety of Inventions*, B1^V.
94. Rovenzon, *A Treatise of Metallica*, C3^V.

Chapter 5

1. Bafour-Paul (ed.), *The Accounts*, VI, p.454; VII, p.357; VIII, p.450; Galloway and Wasson (eds.), *Malone Society Collections*, XI, p.128.
2. Edmund Howes, *The Annales or Generall Chronicle of England*, p.887; Withington, *English Pageantry*, I, p.229; Chambers, *The Elizabethan Stage*, I, pp.138, 172. The *Ironmongers' Court Books* record the following device for use in the *Lord Mayors' Show*:" A whale rounded close wthout sight of the boate and to row wth ffins/ open for ffireworke at the mouth and water vented at the head and the same to be in good and comelie pporcõn /."; Robertson and Gordon (eds.), *Malone Society Collections*, III, p.73.
3. Stokes (ed.), *The Life of Saint Meriasek*, p.228, ll.3941, 3947.
4. Robert Coltman Clephan, *An Outline of the History and Development of Hand Firearms, from the Earliest Period to about the End of the Fifteenth Century* (London: 1906; facs.rpt.: no date), p.5; Samuel Rush Meyrick, *Observations upon the History of Hand Fire-arms and their Appurtenances* (Richmond: 1971), p.61. Reference to "fiery breathing gones" is made in Robert Dodsley and later W.C.Hazlitt (eds.), *Summer's Last Will and Testament* in *A Select Collection of Old English Plays* (London: 1744; rpt.1874), VII, Prologue.
5. S.J.von Romocki, *Geschichte der Explosivstoffe: Geschichte der Sprengstoffchemie, der Sprengtechnik und des Torpedowesens bis zum Beginn der neuesten Zeit* (Berlin: 1895), I, p.199; translation of MS in Partington, *A History of Greek Fire and Gunpowder*, p.20.
6. Stokes (ed.), *The Life of Saint Meriasek*, p.228, l.3949.
7. Detailed dimensions of Hell and its mouth in the Lucerne *Passion Play* are contained in Meredith and Tailby (eds.), *The Staging of Religious Drama*, p.81. Presumably the six or eight devils indicated in the director's plans are capable of being enveloped by the Hell structure. The arrangement may be similar to the one shown in Jean Fouquet, *The Hours of Etienne Chevalier* (London: 1972), pl.45; Richard Southern, *The Medieval Theatre in the Round* (London: 1957; rpt.1975), p.103.

8. Anon, 'The Scenic World' in *Cornhill Magazine* 53 (1886), 291; W.J.Sorrell, *The Amateur's Hand-Book* (London: 1866), pp.23-4; Douglas Gilbert, *American Vaudeville: Its Life and Times* (New York: 1940; rpt. New York: 1968), p.30.

9. Meredith and Tailby (eds.), *The Staging of Religious Drama*, p.121.

10. Robertson and Gordon (eds.), *Malone Society Collections*, III, p.34.

11. *REED: Coventry*, pp.217,221,224,237.

12. Meredith and Tailby (eds.), *The Staging of Religious Drama*, pp.91,103.

13. Meredith and Tailby (eds.), *The Staging of Religious Drama*, p.157.

14. Meredith and Tailby (eds.), *The Staging of Religious Drama*, p.90.

15. See **CHAPTER 1**, n.60.

16. Hell mouth as a property is also recorded at York in the *Mercers' Pageant Documents* for 1433; see *REED: York*, I, p.55; see also the record of "j Hell mought" in "The Enventary tacken of all the properties for my Lord Admeralles men, the 10 of Marche 1598" in R.A.Foakes & R.T.Rickert (eds.) *Henslowe's Diary* (Cambridge: 1968), p.319.

17 *REED: Coventry*, pp.167, 212, 245, 256, 469, 472.

18. *REED: Coventry*, p.478.

19. *REED: Coventry*, p.478.

20. *REED: Coventry*, pp.221, 237, 478.

21. *REED: Coventry*, p.224.

22. *REED: Coventry*, pp.217, 221, 224, 230, 237, 242, 256.

23. Mary Dormer Harris, 'The "World" In The Doomsday Mystery Play', *Notes and Queries* CXLIX (1925), 243; R.W.Ingram, '"To find the players and all that longeth therto": Notes on the Production of Medieval Drama in Coventry' in G.R.Hibbard (ed.) *The Elizabethan Theatre* V (Toronto: 1975), p.30; Reginald W.Ingram, '"Pleyng geire accustumed belongyng & necessarie": guild records and pageant production at Coventry' in Joanna Dutka (ed.) *Proceedings of the First Colloquium* (Toronto: 1979), p.78; Reg Ingram, 'The Coventry Pageant Wagon', *Medieval English Theatre* 2:1 (1980), 11.

24. Norton, *The Gvnner*, p.155.

25. Babington, *Pyrotechnia*, p.46.

26. Jones, *A New Treatise*, pp.246-7.

27. See Peter Meredith, 'The Development of the York Mercers' Pageant Wagon', *Medieval English Theatre* 1:1 (1979), 10; William Donald Young, *Devices and Feintes*, pp.122-4.

28. Cohen, *Le Livre De Conduite Du Régisseur*, p.14; Meredith and Tailby (eds.), *The Staging of Religious Drama*, p.150.

29. *REED: Coventry*, pp.217, 221, 224; cf. Mons where 17 people helped Maistre Jehan du Fayt to produce the effects; Cohen, *Le Livre De Conduite Du Régisseur*, pp.544-5; Meredith and Tailby (eds.), *The Staging of Religious Drama*, p.149.

30. Different statements would have been possible according to whether the audience witnessed the source, its effect or both.

31. *REED: Coventry*, pp.221, 224, 237, 250, 256, 259, 264, 475, 478-9, 481, 506.

32. *REED: Coventry*, p.217.

33. Best and Brightman (eds.), *The Book of Secrets of Albertus Magnus*, p.110. See **CHAPTER 3**, n.2.
34. See **CHAPTER 1**, n.49.
35. J.A.Lavin (ed.), *Friar Bacon and Friar Bungay*, xx; Meredith and Tailby (eds.), *The Staging of Religious Drama*, p.102.
36. *O.E.D.* sb.1 STOPE a. Tow for burning. b. Oakum.
37. McInnes, *The Accounts*, XII, p.405; Philip Butterworth, 'The Baptisme of Hir Hienes Darrest Sone in Stirviling', *Medieval English Theatre*, 10:1 (1988), 46-7.
38. Norton, *The Gvnner*, p.155; Bate,*The Mysteryes of Natvre and Art*, pp.79,80; Babington, *Pyrotechnia*, pp.36-41.
39. Babington, *Pyrotechnia*, pp.36-41.
40. Bate, *The Mysteryes of Natvre and Art*, p.79. Bate required that his dragons should be constructed from "dry and light wood, or crooked-lane plates, or of thin whalebones covered with Muscovie glasse, and painted over.".
41. Cohen, *Le Livre De Conduite Du Régisseur*, p.498. Godeffroy du Pont, coroyer [welder], was paid for 5½ days work to fit out the serpents with metal tubes in order to eject fire. Cohen notes that the serpents were the dragons on top of the Tower of Hell. Another payment is recorded for 12 dozen little tin tubes to fire rockets (p.530). Both these accounts seem to refer to safety methods when dealing with rockets and ejecting fire.
42. Bate, *The Mysteryes of Natvre and Art*, p.75; Brock, *A History of Fireworks*, pp.215-6.
43. Babington, *Pyrotechnia*, p.11; Bate, *The Mysteryes of Natvre and Art*, p.61.
44. Vitale-Brovarone (ed.), *Il quaderno di segreti*, pp.50-3; Cohen, *Le Livre De Conduite Du Régisseur*, pp.498-9.
45. Bate, *The Mysteryes of Natvre and Art*, p.79.
46. Babington, *Pyrotechnia*, pp.10-12; Bate, *The Mysteryes of Natvre and Art*, p.61.
47. Babington, *Pyrotechnia*, p.14.
48. Lucar, *Appendix*, p.83 for recipes of "squibs"; de Malthe, *A Treatise of Artificial Fire-vvorks*, pp.78-9 for method of making "serpents"; Babington, *Pyrotechnia*, p.14 for manufacture of "serpents"; Jones, *A New Treatise*, p.155 on "serpents"; Frederick Bruhl, *The Art of Making Fireworks, Detonating Balls etc* (London: 1844), pp.4-6 for "squibs", "serpents" and "superior serpents"; Kentish, *The Pyrotechnist's Treasury* (c.1976), pp.91-7 on "squibs" and "serpents"; Weingart, *Pyrotechnics*, pp.112-3 on "serpents".
49. William Grant and David D.Murison (eds.), *The Scottish National Dictionary* (Edinburgh: 1931-90), VII, II. n.1 (4) "play-mare, a hobby-horse;".
50. Imrie and Dunbar (eds.), *The Accounts M.W.*, II, pp.90, 92.
51. *The Accounts M.W.*, II, refer to Saint Andrew as Saint George. This is a mistake. It was Saint Andrew who slew the dragon and Saint George was aligned to the Castle of Envy. It is this notion that makes it possible for "the boy fra Bervick" to have also been dressed up as Saint George on his "playmeir".
52. Imrie and Dunbar (eds.), *The Accounts M.W.*, II, pp.79, 84.
53. *The Accounts M.W.*, II, also contain payment for "hair" and "lyme" that could have been used in the plaster work of the dragon.

54. Babington, *Pyrotechnia*, p.55.
55. Bate, *The Mysteryes of Nature and Art*, pp.89-92. Bate describes three kinds of lance.
56. See **CHAPTER 1**, n.54.
57. C.E.McGee, 'Fireworks for Queen Elizabeth', *Malone Society Collections*, XV, pp.204-5.
58. See **CHAPTER 1**, n.55.
59. See **Lances** in **GLOSSARY**.
60. Babington, *Pyrotechnia*, p.49; de Malthe, *A Treatise of Artificial Fire-vvorks*, p.103.
61. Babington, *Pyrotechnia*, p.49; de Malthe, *A Treatise of Artificial Fire-wworks*, p.103.
62. Kentish, *The Pyrotechnist's Treasury*, (c.1976), pp.117-22.
63. Kentish, *The Pyrotechnist's Treasury*, (c.1976), p.108.
64. Bate, *The Mysteryes of Nature and Art*, p.75.
65 Babington, *Pyrotechnia*, p.14.
66. George Plimpton, *Fireworks: A History and Celebration* (New York: 1984), pp.201-2; Peter Milward (ed.), *Hanabi: The Fireworks of Japan* (Tokyo: 1986), p.78; Weingart, *Pyrotechnics*, pp.203-4.
67. Nichols, *Progresses...James*, II, pp.525, 527, 530-7, 587; *B.L.Additional 70518*.
68. Nichols, *Progresses...James*, II, p.532.
69. Brock, *A History of Fireworks*, p.35.
70. Nichols, *Progresses...James*, II, 587.
71. Nichols, *Progresses...James*, II, 537.

Chapter 6

1. Pyrotechnic skill in England and Scotland was initially imported. *The Accounts* for 1506 and 1507 record "Hannis, gunnar" and his involvement in the production and maintenance of gunpowder in "the Castell of Edinburgh".*The Accounts* for 1536 record payment to "Maister Wouff" for fire balls, fire spears and fire arrows.*The Accounts* for 1538-41 further record payment to "Maister Wolf and Cristopheir, Frencheman, gunnaris". It seems from the last payment that "Cristopheir" is the "Frencheman", but it may be possible also that "Maister Wolf" is also a "Frencheman", for it appears that "Hannis" of the 1506 and 1507 records is the same person as "Maister Wolf". "Hans Wolf, foreigner" is recorded as "one of the King's gunpowder makers in the Tower of London and elsewhere" in 1515. See Balfour-Paul (ed.),*The Accounts*, III, pp.332-3, 395; VI, p.454; VII, p.357; Hodgetts (ed.), *The Rise and Progress*, p.185.
2. George R.Kernodle, *From Art To Theatre: Form and Convention in the Renaissance* (Chicago: 1943), pp.76-84; Glynne Wickham, *Early English Stages 1300 to 1660*, I, pp.13-50, 54, 91, 94, 232; John R.Elliott, Jr., 'Medieval Rounds and Wooden O's: The Medieval Heritage of the

162

Elizabethan Theatre' in Neville Denny (ed.), *Medieval Drama* (London: 1973), pp.231-6; Anne Lancashire, 'The Emblematic Castle in Shakespeare and Middleton' in J.C.Gray (ed.),*Mirror up to Shakespeare: Essays in Honour of G.R.Hibbard* (Toronto: 1984), pp.223-41.

3. Eccles (ed.), *The Macro Plays*, pp.1-111; Baker, Murphy and Hall (eds.), *The Late Medieval Religious Plays*, pp.24-95; Lancashire (ed.), *Dramatic Texts and Records of Britain*, p.141 (**707**), 145 (**730**), 187 (**965**); Withington, *English Pageantry*, I, pp.113-4, 116; Mill, *Mediaeval Plays in Scotland*, p.55, n.3.

4. *REED: Cambridge*, I, p.199.

5. Raine (ed.), *York Civic Records*, V, p.117.

6. Scottish Record Office, *SRO E 23/3/45* ; Mill, *Mediaeval Plays in Scotland*, pp.339-43; McInnes (ed.), *The Accounts*, XII, pp.403-9.

7. *A Diurnal of Remarkable Occurrents that have passed within the country of Scotland since the death of King James the Fourth till the year M.D.LXXV.* (Edinburgh: 1833), p.105; Mill, *Mediaeval Plays in Scotland*, p.55, n.1. The following item is recorded in *The Accounts*, XII, p.408: "Item payit to ane man in recompance of his yaird dyk cassin doun at the hors marcat quhair the Quenes majestie and embassadouris stuid iijs.".

8. The items listed in the eye-witness account for entertainment puposes are also recorded for military use in *The Accounts*, IV, p.490; VI, p.454; VII, p.357; VIII, p.450. See also Mill, *Mediaeval Plays in Scotland*, pp.325-6.

9. Michaell Gairdner, "gunnar and poulder maker in the castell of Edinburgh" was another of the key firework men. He was paid "for making of fyreworkis and bying of stuf to that poirpos togidder for his panes and expensis...xli."; *The Accounts*, XII, p.404; Butterworth, 'The Baptisme of Hir Hienes Darrest Sone in Stirviling', 28.

10. Mill, *Mediaeval Plays in Scotland*, p.340.

11. Alexander Warrack (ed.), *A Scots Dialect Dictionary* (London: 1911), TOUR n: "a turf, sod, peat.".

12. *E.D.D.* sb. 4v. TRANT "to act as a carrier".

13. *O.E.D.* TORTIS 2. "A twisted chain; a wreath.".

14. Meredith and Tailby (eds.), *The Staging of Religious Drama*, p.107.

15. Babington, *Pyrotechnia*, p.25.

16. Brewer, Gairdner and Brodie (eds.), *Letters and Papers, Foreign and Domestic*, II, pt.II, p.1505.

17. *Holinshed's Chronicles*, III, p.613.

18. The Earl of Warwick, Ambrose Dudley was well qualified to mount such an entertainment for he was the Master-General of the Ordnance.

19. Trains were thin lines of gunpowder used to convey fire to the "mortyr-pieces". See *O.E.D.* sb. 13. TRAIN.

20. *O.E.D.* sb.1. CALIVER "A light kind of musket or harquebus, originally, it appears, of a certain calibre, introduced during the 16th c; it seems to have been the lightest portable fire-arm, excepting the pistol, and to have been fired without a 'rest'."; *O.E.D.* HARQUEBUS sb.1 "The early type of portable gun, varying in size from a small cannon to a musket, which on account of its weight was, when used in the field, supported upon a tripod, trestle, or other 'carriage', and afterwards upon a forked 'rest'.".

21. Nichols, *Progresses...Elizabeth*, I, p.494.

22. Gascoine devised some of the speeches and dialogue for dramatic sequences but these were not related to the firework displays which appear to have existed in their own right. For synopsis, chronology, authorship and programme of events see Chambers, *The Elizabethan Stage*, IV, pp.61-2; I, pp.122-3.

23. Bate, *The Mysteryes of Natvre and Art*, p.63.

24. The visit lasted three weeks. The Queen arrived on Saturday 9 July and the first firework event was on Sunday 10 July. The second event took place on Thursday 14 July.

25. Nichols, *Progresses...Elizabeth*, I, p.434.

26. Bate, *The Mysteryes of Natvre and Art*, pp.86-8; de Malthe, *A Treatise of Artificial Fire-vvorks*, pp.88-90; Kentish, *The Pyrotechnist's Treasury*, (c.1976), pp.115-6.

27. Lucy Toulmin Smith (ed.), *The Maire of Bristowe is Kalendar, by Robert Ricart, Town Clerk of Bristol 18 Edward IV* (London: 1872), pp.58-9.

28. Nichols, *Progresses... Elizabeth,* I, p.402.

29. Joseph Bettey (ed.), 'Two Tudor Visits to Bristol' in Patrick McGrath (ed.), *A Bristol Miscellany* (Bristol: 1985), p.7.

30. Nichols, *Progresses...Elizabeth*, I, p.402.

31. Bettey (ed.), 'Two Tudor Visits to Bristol', p.10; Smith and Gnudi (eds.), *The Pyrotechnia of Vannoccio Biringuccio*, p.414; Babington, *Pyrotechnia*, p.11; Bate, *The Mysteryes of Natvre and Art*, p.54.

32. Jean Wilson, *Entertainments for Elizabeth I*, (Woodbridge, Suffolk: 1980), pp.100, 161 n.12 [she numbers it 13].

33. Wilson, *Entertainments for Elizabeth*, p.109.

34. Babington, *Pyrotechnia*, p.46.

35. Babington, *Pyrotechnia*, p.46; Norton, *The Gvnner*, pp.152-3.

36. Even though the motion of the planets is not as we understand it today, the source of the inspiration is acknowledged.

37. Bate, *The Mysteryes of Natvre and Art*, pp.76-7; Norton, *The Gvnner*, pp.152, 155; Babington, *Pyrotechnia*, pp16,17; Simienowicz, *The Great Art of Artillery*, pp.164-5.

38. Wilson, *Entertainments for Elizabeth*, p.164 n.93.

39. Brock, *A History of Fireworks*, p.203.

40. *O.E.D.* 3. CATHERINE WHEEL "A kind of firework which rotates, while burning, in the manner of a wheel.". The earliest example offered by the *O.E.D.* is 1760; Babington, *Pyrotechnia*, pp.19-25; Bate, *The Mysteryes of Natvre and Art*, pp.77,78; Brock, *A History of Fireworks*, p.203.

41. Philip, *A Bibliography of Firework Books*, plate 1; Bate, *The Mysteryes of Natvre and Art*, 77-8; Babington, *Pyrotechnia*, pp.19-25.

42. Norton, *The Gvnner*, p.153.

43. Norton, *The Gvnner*, pp.154-5, 155; Bate, *The Mysteryes of Natvre and Art*, pp.97, 98; Babington, *Pyrotechnia*, pp.55-8; de Malthe, *A Treatise of Artificial Fire-vvorks*, p.63; Simienowicz,*The Great Art of Artillery*, pp.174-86.

44. W.J.Hardy (ed.), *The Manuscripts of Lord Kenyon* [A Calendar], Historical Manuscripts Commission, 14th Report Appendix, pt.4 (London: 1894), pp.19-23.

45. The "fort holding" at York conducted by "the honest yong men of this Cittie" makes no reference to pyrotechnics.

46. Imrie and Dunbar, *The Accounts M.W.*, II, p.90.
47. Bate, *The Mysteryes of Natvre and Art*, pp.77-8; Norton, *The Gvnner*, p.153.
48. Babington, *Pyrotechnia*, pp.27-36.
49. Babington, *Pyrotechnia*, pp.34,35.
50. For a description of the nature and function of Kingroad in the eighteenth century, see Patrick McGrath (ed.), *Bristol in the 18th Century* (Newton Abbot: 1972), p.138.
51. Lancashire (ed.), *Dramatic Texts and Records of Britain*, p.202 (**1031**); Mill, *Mediaeval Plays in Scotland*, p.55 n.3.
52. Nichols, John G, *Literary Remains*, II, p.279 n.2: "William Wynter, surveyor of the ships:...".
53. Norton, *The Gvnner*, p.155.
54. *O.E.D.* sb.1. BOMBARD "The earliest kind of cannon, usually throwing a stone ball or a very large shot.". 1.b. BOMBARD "The ball or stone thrown by a bombard.".
55. Feuillerat (ed.), *Documents Relating to the Office of the Revels*, p.345.
56. *O.E.D.* sb. 2. 14. WARD.
57. Nichols, *Progresses...James*, II, p.323.
58. Nichols, *Progresses...James*, II, p.525.
59. Miklos Menis, pyrotechnist, uses a similar technique today when he soaks rope in paraffin and sheathes it in polythene in order to prevent evaporation.
60. Babington, *Pyrotechnia*, pp.34-6.
61. The mechanical figures that are part of the clock arrangement at Wells Cathedral may be compared for possible scale. See Nikolaus Pevsner, *The Buildings of England: North Somerset and Bristol* (London: 1958; rpt. 1979), p.307; Michael Glenny, 'Ingenious and Efficient: The Wells Cathedral Clock' *Country Life* (September 18, 1986), pp.852-4.
62. Plimpton, *Fireworks*, p.203.
63. *B.L.Additional 70518*

Conclusion

1. Nichols, *Progresses...James*, p.535 n.1.
2. Leslie G.Mathews, *The Royal Apothecaries* (London: 1967); G.E.Trease, 'The Spicers and Apothecaries of the Royal Household in the Reigns of Henry III, Edward I, and Edward II', *Nottinghamshire Medieval Studies* 3 (1959), 19-52; Leslie G.Mathews, 'The spicers and apothecaries of Norwich', *The Pharmacutical Journal* 198 (January 7, 1967), 5-9; Leslie G.Mathews, 'Spicers and Apothecaries in the City of Canterbury', *Medieval History* IX (1965), 289-91; Charles H.Hartshorne, 'Bills of Medicines Furnished for the Use of Edward I. 34 and 35 EDW.I., 1306-7', *Archaeological Journal* XIV (1857), 267-71; Leslie G.Mathews, 'Byways of pharmacutical history', *The Pharmacutical Journal* 191 (21 December,1963), 629-31.

3. O'Dea, Thwing and Eveleigh refer to the condenser. The earliest acknowledged evidence is cited by O'Dea to be that of Rovenzon in 1612. Earlier evidence is not produced even though generalised statements are made by each of these authors to the effect that condensers existed in this country in the sixteenth century. In his introduction to *Candle Lighting*, Eveleigh states "that this device (the lacemaker's condenser) is recorded as early as the late sixteenth century.". When I asked David Eveleigh if he could locate his evidence for this statement, he could not, and replied: "All I can say is that it was not a primary source, but derivative - from a relatively recent publication.". Letter from David Eveleigh, Curator, Agricultural and Social History, Blaise Castle House Museum, 4th October, 1991.

4. Glynn Wickham, *Early English Stages 1300 to 1600*, I, I and II, pp.3-50.

5. Thomas Gage, *The English-American his Travail by Sea and Land: or, A New Svrvey of the West-Indias, containing A Journall of Three thousand and Three hundred Miles within the main Land of America* (London: 1648), p.104.

6. The texts and sub-texts, plots and sub-plots of these latterday "fort holdings" have been thoroughly analysed by Max Harris in *The Dialogical Theatre: Dramatizations of the Conquest of Mexico and the Question of the Other* (London: 1993), pp.65-81 and passim; Max Harris, 'Parachicos at Chiapa', *Intergrad* (Summer, 1972), 1-5; Max Harris, 'Muhammed and the Virgin: Folk Dramatizations of Battles Between Moors and Christians in Modern Spain', *The Drama Review* 38 (Spring, 1994), 45-61.

7. Letter from Chris Philip, January 31, 1993.

8. See **CHAPTER 3**, n.51.

Appendix 1

Excerpts From Eye-Witness Accounts

THE eye-witness accounts concerning celebrations for Elizabeth at Warwick, Bristol, Kenilworth and Elvetham are all printed in Nichols' *Progresses...Elizabeth*. Similarly, accounts of the wedding celebrations for Frederick and Elizabeth on the Thames are contained in Nichols' *Progresses...James*. The eye-witness account of pyrotechnic celebrations in Edinburgh for James' birthday occur in the *Kenyon MS*, printed by the Historical Manuscripts Commission. The transcription of *MS BL Additional 70518* is printed here for the first time.

Some reliance is clearly placed upon the accounts in Nichols' "monumental anthology", as Wilson describes *Progresses...Elizabeth*. In her *Entertainments for Elizabeth I*, Wilson compares most of the extant manuscripts in this area. Some of the documents that Nichols originally used were not available to Wilson, yet she was still able to refer to Nichols as "the usually reliable Nichols".

Appendix 1A
Warwick 1572

Nichols, *Progresses...Elizabeth*, I, pp.319-320.

That afternone passid, and supper done, a showe of fireworks, prepayrid for that purpose in the Temple felds, was sett abroche, the maner wherof this writer cannot so truly set furth as if he had bene at it, being sick in his bed. But the report was, that there was devised on the Temple diche a fort made of slender tymber coverid with canvas. In this fort were appointid divers persons to serve as soldiers, and therefore so many harnesses as might be gotten within Towne were had, wherewith men were armed, appointed to shew themselfs; some others appointid to cast out fire-woorks, as squibbes and balles of fyre. Against that fort was another castlewise prepared of like strength whereof was Governor, the Earle of Oxford, a lusty gentleman, with a lusty band of Gentlemen. Between thies forts or against them were placid certen battering-pieces, to the nomber of twelve or fourteen, brought from London, and twelve faire chambers or mortyr-pieces, brought also from the Towre, at the chardge of the Erle of Warwik. Thies pieces and chambers were by traines fyred, and so made a great noise as though it had bene a sore assault; having some intermission, in which time the Erle of Oxford and his soldiers, to the nomber of 200, with qualivers and harquebuyces, likewise gave dyvers assaults; they in the fort shoting agayn, and casting out divers fyers, terrible to those that have not bene in like experiences, valiant to such as delighted therin, and in dede straunge to them that understood it not; for the wildfyre falling into the ryver Aven, wold for a tyme lye still, and than agayn rise and flye abrode, casting furth many flashes and flambes, whereat the Quene's Majesty took great pleasure; till after, by mischances, a poore man or two were much trowbled: for at the last, when it was apointid that the overthrowing of the fort should bee, a dragon, flieing, casting out huge flames and squibes, lighted upon the fort, and so set fyere thereon, to the subversion thereof; but whether by negligence or otherwise, it happned that a ball of fyre fell on a house at the end of the bridge, wherin one Henry Cowper, otherwise called Myller, dwellid, and set fyre on the same house, the man and wief being bothe in bed and in slepe, which burned so, as before any reskue could be, the house and all things in it utterly perished, with much ado to save the man and woman; and besides that house, another house or two nere adjoyning were also fyred, but reskued by the diligent and carefull helpe, as well of the Erle of Oxford, Sir Fulk Grevile, and other Gentlemen and Townesmen, which reparid thither in greater number than could be orderid. And no marvaile it was that so little harme was done, for the fire-balles and squibbes cast upp did so flye quiet over the Castell, and into the myds of the Towne, falling downe, some on houses, some in courts and baksides, and some in the streate, as farre as almost to Saint Mary Churche, to the great perill, or else great feare, of the inhabitants of this Borough: and so as, by what meanes is not yet knowen, foure houses in the Towne and Suburbes were on fyre at once, wherof one had a ball cam thorough both sides, and made a hole as big as a man's head, and did no more harme.

"This fyre appesid, it was tyme to goo to rest; and in the next morning it pleasid her Majesty to have the poore old man and woman that had their house brent brought unto her; whom so brought, her

Majesty recomfortid very much; and, by her Grace's bounty, and other courtiers, there was given towards their losses that had taken hurt £.25. 12s. 8d. or therabouts, which was disposid to them accordingly.".

Appendix 1B

Bristol 1574

Nichols, *Progresses...Elizabeth*, I, pp.393-407.

p.399.

A Fort was made beyond the water in a ground fit for that purpose, and to the saem as a frind (called Feeble Pollecie) joyned by a littell Bastillion, builded on a hil, which was not strong by reason of the weak mayntenance belonging therunto, to the which piel the soulders of the main fort did repayre. Now must be understood that Dissension passying between Wars and Peace (warrs being placed in sight) had certayn Speeches as follows, which Speeches could not be sayd in the heeryng of the Prynce, wherefore they wear put into a book, and presented as heer after you shall kno. Dissencion to the Citie, to move them to arms, hath his Speeches as these things wear don in action.

The Sunday next the Queen went to the Colledge, to hear a Sarmon, whear thear was a Speech to be sayd and an imme to be songe; the Speech was left out by an occasson unlooked for, but the imme was songe by a very fien Boye.

[The Speech and the imme follow].

p.400.

A skafold the next day was set up full over agaynst the Fort; and the Prince beynge placed, the Speeches shold have bin spoken for the better understanding of the devised Triumphe; so you must heer the Speeches, or els shal you be ignorant of the hoel matter.

Dissension to Peace (which was the mayn Fort) speaketh in furie these words that follow:

[The Speech]

p.401.

Now Dissension went to the warrs, which was set out in open view (with all orders of marshall manner) and spake as follows:

[The Speech]

169

p.402.

On thoes words was warres in sutch a stoer that you might see the feeld all over spred with soldiers, and so they marched down a hill, and maed a goodly shoe full against the littel Fort (called Feble Pollecie); and repolsing in all the soldiours of the same, wan it with great fury, and so rased it, and overthrow hit down to earth.

The mayn Fort in the mean while did send sutch sucker as they might; but prevaylyng not, they wear in like sort driven back, and their Fort besieged, and mutch ado about the saem, which drove out that day, and then by tortch light the Prince from her skaffold went to her lodgyng, and in the mean season som fierworks wear seen, and so the watch was charged.

The second day was thear maed a new aproetch to the mayn Fort; for a better order of warre, and to the ayde of the Fort, cam divers Gentilmen of good callynge from the Court, which maed the shoe very gallant, and set out the matter mutch.

Now sarved the tied, and up the water from Kyng-road cam three brave galleys, chasing a ship that cam with vittayls to the Fort. The Fort seyng that their extremetie within was great, sent a Gentilman to the Prince for aid, who brought her a book covered with green velvet, which uttred the whoell substance of this device. The Gentilman had a Speech of his own makyng, as follows. After he had swam over the water in som danger, cloes and all, he speak his part to the Prince.

[The Speech]

p.403.

So he departed, and all this while the businesse was great about the Fort (which hazarded the Gentilman's lief), and in a wonders bravery the broyll continued, with a shoe of fight on land and sea, till the very night approtched, at which time the Prince partted, and stoed marvelously well contented with that she had seen.

Now you must conceyve that Warres (with blodsheds, mizeries, and other horly borlees) waxt a weery; and that neither the Fort, nor the wickednes of the World (which warres represented), was desirous of further trobuls, but rather glad to have the matter taken up in any reasonable condicions, for the which purpose was devised that Perswasion should go and tell his taell, and unfold what follies and conflicts rises in civill broyle, and what quietnesse coms by a mutual love and agrement. This Perswasion had a Speech, as hereafter follows:

Perswasion to the Citie, called the Main Fort.
[The Speech]

170

p.405.

This was to be don and put in exersies befoer the Queen cam to the knitting up of the matter; but Perswasion beyng dismist, the battry was planted befoer the Fort, and they within so straitly enclosed, that they must needs abied the mercy of the sword and cannon. At which instant, in the afternoon that present day, the Prince was in her skaffold to beholde the successe of these offers of Warre; and so went the Battry of, and the assaut was given in as mutch order as might be; the Enemie was three times repolsed, and beholdyng nue suckors commyng from the Courte to the Forts great comfort, the Enemye agreed on a parley, whearin was rehersyd that the Cortain was beaten down, and the Fort maed sawtable; and yet the Enemye, to save the lives of good Citizens and soldiors thereof, would give them leave to depart with bag and bagaeg, as orders of warres required. To the which the Fort maed answer, that the Cortayns nor bulwarks was not their defence, but the corrage of good peple, and the force of a mighty Prince (who saet and beheld all these doyngs), was the thyng they trusted to, on which answer the Enemie retired, and so condicions of peace were drawn and agreed of; at which peace both the sides shot of their artillery, in sien of a triumphe, and so crying "God save the Queen," these triumphes and warlik pastimes finished. The Prince, liking the handlyng of these causes verie well, sent ij hundreth crowns to make the souldiours a banket. Now heer is to be considered that the Prince went into the gallees, and so down to Kyngroed, aer these things wear brought to an end.

Appendix 1C

Kenilworth 1575

Nichols, *Progresses...Elizabeth*, I, pp.434-435.
[Laneham's account of the Queen's arrival on Saturday].

So passing intoo the inner Coourt, her Majesty (that never ridez but alone) thear set doun from her pallfrea, was conveied up to chamber: When after did follo so great a peal of gunz, and such lightning by fyrwork a long space toogither, as Jupiter woold sheaw himself too bee no further behind with hiz welcum then the rest of hiz gods; and that woold he have all the countrie to kno; for indeed the noiz and flame were heard and scene a twenty myle of.

Nichols, *Progresses...Elizabeth*, I, p.435.
[Laneham's account of the Sunday evening firework display].

 At night late, az though Jupiter the last night had forgot for biziness, or forborn, for curtezy and quiet, part of hiz wellcoom untoo her Highness appointed, noow entrins at the fyrst intoo hiz purpoze moderatly (az mortalz doo) with a warning peec or too, proceding on with encres; at last the Altitonant displayz me hiz mayn poour; with blaz of burning darts, flying too and fro, leamz of starz coruscant, streamz and hail of firie sparkes, lightninges of wildfier a water and lond, flight & shoot of thunderboltz, all with such continauns, terror, and vehemencie, that the Heavins thundred, the waters soourged, the earth shooke; in such sort surly, az had we not bee assured the fulminant Deitee waz all but in amitee, and could not otherwize witnesse hiz wellcomming untoo her Highness; it woold have made mee, for my part, az hardy az I am, very veangeably afeard. This adoo lasted while the midnight waz past, that well waz me soon after when I waz cought in my cabayn: and this for the secund day.

Nichols, *Progresses...Elizabeth*, I, p.494.
[Gascoine's account of the Sunday evening firework display].

 On the next day (being Sunday) there was nothing done until the evening, at which time there were fire-works shewed upon the water, the which were both strange and well executed; as sometimes, passing under the water a long space, when all men had thought they had been quenched, they would rise and mount out of the water againe, and burn very furiously untill they were utterly consumed.

Nichols, *Progresses...Elizabeth*, I, p.440.
[Laneham's account of the Thursday evening event].

 As this sport was had a day time, in the Castl, so waz thear abrode at night, very straunge and sundry kindez of Fier-works, compeld by cunning to fly too and fro, and too mount very hye intoo the ayr upward, and also too burn unquenshabl in the water beneath; contrary, ye wot, too fyerz kinde: this intermingld with a great peal of guns, which all gave both to the ear and to the ey the greater grace and delight, for that with such order and art they wear tempered, toouching tyme and continuans, that waz about too hours space.

Appendix 1D
Elvetham 1591

Nichols, *Progresses...Elizabeth*, III, p.118.

First, there was a peale of a hundred chambers discharged from the Snail Mount; in counter whereof, a like peale was discharged from the Ship Ile, and some great ordinance withal. Then was there a castle of fire-works of all sorts, which played in the Fort. Answerable to that, there was in the Snail Mount, a globe of all manner of fire-works, as big as a barrel. When these were spent on either side, there were many running rockets uppon lines, which past between the Snail Mount and the castle in the Fort. On either side were many fire-wheeles, pikes of pleasure, and balles of wilde fire, which burned in the water.

During the time of these fire-workes in the water, there was a banket served,...

Appendix 1E
London – Thames 1613

Nichols, *Progresses...James*, II, p.525.

The preparations for Fire-works and Fights upon the water are very great, and have already consumed above £.6000,...besides four Floating-Castles with Fire-works, and the representation of the town, fort, and haven of Argier upon the land.

p.527.
Heaven's Blessing and Earth's Joy; or, A True Relation of the Supposed Sea-Fights and Fire-Workes as were accomplished before the Royall Celebration of the All-Beloved Marriage of the Two Peerlesse Paragons of Christendome, Fredericke and Elizabeth. By John Taylor, the Water Poet.

pp.530-535.
For the Fire-workes were performed on Thursday night the 11th of February, and the Fight [This referred to the sea-fight] was upon the Satterday following. At the which Fire-workes the Maister-gunner of England on the shore did performe many skilfull and ingenious

exploits with great bumbards, shooting up many artificiall balls of fire into the ayre, which flew up in one whole fierie ball, and in their falling dispersed into divers streams like rainebowes in many innumerable fires. After all which was discharged a great peale of chambers, to the contentment of the Royall Spectators, and the great credit of the performers.

The True Description of such part of the Fire-workes as were devised and accomplished by Mr. John Nodes, Gunner and Servant to the King's most excellent Majestie.

The imperiall and beautious Lady Lucida, Queene of the feminine territories of the man-hating Amazonians, with whose bright eye-dazeling corcuscancie, and whose refulgent feature, the black-sould, hell-commanding magitian Mango (a Tartarian borne) was so ensnared and captivated, that for her love, and to be assured to enjoy her, he would set all hell in an uprore, and pluck Don Belzebub by the beard, assuredly perswading himselfe that without her he could not live, and for her he would attempt any thing; but she having vowed herself ever to be one of Vesta's votaries, always kept Cupid out at the arme's end, and bad Madam Venus make much of stump-footed Vulcan, and keepe at home like a good huswife, for she had no entertainment for her.

Whereupon this hellish Necromancer Mango, being thus repulst, converts all his love to outragious rigor, and immediately, with his charmes, exorcismes, and potent execrable incantations, he raises a strong impregnable pavilion, in the which he immures and encloses this beautiful Amazonian Queene with her attendant Ladies, where, though they lived in captivitie and bondage, yet they had variety of games and pleasant sports allowed by the Magitian, in hope that time would make an alteration in her faire flinty breast. And, for her sure gard in his absence, he had erected by magick another strong tower as a watch-house, wherein he had placed a fiery dragon and an invincible giant (of whom I will speake in another place hereafter).

Now to this aforesaid pavillion, wearyed with toyle and travaile, the great unresistable Champion of the world, and the uncontrolable Patron, Saint George, comes; and seeing so bright and luculent a goddesse, according as his necessitie required, demanded entertainment, whereby he might be refreshed, after his laborious atchievements and honorable endeavours.

The curteous Queene, although she cared not for the society of man, seeing his outward or externall feature and warlike acouterments, did presently resolve with herselfe that so faire an outside could not be a

174

habitation for fowle trechery, and with most debonayre gesture, admits his entrance into the pavilion; where, after he had feasted awhile, she relates unto him the true manner and occasion of her unfortunate thraldom; Saint George, ever taking pleasure in most dangerous attempts, and holding it his chiefest glory to helpe wronged Ladies, vowes, that as soone as Phoebus rouz'd himselfe from the Antipodes, he would quell the burning Dragon, conquer the big-boned Giant, subvert the inchanted castle, and enfranchise the Queene with her followers, or else die in the enterprise thereof. After which promise of his, the Queene, to passe away the time, delights him with these pastimes following, being all Fire-workes:

First, the pavilion is beleaged or invironed round about with fires, going out of which many fiery balls flie up into the ayre, with numbers of smaller fieres ascending; that cemicircled Cinthia is as it were eclipsed with the flashes, and the starres are hood-winckt with the burning exhalations.

Secondly, is seene a Royall hunting of bucks, and hounds, and huntsmen, flying and chasing one another round about the pavilion (as if Diana had lately transformed Acteon and his ignorant dogges ready to prey on his carkas), from whence continually is flying many fiers dispearsed every way; the lower part of the pavilion alwayes flying round about, giving many blowes and great reports, with many fires flying aloft into the ayre.

Thirdly, there doth march round about the pavilion artificiall men, which shall cast out fires, as before, as it were in skirmish; another part of the pavilion is all in a combustious flame, where rackets, crackers, breakers, and such like, give blowes and reports without number.

Fourthly, the Queene of Amazonia with all hir Traine of virgin Ladyes, with fires marcheth round as the men did before, with the fire flying dispearsedly divers wayes; the whilst another part of the pavilion is fired with many blowes and reports, and fiers flying aloft into the ayre, from whence it comes downe againe in streaming flakes of flashing fire.

Fifthly, aloft within the turret shall runne, whirling round, a fyerie globe, with the turret and all on fire, with many more greater blowes then before had bin heard, and divers and sundry other sorts of fires than any of the former, proceeding from thence, and flying into the ayre in great aboundance.

All which things being performed, and the undanted Knight Saint George taking his leave of the Amazonian Queene Lucida, he mounts uppon his steede and adventurously rides towards the inchanted Towre of Brumond.

Now these disports being ended, wherein Saint George's entertainment was onely expressed, with the Queene's relation of her bondage, this brave Champion was seene to ride over the bridge to combat with these aforesaid monsters, the Dragon and Giant. All which was expressed in the next devise of Mr. Thomas Butler; and so I end, with my harty invocations to the Almighty to send the Bride and Bridegroome the yeares of Methushalah, the fortitude of Joshua, the wisedome of Solomon, the wealth of Cressus, and last of all an endless crowne of immortalitie in the highest Heavens. John Nodes.

A true Description of the Platforme of a part of the Fire-workes devised and made by Mr. Thomas Butler, Gunner and Servant to the King's Royall Majestie.

This inchanted Castle or Tower of Brumond is in hight forty foote and thirty square, betweene which and the Pavilion of the Amazonian Queene is a long bridge, on the which bridge the valiant and heroicke Champion, Saint George, being mounted on horseback, makes towards the Castle of Brumond; which being perceaved by the watchfull dragon, who was left by Mango the Conjurer as a centinell, is encountered by him; whereas Saint George, being armed at all points, but especially with an unrebated courage, having in his helmet a burning flaming feather, and in one hand a burning launce, and in the other a fiery sword, with which weapons he assailes the dreadfull Dragon with such fury and monster-quelling stroakes, as if the Cyclops had bin forging and beating thunder-bolts on Vulcan's anvile; where, in conclusion, after a terrible and long-endured combat, with his launce he gores the hell-hound under the wing, that he presently, after most hideous roring and belching of fire, is vanquished and slaine.

At which the terrible-shaped Giant rises, having sate as a spectator of this bloody battel upon a great stump of a tree at the castle-gate, and addresses himselfe towards Saint George, meaning to revenge the death of the Dragon, and to swallow his enemy for a modicum; but at their first encounter the blowes on both sides fell like thunder-clappes, enforcing lightning and fiery exhalations to sparkle from whence their powerfull stroakes lighted; at last the monster, gaping wide as an arch in London Bridge, runnes furiously, intending to swallow his adversary at a bit; which Saint George seeing, upon the suddaine thrust his sword into his greedy throat, and overthrewe him; at which the Monster yelles and rores forth such a terrible noyse, as if the centre of the earth had crackt, that with the uncouth dinne thereof the neighbouring hills, woods, and valleyes seemed to tremble like an earthquake. The Gyant lying at the mercy of Saint George, entreats him to spare his life, and he will shew him the way how he shall conquer the Castle, and bring the Inchanter to his everlasting downefall. Upon which promise Saint George and the Gyant walke into the Castle together, where he tells Saint George that there is an enchanted fountaine, and whosoever can attaine to drinke of it shall be he whome the Fates have ordained to be the conclusion of the Castle's glory.

In the meane space, whilst these things were doing, the Magitian Mango, having intelligence of the dangerous estate of his Castle, and fearing the losse of his Lady, suddainely mounts him on a flying invisible devill, and in a moment alights within the Castle; upon whome St.George makes a present conquest. The Castle hath on the top thereof a fiery Fountaine, which burnes and sends up rackets into the ayre, with many reports and blowes, some greate and some lesse, and fire dispearsed many wayes in great abundance, with innumerable lights round about.

Secondly, the Magitian is taken with his conjuring scepter in his hand, and bound to a pillar by Saint George, and burned with fire and lights as before, with fiers and rackets ascending and descending to and fro in the ayre.

Thirdly, the foure squares of the Tower are fiered with abundance of lights, with rackets flying into the ayre, with fiers dispearsed and scattered divers and sundry wayes, and with reports and blowes, some great and some lesse, according to their making.

Fourthly, the foure turrets are fyred with fire and innumerable lights, with aboundance of rackets flying to and fro in the ayre, giving divers reports as before.

Then the maine Castle is fyered, and upon two of the corner turrets are two globes fyered, and betwixt each globe, at two other corner turrets, are two men, catching as it were at the globes which still turn from them, and they chasing and following the globes, still burning and turning till all be extinguished with fire; always rackets flying, and reports thwacking, and lights burning.   Thomas Butler.

William Bettis his invention of such part of the Fire-workes as were performed by him at the Royall Celebration, which he had contrived in such sort, that if the weather had bin rainy or windy, yet his dessignments should have beene accomplished.

A Castle with divers Fier-workes, representing and assuming divers variable shapes and imaginary formes, which continued the space of an houre or thereabouts; the nature and quality of which Fire-worke was performed as followeth:

beholders of it; I myselff was one. The play breifflie was thus. It was actet in the nicht. Their was 2 castles erected in the utter court, one castle at the one end off the court and another castle at the uther end, the one called the pallace of St.Androis, the other the Castle of Envy. It was acted and played by the yong men of Edenborrow. Their was so many fuilles with their belles, so many daunceres, a playmeir casting fyr both behind and befor, a maid, so many hagbuttes, so many muscetters, thair ensignes, thair horsmen, thair footmen runing with speires off fyr, the one castle schuiting fyrballes at the other, quheilles [wheels ?] runing round about of fyr and so many schotes into it, so many twix the Castles fychting, so many keiping every Castle, sumtymes the one syd winning, then agane retyring bak and flying. Thair was a devys maid, that out off the pallace off St.Androis cam Sanct Andrew ryding on a hors, with a speir off fyr in his hand, and met the dragon midway, that came out of the Castle of Envy, and out of hir mouth cam fyr spouting, so they foght aspace togither; bot Sanct Andrew did overcome the dragon and cam home ryding, and was welcomed home by the men of the pallace. In the mids, betwix the two castles, was a devys set up that schot so many schotes, and a thing going about with horsmen and footmen; then the quheill wald [wheeled ?] about agane and persew theis men, and at a certaine space so many schottes, and ane man maid of timber in the mids of the quheill, that went ay about as the two troupes of men, did, having an ensigne in his hand, and on it St.Androis cros. Then their was four hieland men, dressed up so of purpos, that came out of the pallace of St.Androis with their boues and arrowes of fyr, that did win the Castle of Envy, quilk castle had for their badge, St.George. The castle was throuen down, the men taken prisoners, and the captain sould have bein, as it wer,hanged.Giff so be the King had stayed longer, thair was many more toyes in it nor I can tell.

Appendix 2

Appendix 2A
Firework Accounts – Stirling 1566

This account contained in H.M.Register House SRO E 23/3/45 at the Scottish Record Office, Edinburgh and published in *The Accounts of the Treasurer of Scotland 1566-1574,* ed. Charles T. McInnes, volume XII, Edinburgh, H.M.S.O., 1970, pp.403-409, constitutes the most comprehensive list of firework expenses in either England or Scotland in the sixteenth century. The details indicate and confirm a number of processes and techniques discussed throughout this work. Excerpts of the account are contained in Anna J.Mill, *Mediaeval Plays in Scotland,* St.Andrews,1924, pp.339-343. An analysis of the document has appeared in my "The Baptisme of Hir Hienes Darrest Sone in Stirviling", *Medieval English Theatre,* vol.10:1 University of Lancaster, 1988, pp.26-55.

p.1. "Expensis maid be Johnne Chisholme, comptrollar of the artailyerye, upoun certane nummer of fyreworkis ordanit be the Quenes majesties precept directit to the said Johnne thairupoun, to be maid and put to executioun at the baptisme of hir hienes darrest sone in Stirviling, the said expensis beginning the xix day of November 1566 and ending the xxij day of December nixt eftir following as at mair lenth is contenit in every article of this present comt".

"*Item* in the first payit to James Barroun, carter of Leyth, for his passing out of the said toun to the castell of Dunbar and thairfra brocht upoun his cart to the said toun of Leyth four barrellis of cannoun poulder to serve for making of the fyreworkis and ane littill barrell with bruntstane and roset to the same affect   1 s.

Item payit to James Hector, ordinar gunnar, send to Dunbar for getting of the said poulder be ane precept of the Quenes majesteis to the laird of Quhitlaw, for his expensis and hors fee   xxiiij s.

Item payit to Michaell Gairdner, gunnar and poulder maker in the castell of Edinburgh, passing from the samin to the toun of Stirviling for making of fyreworkis and bying of stuf to that poirpos togidder for his panes and expensis the soume of   x li.

Item payit to the said James Hector at ane uthir tyme passing towartis the Quenes majestie than being in Dunbar with letters to informe hir hienes of the proceiding of the foirsaid fyrework conforme to hir grace precept p.2. thairupoun, and als to require of hir majestie fourneissing of silver for making of the said fyrework and expensis quhilk convenit to be maid thairfoir, lykwis for his expensis and hors fee   xxij s. vj d.

Item mair to him passing to Craigmillar to advertis hir majestie of the beginning and making of the saidis fyreworkis, and how that Johnne Cheisholme had sa far advancit that labour of his awin monney that he was nocht able to do ony farder without help of hir majestie and fourneissing to be maid to him, quhairupoun hir grace ordanit my lord thesaurer to tak ordour thairwith, as he did, for the said James expensis during twa dayis remaning thair upoun hir hienes answer   x s.

Item in the first coft four stane ten pundis wecht of salpeter at iij li. xiij s. viijd. the stane, summa   xvij li. v s. iiij d.

Item coft fyve stane twelf pundis wecht of bruntstane at xxxvij s. iiij d. the stane summa   x li. xiiij s. viij d.

Item coft thre stane aucht pundis wecht of cannoun poulder of the waikest sort meit for mixing of fyreworkis, price of the stane xlviij s. summa   viij li. viij s.

Item for half ane unce quarter and half quarter of oyle petrole with ane glas, price   iij s. iiij d.

Item for nyne unce of gume of Arabye   ix s.

Item for twa unce of colophone   xii d.

Item for ten unce of orpyment   v s.
p.3.

Item for four unce of terpentyne with ane pig   xij d.

Item for fyve unce quik silver   xv s.

Item for ane unce of camphor   xij s.

Item for twa unce of oleum laurinum with ane pig   xviij d.

Item for ane quart of oyll linget   xxiiij s.

Item for thre dosone and ane half of skenyeis of pakthreid of thre plettis at iiij s. vj d. the dosone   xv s. ix d.

Item for twa quair of Lumbard paiper   viij s.

Item for fyftein ellis of Poldavid cannevas at ij s. vj d. the ell   xxxvij s. vj d.

Item for twa daillis of collis and bearing of thame   xiij s. vj d.

Item for alevin lem pottis of sindry sortis   vj s. v d.

Item for ane stane and ane half of hardis   xxiiij s.

Item for ane barrell of tar   iij li. x s.

Item for ane dosone of small lem piggis for halding of fyrework   vj s.

Item for twa piggis quhairin at sindry tymes was put and caryit to Leyth the said oyll linget   xij d.

Item for sax uthir les piggis to the affect above writtin   ij s.

Item for twa stane and ane half of talloun at xviij s. the stane   xlv s.

Item for ane stane of leid   xvj s.

Item for twelf trein dischis or coppis   vj s.

Item for ane dosone of lang fedderit arrowis   xxiiij s.

Item for auchtein girthis of haisill   vj s.

Item for ane bourding of unbrunt lyme furth of Cousland   ij s.

Item for alevin hankis pakthreid   v s.

p.4.

Item for threttie sax ellis of wyre   vj s.

Item for thre uthir littill piggis als for halding of fyrework   xij d.

Item for ane hundreth takketis   x d.

Item for twa peices of treis to mak fyre pompis and bearing thame to the hous   ix s. iiij d.

Item for fyftie sevin faldomis of merlin cord   vij s. j d. obolus.

Item for sax skenyeis of uthir pakthreid   ij s.

Item for ane hank of wyre   xiiij s.

Item for xxviij ellis of uthir wyre   iiij s. viij d.

Item for four torches   x s.

Item for four uthir gritter torches   xiij s. iiij d.

Item for xvij plaittis of quhit yron quhairof was maid fyve flambeantis   xix s. x d.

Item for twa hundreth dur naillis   iij s. iiij d.

Item for ane hundreth planscheour naillis   ij s. viij d.

Item for fyve pyntis of tar   x s.

Item for half ane galloun of fische oyll   xiij s. iiij d.

Item mair for talloun   ij s. viij d.

Item mair for sax skenyeis of pakthreid   ij s.

Item for nyne littill girthis quhairof was maid balles coverit with canevas   iij s.

Item for four new fyre pannis togidder with ane fork of yron to schaw lycht in the nycht   lij s.

Item for thre tuyme puncheouns quhairin was pakkit the maist pairt of the small fyreworkis and tourteantis send out of Leyth to Stirviling   xv s.

Item for ane tuym barrell   iij s. vj d.

Item for twa pundis and ane half of coulvering poulder   xv s.

Item for thre dosone of daillis quhairwith was maid the closing of the

forth haldin in Stirviling aganis the men of warre, price of the dosone iijli. vj s., summa ix li. xviij s.
p.5.
Item for ane dosone and aucht double fir spars to serve for upstanders to the said closing of daillis and als for gibettis to hing the fyre cransis on schawing lycht in the forth, price of the dosone xviij s., summa xxx s.
Item for aucht littill peices of aykin tymmer alsua serving for uphald to the saidis daillis quhilkis closit the forth in sindry places, price of the peice iij s., summa xxiiij s.
Item for twenty aucht gaitt skynnis quhairof was maid four hieland wyld mens cleithings from heid to fute, price of the peice iij s., summa

v li. xij s.
Item for twenty aucht ellis thre quarters of bougrem, coullouris reid, blew, blak and quhit, price of the ell iiij s. vj d., summa

vj li. ix s. iiij d. obolus.
Item for four ellis and ane half of uthir bougrem, price of the ell v s., summa xxij s. vj d.
Item mair for auchtein ellis of uthir bougrem being of the saiddis coullouris, price of ell iiij s. iiij d., summa iij li. xviij s.
All this bougrem abone writtin maid in fyftein cleithingis, to wit four lansknychtis, four for morres, four for horsmen and thre for contrefait devillis, quhilkis cleithingis war distributit to fyftein soldiouris of the companyes quha combattit within and without the forth togidder with the foirsaidis hieland men having the executioun of the fyreworkis in thair handis
Item for thre lamis skynnis quhairof was maid four bonnetis of fals hair to the saidis mores, price of the peice ij s., summa vj s.
p.6.
Item payit for litting of ane pairt of the said bougrem, quhilk was blew, into blak for parfitting of the saidis cleithingis dewlie iij s.
Item for hardin quhilk was stuffing to ane pairt of the saidis cleithingis quhair it was necessar ix s. iij d.
Item payit for the making of the saidis fyftein stand of cleithingis togidder with the four hieland cleithingis of gait skynnis making in the haill xix stand, price of the peice viij s., summa vij li. xij s.
Item payit in drink silver to the boyis that helpit to mak the saidis cleithingis v s.
Item payit for the cariaige of the haill cleithingis abone writtin from Edinburgh to Stirviling x s.
Item payit for the len of ane pik pot xv dayis quhairin was maid the tourteantis ij s.
Item for bearing of ane barrell of pik fra the place it was coft in to the

hous quhair the fyrework was maid   iij d.

Item to ane man for fetching afeild and bearing haym of ane borrowit tar trough quhairin was tarrit the cransis   iij d. obolus.

Item payit for stray to the pakking of the small fyreworkis alswele within the puncheouns as in the boit   ij s.

Item payit for bringing down of the foresaid talloun and certain potis of Edinburgh to Leyth   x d.

Item payit to ane man for bringing furth of the castell of Michaell Gairdners fyrework buyrd with certane auld fyre potis to Leyth   x d.
p.7.

Item payit to ane man passing to the laird of Roslyne with ane letter fra Johnne Chisholme at the said Michaellis desir to have gottin knowlege of sum waik poulder meit for mixing of fyrework   ij s.

Item payit for bearing doun of all the saidis lem potis from Edinburgh to Leyth   viij d.

Item payit to twa men for fetching furth of the castell of sum auld towis, twa lenternes and twa fyre pannis to Leyth   xvj d.

Item for the making of the saidis fyve flambeantis of quhit yron   xvj s.

Item payit to ane tailyeour of Leyth for making and sewing of thre dosone lang pokkis, threttye round pokkis, twelf bodomit pokkis, twa dayis labour of him and his servandis in making and sewing of the fyre cransis and sindry uthir thingis doing to the parfitting of the fyreworkis   xxij s.

Item payit to ane cowppar for girthis and heiding of thre puncheouns full of fyreworkis and girthing of ane barrell of brokin poulder and small munitiouns   x s.

Item payit to ane man that wrocht about the fyreworkis to and fra the space of ane day   xviij d.

Item payit to James Hector, ordinar gunnar of Dunbar, for his awaitting and labouring continnuallye upoun the making of the fyreworkis in Leyth be the space of threttye dayis endit the xiij day of December 1566, ilk day for his waiges v s., summa   vij li. x s.

Item payit to James Roknow and Johnne Mylne, alsua ordinar gunnaris and wrychtis, for thair labouring and awaitting with the said James Hector in p. 8. helping him to work and mak the saidis fyreworkis alswele as working of sindry sortis of tymmer necessar thairto during the space of xv dayis endit the said xiij day, takand be day for thair waiges ilk man iij s. vj d., summa   v li. v s.

Item payit to Clowis Helyot, Johnne Smyth and Robert Bikertoun, alsua ordinaris, for thair labouring the space of thre dayis endit the said xiij day with the foirsaidis in helping thame for the mair dilligence making, ilk ane on the day iij s. iiij d., summa   xxx s.

Item payit to Johnne Lamy and Henry Scherar, marinellis, for thair labouring during the space of four dayis endit the foresaid xiij day in heitting pik and tar, oppinning out towis and dipping of nummer of toureantis and cransis, ilk ane on the day ij s., summa xvj s.

Item for sawing of twa dosone of the foirsaidis daillis quhairwith the forth was closit, price of the peice xiiij s., summa xxviij s.

Item payit to aucht men passing fra the castell to Leyth with chalmeris of gunnis, pikkis, schuyllis and uthir munitiouns viij s.

Item payit to Charles Bourdeous for twelf dosone of fusees double and single, and half ane hundreth pettaratis, the poulder fourneist to him be the said Johnne Chisholme, for his fassoun and expensis of ilk dosone of fusees x s., and for the half hundreth petteratis xl s., summa viij li.

Item payit to Johnne Reid for the fraucht of ane boit from Leyth to Stirviling laidin hayllie with the fyreworkis preparit for the baptisme, togidder with p.9. daillis and uthir tymmer, with sindry uthir thingis dependuing of the saidis fyreworkis iiij li.

Item payit for two hors feis of Edinburgh to Stirviling the xiiij day of December quhairon raid the said James Hector and Charles Bourdeous quha war send to the said toun for gydding and principall handilling of the fyreworkis and asseiging of the forth xxxij s.

Item for expensis maid be the way betuix Edinburgh and Stirviling for thame and thair twa hors xiiij s.

Item payit to twa men that waid in and los the boit arrivit at Stirviling with the fyrework upoun the xv day of December iij s.

Item payit to twelf men for ilk ane bourding of fyrework borne in the nycht for feir of knawlege thairof from the place the boit lay in the toun of Stirviling, ilk ane vj d., summa vj s.

Item to carters of the said toun for ten drauchtis of the foirsaid fyrework and munitioun upoun thair cartis from the boit to the toun x s.

Item payit for the cariaige of thre dosone of daillis from the boit to the toun, ilk dosone xviij d., summa iiij s. vj d.

Item payit to sax workmen quha helpit to lois ane grit pairt of all that was in the said boit, als labourit at the buylding of the forth carying of tymmer to the same and bearing chalmeris of gunnis and all uthir munitiouns necessar to the said forth, and that be the space of ane day and ane half, ilk ane iij s., summa xviij s.

Item for collis to the fyre in the forth xxiij d.

Item for having doun of twa faulcons furth of the castell to the asseigeing of the forth and taking of thame up agane xv s.

p.10.

Item payit to twa tailyeouris in Stirviling quha helpit the tailyeour that maid the play claythis to translate thame and augment quhair it was necessar togidder with the helping on of thame upoun the souldiouris

the tyme of the asseiging of the said forth and that be the space of twa
dayis   xvj s.

Item for carying doun out of the toun of Stirviling to the boit of the rest
of the munitiouns that war left eftir the forth asseiging as chalmeris of
gunnis and sindry uthir munitiouns alswele upoun cartis as be men
bearing   vij s

Item payit to ane man in recompance of his yaird dyk cassin doun at the
hors marcat quhair the Quenes majestie and embassadouris stuid   iij s.

Item payit to Clowis Helyot, Johnne Smyth, James Roknow, Robert
Murray, Johnne Hunyman, Robert Bikertoun and Johnne Mylne,
ordinar gunnaris, for ten dayis endit the xxij day of December foirsaid
for thair passing of Edinburgh and awaitting in Stirviling during the
said space upoun the executioun of the forth asseigeing and handilling
of fyrework, ilk ane on the day iij s. iiij d., summa   xj li. xiij s. iiij d.

Item mair payit to James Reid, wrycht, for his awaitting and serving of
wrycht craft during the foirsaid space of ten dayis at the
constructioun of the said forth and uthir labouring, ilk day iij s.,
summa   xxx s.

Item alsua payit to the said James Hector and Charles Bourdeous,
principall ordinaris, for thair expensis awaitting in Stirviling upoun the
said service the lyk space of ten dayis endit the said xxij day of
December, ilk ane on the day v s., summa   v li.
p.11.

Item payit for ane hors fe to the said James Hector fra Stirviling to
Edinburgh passing haym   xvj s.

Item payit to the said Johnne Reid, boitman, in compositioun of fraucht fra
the said Stirviling to Leyth with certane chalmeris of gunnis, fyre pannis
brokin daillis, pikis, schuyllis and sindry uthir littill munitiouns   xx s.

Item amir payit to Johnne Chisholme, comptrollar of the said
artailyerye, for his awaitting and extraordinar service making in the
dressing and overseing and causing to mak this triomphe of fyrework
above speciffyit be the space for fourtye dayis, to wit xxx dayis in Leyth
and ten day in Stirviling for his panis and extraordinar waigis, ilk day
vj s. viij d., summa   xiij li. vj s. viii d.

Summa quhaironto extendis this haill compt is j^{C}iiij^{XX} x li. xvij s. v d.
obolus.

JOHNNE CHISHOLME

Endorsed: "Expensis maid be Johnne Chisholme, comptroller of the
artailyerie, upoun the fyreworkis spendit at the triomphe of the
baptisme of my lord Prince in Stirviling in December 1566."

"Ressavit fra my lord thesaurer Maister Robert Richartson the vj day of December 1566 upoun this compt lxvj li. xiij s. iij d."

[1]-"*Item* mair ressavit at ane uthir tyme fra my lord thesaurer j^{c}v li. vii s. xj d. Restis to pay to Johnne Chisholme of this compt xviij li. xvj s. ij d. obolus."-[1]

"xij Februarii anno lxvij. This compt producit be Johne Chesholme this day".

Paper enclosed, giving totals for each page and "attour to be considderit my awin extraordinar waiges for xl dayis untaxit in the compt £13 6s. 8d".

46. Receipt by James Inglis "for abiliamentis to the prince" [ante p.67]. 26 July 1567. Attested for signature by Peter Hewat notary public. At foot of page: "Incript. cum preciis."

Appendix 2B

Firework Accounts – Edinburgh 1617

Like the previous account this is an exceptionally full one in which some of the same key materials are documented. However, some interesting additional detail is recorded here which bears upon adopted processes and further indicates the character of the event. The expenses are contained in the Scottish Record Office, SRO Exchequer Records E.36 and published in *Accounts of the Masters of Works For Building and Repairing Royal Palaces and Castles*, volume II 1616-1649, eds. John Imrie and John G.Dunbar, Edinburgh, H.M.S.O., 1982, pp.89-93.

68 r.

The expenses maid upoun the fyirwarkis within the castell of Edinburgh and in the utter clois of the palace of Halyruidhous 19 June

27 Aprile 1617

Inprimis to Johne Prat for his paynes taken in the saidis warkis be the space of sevin dayes haifing daylie xxiiii s. inde

		viii lib. viii s.
To Johne Schort	sevin dayes	viii lib. viii s.
Thomas Smyth	7	viii lib. viii s.
Anthony Achesone	7	viii lib. viii s.
Robert Dickesone	7	viii lib. viii s.
To Johne Ewnes	7	viii lib. viii s.
Elias Pratt	6	vii lib. iiii s.

Provisionis

For threscoir elnes of canves	xxiiii lib.
For xx pond wecht of rossen	liii s. iiii d.
For merling cord	liiii s.
For xxiiii bowstringis	xxiiii s.
For ten paisboordis	xxx s.
For xx pond wecht of pick	iii lib.
For xx pond wecht of brinstane	iiii lib.
For pack threid	iii lib.
For tailyeour threid and neidles	xviii s.
For cork	v s.
For tua ryme of paper	v lib. xiii s. iiii d.
For a pair of tailyeouris scheiris	xxx s.
For a pond of vergeis	iiii lib.
For a pynt of lynseid oyle	xxxvi s.
For vinager	x s.
For tua pond of tarpettyne	xlviii s.
For ane irone pott	iii lib. vi s. viii d.
For four pond of talloun	xvi s.
For a pound of small Flanders wechtis	xxxii s.
For a pynt of aquavitye	xxxvi s.
For a stane of saltpetir	xxvii lib. iiii s.
For vi lib. x unce of saltpetir	viii lib. xi s. ii d.
For nyne unces brunt wax 16 s.unce	vii lib. iiii s.
For transporting of the saidis sevin fyrewark men fra Bervick to Edinburgh haifing 8 horssis	xxx lib.

5 May 1617

68 v.

(Firework men as last week, Elias Prat being absent.)

Provisionis

Item for xxxvi elne of canves at 8 s. elne	xiiii lib. viii s.
For thrie tymber plaittes	xxx s.
For great salt	ii s. viii d.
For tuelf pond of pick	xxxvi s.
For xii pund of brinstane	xlviii s.
For xii pond of rosen	xxx s.
For threid	xx s.
For tua ryme of paper	v lib. xii s.
For pack threid	xx s.
For tua great reames quheillis	xl s.

For tua litle reames quheillis xxxvi s.
For xii ringis of bras iiii s.
For tua quair of Lumbard paper xxxii s.

12 May
(Firework men as last week, Elias Prat returning, and Ralff Dryden coming on at £6 6s. for 7 days.)
Item for transporting of Elias Prat fra Bervick to Edinburgh with hors hyre iiii lib.
For careing the hobby hors and the boy fra Bervick to Edinburgh
iiii lib. iiii s.

19 May 1617
69 r.
(Firework men as last week, working 7 days.)

Provisionis
Item for 19 pond of pick lvii s.
For xxviii pond of rosen xlii s.
For xxii elne and a half of hardin vii lib. xix s
For lunt xii s.
For a chopin of vinager iii s.
For pack threid and merling cord iii lib. xiiii s.
For thrie mutchkins of aquavitye xxiiii s.
For xii pond of brimstane lii s.
For tackettis to the hobbie hors iii s.
For paper iiii lib.
For neidles and tailyeour thried vii s.
For sex lib. of brimstane xxvi s.
For xii bowstringis xii s.
For tua scheipis skynnes xviii s.
For mae paisboordis weyre and vinager xx s.
For towes and merling cord xiiii s.
For a plaitt of wheat irone iiii s.
For tua dart heidis vi s.

26 May 1617

69 v.
(Firework men as above.)

Provisionis

Item for aucht paisboordis	xxiiii s.
For pack threid and merling cord	l s.
For v pair of bellis at 18 s. pair	iiii lib. x s.
For 8 pair of bellis at 8 s. pair	iii lib. iiii d.
For 24 pair bellis at 6 s. pair	vii lib. iiii s.
For nyne powder hornes	iii lib. iiii s.

7 (sic) June 1617

(Firework men as above.)

Provisionis

Item for xxi elne of canves	viii lib. viii s.
For tailyeour threid and pack threid	xxx s.
For 24 pund of pick at 3 s. pund	iii lib. xii s.
For 8 pund of brinstane	xxxvi s.
For 8 pond of talloun	xxxii s.

9 June 1617

70 r.
(Firework men as above.)

Provisionis

Item for ten pond of brinstane	xliiii s. iiii d.
For pack threid and fyve quair paper	li s.
For four pund of talloun	xvi s.
For xii elne of hardin	iiii lib.
For 3 mutchkins of aquavitie	xxiiii s.
For 4 pund of brimstane	xvii s. iiii d.
For 3 pund of pick	ix s.
For 5 pond of rosen	vii s. vi d.
For ten bowstringis	x s.
For 19 paisboordis	iii lib. ii s.
For xliiii hankis of skanyie and merling cord	iiii lib. vi s.
For x quair of paper	xxxiii s. iiii d.
For a pond of glew	vi s. viii d.
For i^c faddum towes at 2 s. faddum	xii lib.
To Ralf Dryden for his hobbie hors	iiii lib.

16 June 1617

70 v.
(Firework men as above.)

Provisionis

For aucht elnes of canves	iii lib. iiii s.
For four scheip skynnes	xlviii s.
For sex elnes of linning	iii lib. xii s.
For glew	viii s.
For pack threid	xxx s.
For paisboord and tailyeour threid	xxvi s. viii d.
For tuyne	xxiiii s.
For a ryme	iii lib.
For weyir of sindrie sortis	iiii lib.
For a wissoren	xxx s.
For a pynt of double aquavitye	iiii lib.
For a glas to put it in	vi s. viii d.
For a bowett and candle to the hill	xii s.
For sex torches	iiii lib.
For i^{c}xl wavers to the Hielandmen	iiii lib. vi s.
For tuyges	xxx s.
For a stane of pick	xlviii s.

[23 June 1617]
(Firework men as above, but working only 2 days.)

Provisionis

71 r.

To the maister of cunyehous for a stane wecht of saltpetir at 34 s.ilk pond .... xxvii lib. iiii s.

For 3 stane half pick at 3 s. lib. .... viii lib. viii s.

For ten lib. of rosen .... xv s. vi d.

For a pair of schone to the Captain of Envie .... xl s.

To the Earle of Abircornes tabernour and quhisler for attending the youthes at the moreis dance the nycht of the fyrwarkis .... viii lib. xii s.

To a man that brocht lyme .... xxiiii s.

To the fyrewarkmen to drink .... vi lib. xiii s. iiii d.

For the fyrewarkmenis beddis 15 nychtis haifing 16 s.ilk nycht inde .... xii lib.

To Johne Pratt and sevin with him for transporting them with thair hors hyre fra Edinburgh to Bervick and for thair charges .... i^{c}i lib.

Summa of the haill expenssis debursit in fyrewarkis according to this preceiding compt extendis to ane thousand fourtene pundis fourtene schillingis sex d.

Tenet CLERICUS REGISTRI.

Summa of the haill expenssis maid upoun new buildingis and reparationis in and about the castell of Edinburgh and upoun fyrewarkes fra the fyft of August 1616 exclusive to the xiiii of Merche 1618 inclusive according to thir preceiding comptis extendis to the soume of tuentie fyve thousand fyve hundereth fourscoir four pundis thrie schillingis tua pennyes.

Tenet CLERICUS REGISTRI.

AL.CANCELLARIUS;   MAR   THESAURARIUS;   CARNEGY; LOTHIANE; GEO.ARESKYN; KILSAYTH; Sir R.COKBURNE; Sir A.DRUMMOND; P. ROLLOK; Sir G.MURRAY; Sir A.HAMILTON.

Appendix 2C

Firework Ingredients
For The Earl of Leicester 1572

This previously unpublished account of firework materials is perhaps the most detailed of the English sixteenth-century records. The ingredients are itemised for celebratory purposes on behalf of the Earl of Leicester. The list is contained in The Longleat Dudley Papers, volume III, fols.55^r and 55^v and reproduced on microfilm as The Dudley Papers, pub. no. 96700, 3 reels, by Microform (Wakefield) Ltd., Main Street, East Ardley, Wakefield, West Yorkshire. This item is on reel 2. The transcription has been completed by Peter Meredith and myself.

fol.55^r.

For therle of Leicestre to be vsed at
Killingworthe. mens*e*Augustie. 1572

Serpentine powdre	di last.
Corne powdre	I lb
Saltpetre in roche	xl lb
Sulphur in meale	xx lb

Rozen	xx lb
Turpentine	iii lb
Grene copperas	ii lb
Camphire	i lb
Mastick	v lb
Verdigrew	ij lb
Salarmoniack	iii lb
Mercurie sublimat	iv lb
Aquavite'	i quarte
Portingale salt	i (?)pynte
Foundur dust	i lb
Traine oyle	i quart
Linced oyle	i pottle
Canvas	x elles
Soultage	vi elles
Browne threde	i quar lb
Sewing nedles	xii
Towe	ii lb
Paper royall	vi quires
Stone pitche	qrt barʒ
Small lyne for trunckes	xx lb
Marlyne and Twyne	xx lb
Trunckes for Staves	ii dozens
fol. 55 v.	
Pins	ii dozens
Tampions	di ^c (?)
Cains	
Roddes for rocketes	xvi dozen
Matche	iii lb

Appendix 3

Appendix 3A
John Hestor's Stock-List 1588

This document is a two-page broadsheet that contains a list of ingredients and compositions sold at "Paules wharfe" by the distiller and Paracelsian, John Hestor. Much of his stock consisted of items to realise the remedies defined by Leonardo Fioravanti, the Italian surgeon. There are,however, many pyrotechnic materials in the list that were included for the express purpose of making fireworks. The outer edge of the right-hand collumn has been lost in the original document, thus leaving a number of incomplete words. Typography represents the original.   *BL C.60.o.6.*

These Oiles, vvaters, Extractions, or Essence
Saltes, and other Compositions; are at Paules wharfe ready made to be solde, by
IOHN HESTER, practitioner in the arte of Distillation; who will also be ready for reason-
ble stipend, to instruct any that are desirous to *learne the secrets of the same in few days, etc.*

I

Oyles of

Cinamon
Cloues. (Maces.
Nutmegges.
Pepper:(Ginger.
Anniseedes.
Fennell seedes.
Dyll seedes.
Carraway seedes.
Commin seedes.
Baie berries.
Iuniper berries
Mustard seedes.
Orange pilles.
Lemmon pilles.
Sweete margerum
Rosemary flowers.
Sage (Time.
Origanum.
Hysope.
Mintes.
Lauender.
Penniroyall.
Camomill flowers.
Waxe.
Honnie.
Turpentine.
Frankensence.

Carabe or Amber.
Gagates or Jett.
Aqua fortis.
Aquaregis.
Aqua spermatis Ra-
narum.
Vineger distilled.
The spirit of wine.
Aqua fragrariae cum
spiritu vini.
Aqua Cranij hu-
mani.

3. Saltes of

Cinamon.
Cloues.
Nutmegges.
Ginger.
Pepper.
Rosemary
Sage.
Time.
Marioram.
Origanum.
Mintes.
Hysope.
Briony
Centuary.

4. Extractio vel Essentia

Rhabarbari.
Eloborni gri.
Hermodactilorum.
Seenae Alexandriae.
Polipodij.
Brioniae.
Gentianae.
Angelicae.
Sabinae.
Agrimoniae.
Vnicae peruincae.
Betonicae.
Chellidonij.
Absinthij.
Chamomillae.
Saluiae.
Rutae.
Parthenenionis.
Pioniae.
Inipereri.
Florum genistae.
Colocynthidae.
Soldanellae.
Laureolae.
Alloae.

Agarici.
Cnici feu Carthami.
Euforbij.
Segatpeni.
Squillae.
Sarcocollae.
Aristolochiae.
Cantharides.
Tanacetum.
Marubij.
Eufragiae.
Calendulae.
Tormentillae.
Philopendulae
Hiosciami.
Fumi terrae.
Chamipiteos.
Spicae nardi.
Zedoariae.
Zinziberis.
Croci.
Piperis.
Corticis aurantiae.
Extracio Amuleti.
Palmarij.

AquaTheriacalis.
Calx testarum ouorum, & lymarum.
Emplastrum fodicationis, vel stictio.
Amuletum Palmarij   (Para...
Aqua aluminis magistralis.
Oleum benedictum Phalopii   (Fer...
Gibsons Balme.

6.

Certaine Compositions of
Leonardo Phirouanti.

La Petra philosophale nostra.
Pillole Aquillone.
Electuario Angellica.
Dia Aromatio.
Aqua Balsami.   Oleum Balsami.
Balsamum artificiale.
Oleum Hipericionis compositum.
Electuarium magistrale, for the cough.
Magno licore. Vnguento magno.
Elixer vitae. Aqua preferuans.
Cerote magistrale.
Oleum benedictum nostrum.
Oleum philosophorũ de terebinthina
Vnguentum ex litargiro.   (ce...
Dur Causticke.
AquaReale, which maketh the teeth
w[hite?] presently.   decoratiue
Water and oyle of Petra vegetabile.

[contd.]

Colophoni.
Carabe or Amber.
Iet or Gagates.
Benzoin.
Storax liquida.
Labdanum.
Amoniacum.
Galbanum.
Sagapenum.
Masticke.
Castoreum.
Egges. (Butter.
Tartar.
Cranij humani.
Lignum vitae.
Fraxini
Genistae
Oleū tartari faetens.

2.
VVaters of
Cinamon.
Cloues.
Nutmegges.
Frankensence
Turpentine.
Honnie (Waxe.
Egges.
Harteshorne.
Amoniacum.

Fumitory.
Penniroyall.
Hipericō or S.Iohns
worte.
Mugwort.
Polipodie.
Piony.
Fetherfewe.
Chamnipitheos.
Eye bright.
VVormewood.
Broome.
Ashe.
Beane stalkes.
Iuniper.
Lignum vitae.
Zarsa perilla.
Eleborus niger.
Sal vini.
Sal vrini.
Sal cranij humani.
Sal aceti.
Sal tartari .
Sal tartari christallini.
Sal vitrioli.
Sal vel saccharum
plumbi.
Sal bythargirij
Salconditum ? Phiro-
uanti.

5. Compositions of diuers
Authors.

Phlegma,spiritus,Oleum,&sal vitrioli.
Mūmia vel Balsamum vitrioli.
Creta vitrioli. (Crocus martis.
Oleum tartari faetens.
Oleum aceti. (Oleum sulphuris.
Balsamum sulphuris, Rulandi.
Emplastrum Diasulphuris, eiusdem.
Rubinum sulphuris, cum spiritu vini.
Flos sulphuris.
Sulphur vitriolatum.
Oleum Camphorae.
Oleum ligni Heracle, Rulandi.
Magisterium, vel essentia perlarum.
Corrall dissolued.
Vitrum Antimonij.
Mercurius Antimonij.
Flores Antimonij.
Aquila Caelestis, Phedronis.
Turpetum minerale, Quertcetani.
Turpetum Leonificatum diaphoreticū,
specificum Parac.
Panchimagogon specificum, eiusdem.
Laudanum Anodinum specificū, eiusdē.
Mercurius sublimatus.
Mercurius precipitatus.
Oleum siue munia tartari.
Aqua oleum, & sal ligni vitae.

Pillulae contra morbum gallicum.
Oleum de lateribus vel philosophori...
Sirōpo del Ebulo Compostum.
An vnction against contraction of sinowes
Diuers and sundrie vernishes, both for...
ners, Paynters, and Limmers.
Also liquid gold and siluer to write with
Diuers compositions of most strange...
terrible fireworkes, made by the Sp...
ricall arte, not heretofore knowen of
[ma?]ny . pyrotechnie.
A deuise to make fresh water out of the
[sea?] as the ship sayleth, in great abounda...
[nce?] to serverr. orrrr.mēaday, for one shil
[ling?] charge: and is most holesome, espec[ially]
for those that are troubled with moyst...
mors: as, the dropsie, and such like...
may be kept sweet a yeare.
Also a certaine kind of pitch for trimmin[g?]
ships: Which water, nor sunne, nor w
[ind?] can consume in long time.
With diuers other secretes not her
[before set?] downe.
Nowill. Keymis, the great Alchymi[st].
of London.   FINIS.   I.H.

gabriel harvey. 1588.

Appendix 3B

The Grocers' Company – Tariff of Charges 1453

The Grocers' Company of London had the responsibility of managing the public scale, or the King's Beam. The tariff of charges listed here identifies some of the ingredients itemised in John Hestor's stock-list and indicates the range of materials that could be weighed by the King's Beam in 1453. The list also implies the scope of the Grocers' trade and is contained in Baron Heath, *Some Account of the Worshipful Company of Grocers of the City of London* , London, 1869, pp.421-422.

In the tyme of Rich^d. Lee, Will.Taylor, & John Basingthwayte beynge Wardeyns,

This imposicion was maad & ordeyned by the Wardeynes & the feleshepe associed, the xxi daye of Juin in the yere of owre Lord m.cccc.liij, and alle the names of them folowe in wrytinge that were at this ordenaunce makyng, for wele of the beem.

	d.
Furste, for Pepper, 1 bale	xx
Safron, 1 cak	xx
Clowes, 1 bale, ye C.	viij
Mac, 1 bale or barel	viij
Greynes, 1 balet, ye C.	xij
Cynamon, 1 kase be it gret or smal	vj
Gynger, case or bale, ye C.	iiij
Nottemeg, 1 bale, ye C.	iiij
Long Pepper, d. ye C.	iij
Flowre of Alman, eny draught	iiij
Reysens of Corent, ye butte, }	
} ye C.	j
Reysens of Corent, ye barell,}	
Gynger, ye barel, ye C.	vj
Galyngale, ye bale, ye C.	iiij
Drugges, eny draught	ij
Woode, ye balett	ij
Mader, ye bale	v
Alum, foyle or rooch, ye bale	iiij
Yorns (horns) ye tunne	iiij
Tyn, ye peece	ij
Leed ye ffodder	iiij

Coton, ye bale .... iiij
Coton, Cyprus or basselan, ye C. .... ij
Ryse, ye bale .... ij
Comyn and Anneys, ye bale .... iiij
Soope, ye pype .... iiij
Almaunds, ye bale .... iij
Wex, ye bale .... ij
Dates, ye bale .... ij
Saunders and Brasile, ye C. .... iij
Argent Vyff, ye bolyon .... iiij
Vermelion, ye lof .... iiij
Verdegres, ye C. .... iiij
Salt Peter, ye C. .... ij
Brymston, ye C. i
Reed Copper, ye C. i
Grey Copper, ye C. i
Flex, ye C. ii
And al maner other merchandises y^t comyth
to ye beem and is not comprehendid in this
wrytynge, to paye for the bales
of ev'ry xxlb i

Signed by the members in the manner following, viz.

        I, RICH.LEE, am content.
        I, WILL.MAROWE, am content.
        I, WILL.TAYLOR, am content.
            &c^e. &c^e.

Appendix 4

Recipes From Babington

Three of the recipes presented here are concerned with "dragon on the line" techniques. The fourth recipe is Babington's version of the "trunck of fire".

Babington's recipes are perhaps some of the most comprehensive of those offered by early firework writers. Hodgkin in his *Rariora* regards Babington's *Pyrotechnia..* as "The most covetable, I think, of all *English* Books, at any rate, on this subject...But Babington is greatest when he comes to the elaboration of the various complex devices in which the age delighted and in which he has evidenced more proficiency than any other of the writers..". Philip in his *Bibliography...* declares that "This book is without doubt the most important in Firework bibliography. It was the first work in English to deal exclusively with the subject of display fireworks, a fact often acknowledged in later works. All previous books which dealt with the subject concerned themselves primarily with the military uses of fireworks.".

Appendix 4A

[**FIG. 21**]

pp.36-37

How to make a Dragon, or any other creature to run on the Line, by the help of fire:

LET your Dragon be made either of pasteboard, or else of fine rods, such as your Basketmakers use; which must bee made hollow, with a place in the belly to put in two rockets, and shall bee so ordered, that there may come a small pipe from the tayle of one, to the head of the other; then make a place in the eyes, and mouth, to put into each hole fire, which shall be made up in rowled paper, and thrust in; then on the top of the back let there bee fastned two small pulleys for the line to run in, which being done, your Dragon is finished, to firing, which must be thus; first fire it at the eyes, and mouth, (always noting, that this receipt must be some slow mixture, such as your starres) then fire that rocket which is placed with his mouth toward the tayle of the Dragon, which will make it seem to cast fire from thence, till hee come to the end of his motion; and then on a sudden, as a creature wounded with some accident, shall return with fire coming forth of his belly, which being well ordered, will give great content.

The form of this you shall finde in the tenth figure, by the letter B.

B	*represents a dragon to bee forced with rockets, which are placed in the belly.*
C	*a place made to put in a rocket, which must be put in at the tayle, with the mouth of the rocket outward.* [not marked in drawing].
D	[marked *E* in drawing]. *is a conveyance from the tayle of that rocket, to the mouth of the next, which commeth out at the belly.*
E E	*two small brasse pullees, fastened in a frame on the back, for the line to run in.*

Appendix 4B

[FIG.22]

p.37

Another way for making a fiery Dragon to passe on the line without the help of fire.

IN the former Chapter, I spake of a Dragon of a small size, of a foot in length, or thereabout; now I come to speak of those of a greater magnitude, which cannot so easily bee forced with fire, in a straight line, without some artificiall help; for Art must bee always as a handmaid attending on Nature, to help her in her work; therefore having prepared a large dragon, you must make divers hollow truncks of wood, within the body, which shall bee to cast out fire, and on a sudden divers small bals of fire, other times a great number of small fisgigs. Now to make this run on the line, you must have a hollow trunck fastned on the back, between the wings of your dragon, which must bee somewhat bigger than your cord, with a small hole thorow each end; the use of those small holes is, to fasten a small cord, which must be so fastned, that one end thereof must bee fastned at the head of the Dragon, and so passe over a pulley; (which pulley shall bee fastned at the end of the line) and returning thorow that hollow trunck in the back, it shall be put over another pulley at the other end of the line, and so making a return, shall be fastned to the hole in the hinder part of the trunck. Now one of these pulleys shall have a handle or winch to turn it about, which shall cause the dragon to move, and shall be a help to the drawing of it backward and forward at your pleasure; after this manner you may form many works on the line, which otherwise cannot be done. The form of this is set down in the eleventh figure, by the letter *A*.

A   *representeth the dragon ready finished, with all his works.*
B C   *the manner of the hollow trunck which the cord must passe thorow.*
B   *the place for fastning of a small cord, which must passe over the pulley marked D*
D   *the manner of fastning that pulley which must bee at the further end of the line.*
OOOO   [the shapes of the pulleys and the ends of the trunck in the drawing] *the manner of the passing of the sayd line which is thorow the hollow trunck, and so over the pulley marked E, and then fastned to the other end of the trunck marked G.* [C in drawing].
F   *a handle or winch belonging to one of the pulleys which maketh the dragon move forward and backward, as occasion profereth.*
H H   *the great line on which the dragon passeth, and is only for keeping it steaddy in the motion.*

Appendix 4C

[**FIG. 23**]

pp.37-41

How to represent S.George fighting with a Dragon in fire on the Line.

HAving prepared your figures artificially made, you must make a hollow trunck thorow the body of each figure, for a great line to passe thorow, and likewise for a smaller line to draw them to and from each other; which must bee fastned in this manner: at the breast of the dragon let one end of one cord be tied, which shall passe thorow the body of the George, and returning it about a pulley at the other end, fasten it to the back of the George, and at the breast of the George let another cord be tied, which shall passe thorow the body of the dragon, or a trunck on the back, and so returning about a pulley at that end shall be pulled straight, and fastned to the tayle of the dragon, so that as you turn that wheele, the George and dragon will runne furiously at each other; and when you please you may cause them to make a retreat, and come on againe divers times; but in all these works forget not to sope your line extraordinary well, and likewise have a care that your work be not too heavy above the line, but that they may hang *equilibrio*, otherwise they will turn their heeles upward, which would bee a disgrace to the work and workman: there might bee much written upon this same subiect, but to the ingenious, I think it is sufficient, they may order their works according to their own fancies; only here is the ground of the matter. The manner of this is represented in the eleventh figure, by the letter *B*.

C   *representing the George.* [not labelled in drawing].
D   *the dragon.*
E   *the small line fastned to the head of the dragon, and passeth thorow the body of the George.* [not labelled in drawing].
F   *the pulley which guideth the said line.*
G   *the place of fastning the other end of that line.* [not labelled in drawing].
H   *another line fastned to the breast of the horse, which passeth thorow the hollow trunck of the dragon.* [not labelled in drawing].
I   *the pulley about which it passeth, and is fastned to the tayle of the dragon.*
K   *the place of fastning the said line to the dragon.*
L L   *the great line which guideth these two figures.*
M   *the winch or handle fastned to one of the pulleys, and is for the moving them forward or backward.*

Appendix 4D

[**FIG. 30**]

pp.41-42

How to make a trunck of fire, which shall cast forth divers fire bals.

PRovide a trunck of foure inch boare, and two foot long, with a hollow place in the bottom, of two inch boare, & as much deep, to the end it may be put on a strong post; let there be a bottom left between the two boares, which shall be two inches thick, so that there will be twenty inches left for your work, which shall bee filled as followeth; first fill it with corne powder one inch, then put in your ball, which shall bee five inches and a halfe, and round about it put powder dust, till you come to the top, then fill it two inches and a halfe with slow mixture, and on that two inches of corn powder: then put in another ball, and after it slow mixture, which shall be filled to the top, and so reserve it for your use; note that you must turn three places for arming of it, which must be done either with iron hoops or else with cords, to the end the violence of your corn powder burst it not; your upper ball shall be made after this manner: Having made ready a case of canvas, fill it with this mixture following.

Take   *1 l. of saltpeter.*
          ¹/₂ l. of powder dust.
          ¹/₄ l. of sulphur vive.
          2oz of camphire.
          1oz of oyle of peter.

Mix these very well, till it become somewhat tough, and then fill your ball, and arm it, leaving foure vents, into which you shall put foure small sticks, till such time you have coated; the manner of coating is, to dip the ball in a mixture of pich, rosin, tallow, and sulphur, but this is for bals of longer continuance; the coating for this ball shall be as followeth;

The receipt for coating,

          ¹/₂ l. of pitch.
          ¹/₄ l. of vernish.
          1 oz of sulphur vive.
          2 oz of powder dust.

Melt your pitch and sulphur, and then poure in your vernish and powder dust, and while it is hot dip in your ball, and then cast a little fine powder dust over it, and so let it coole a little, and then dip it lightly againe, and so you have it ready; when you use it, pull out your foure sticks out of the vents, and fill them with powder dust, and so put them in. The lower ball which is last fired, shall be full of starres, with powder dust intermixed, to break the ball, these shall be primed with cotton wick made of purpose, to the end it may not fire the bal til it be up a good heighth, and then to break into a showre of starres.

The receipt of the composition for the trunck.

> *1 l. of roch peter.*
> *$^1/_4$ l. of fine powder dust.*
> *$^1/_2$ of sulphur vive.*
> *2oz of camphir.*
> *1 oz of linseed oyle.*

The forme of this trunck is represented in the twelfth figure by the letter A:

A	*represents a trunck ready finished, with two bals.*
B	*the ball which lieth uppermost, and is filled with slow composition.*
C	*the lower ball ,which is filled with starres,*
D	*the slow mixture at the top of the trunck.*
	[not labelled in drawing].
E	*the corn powder to send forth the upper ball.*
	[not labelled in drawing]
F	*the second lay of composition.*
	[not labelled in drawing]
G	*the powder for sending forth the lower ball.*
	[not labelled in drawing].
OOO	*three places left for arming the said trunck.*
	[not labelled in drawing].
H	*the bottom of the trunck, which must be two inches thick.*
I	*a place left to put in a post of wood for it to stand on.*

Glossary

THE GLOSSARY is of necessity a full one. There are many ingredients, materials and processes that require explanation and some extended contextual information occurs with some entries. Items recorded here exist by virtue of their initial inclusion in one or more of the five forms of evidence considered in this work. A number of these items are no longer used in firework manufacture. Reasons for such discontinuation usually relate to the doubtful efficacy of the ingredient. In some cases the supposed or intended value is unknown. No attempt has been made to discriminate between the successful or unsuccessful use of ingredients and processes. The following form is adopted:

Name [Forms]: Definition/Description: Sources/Commentaries

All the sources may be found in the **BIBLIOGRAPHY**.

Alum *O.E.D.* 1. ALUM "A whitish transparent mineral salt, crystallizing in octahedrons, very astringent, used in dyeing, tawing skins, and medicine, also for sizing paper, and making materials fire proof; chemically a double sulphate of aluminium and potassium ($AlK(SO_4)$ + $12H_2O$ water of crystallization).". Alum was painted or pasted on to those parts of the body that needed protection from fire. Sources: Best and Brightman, p.105; Platte, p.31; Partington, pp. 5,286; Hopkins, p.150; Cannell, p.118; Jay, pp.261-265.

Amber *O.E.D.* II. 3. AMBER "A yellowish translucent fossil resin, found chiefly along the southern shores of the Baltic.". The resin was included in many recipes, presumably because it would ignite readily and thus help with the combustion of other materials. It also possessed colour producing ability for Simienowicz declared, "If the Raspings of Yellow Amber, it [the colour of the flame] will appear the same, but inclining to the Citronish.". Sources: Lucar Appendix, pp.82-83; Simienowicz, p.168; Ruggieri, pp.74-75; Brock, *History of Fireworks*, p.196; Church, p.48; Shimizu, p.116.

Antimony (Sb) The black or dark grey metallic form was powdered and used as a colour-producing agent to produce a white colour that inclined towards yellow. Simienowicz described the colour as "sad Yellow, or of an Honey or Box-

Colour.". Sources: Simienowicz, p.168; Ruggieri, p.74; Weingart, pp.8-9; Brock, *History of Fireworks*, p.196; Lancaster, pp.28-29.

Aqua-ardens See **Aqua-vitae**.

Aqua-vitae [Water of life; spirits of wine; aqua-ardens; brandy]. *O.E.D.* 1. AQUA-VITÆ "A term of the alchemists applied to ardent spirits or unrectified alcohol; sometimes applied, in commerce, to ardent spirits of the first distillation.". The distillation produced when wine is heated. Aqua-vitae seems to have been used for two main purposes: one was to "bind" a mixture and the other was to act in a mixture, as Brock says, "as an extra assurance of inflammability.". When ignited on its own, it burns with a colourless flame. If fabric is soaked in aqua-vitae and set alight, the aqua-vitae will burn without affecting the host material. [**CHAPTER 2**]. Don Alessio Ruscelli offers the following recipe for the creation of aqua-vitae:

> To make very good Aqua vitae
> Take Wyne that is not to olde, that is to saye of a yere or somewhat more or lesse, and let it be very good, hauyng a good odour: and distill it in a vessell of glass hauyng a longe necke aboute syxe foote long, wyth a very small and slowe fyer, and take it up together whyles it commeth furthe faste, that is to saye when one droppe tarieth not for another, and it shalbe very good and pleasaunt, for there shalbe nothing els but onely the part of the Wyne verye subtile and fine, true it is that it shalbe not very hote, nor burne so much as other Aqua vitaes do.

Sources: Alessio, *The second part of the Secretes*, f.1; Lucar, p.72; Lucar Appendix, pp.80, 81, 82, 83, 86; Bate, pp. 55, 61, 62, 65, 66, 71; Babington, p.11; Serlio, f.26ᵛ.; Hyll, C8ʳ and D1ᵛ; Simienowicz, pp. 122, 125; Feuillerat, *Revels...Edward VI and Queen Mary*, p.110; *REED:Cambridge*, I, p.185; Feuillerat, *Revels...Elizabeth*, p.308; *Calendar of State Papers, Venice*, VIII, p.535; *Accounts M.W.*, I, p.233; II, pp.90, 91, 92; *Calendar of State Papers, Domestic*, III, p.203; *The Accounts*, VII, p.357; *Malone Collections*, III, p.34; Gwei-Djen, pp.69-112; C.Anne Wilson, pp.45-93; R.J.Forbes, pp.60-69.

Arsedine [Arsowde; Assidue; Asidew; Orsidue; Ossidewe]. A form of gold leaf made of an alloy of copper and zinc and used for decorative purposes. The material may well have been used in Serlio's recipe for the production of lightning where the firework required to create the effect was "couered ouer with pure gold or shining lattin...". Sources: Serlio, f.26ᵛ; Crawford, *Howard Household Books*, p.339; *REED: Shrewsbury*, I, p.184; *Malone Collections*, VII, pp.190, 191, 201; XIII, pp.10,17, 23, 28, 33, 38, 43, 50, 57, 64, 70, 77, 84, 92, 98, 104, 116, 121.

Arsenic See **Orpiment** and **Realgar**

Asphalt [bitumen] This is a blackish brown solid which is thought to be created, according to Lancaster, through "chemical changes and the oxidation of high boiling point mineral oils". It is said to produce excellent colours when finely ground, although the high sulphur content and/or its propensity to decomposition, renders it liable to spontaneous combustion in some mixtures that contain potassium chlorate ($KClO_3$). In modern firework manufacture potassium chlorate has largely superseded saltpetre as the principal oxidising agent in mixtures. Sources: Bate, p.64; Partington, pp.4,5,48; Weingart, p.4; Lancaster, p.30.

Asafoetida [assafetida] *O.E.D.* ASAFOETIDA "A concreted resinous gum, with a strong alliaceous odour, procured in Central Asia from the *Narthex asafœtida* and allied umbelliferous plants; used in medicine as an antispasmodic, and as a flavouring in made dishes.". This gum-resin was possibly used, like shellac, to bind mixtures or to damp stars. Sources: Lucar Appendix, pp.80,89; Kentish, (1879), p.175; Kentish, (c.1976), pp.6-9.

Bees-wax [wax] *O.E.D.* BEES-WAX "The wax secreted by bees as the material of their combs, and used for various purposes in the arts.". Bees-wax was used in preference to tallow or rosin in candle making because it burned more cleanly. However, it was a more costly product. It was sometimes mixed with other gums, resins and tallow to create the combustible parts of torches. Sources: *REED:Coventry,* p.110.

Benjamin [gum benjamin, *O.E.D.* 1.GUM BENZOIN]. Jones describes benjamin as follows: "Benjamin is a resin (much used by perfumers, and sometimes in medicine); it is brought from the Indies, where it is found of different sorts; and distinguished by the following colours, viz. yellow, grey, and brown, but the best is that which is easy to break and full of white spots. Benjamin is also one of the ingredients in odoriferous fireworks, when reduced to a fine flour;...There is also an oil of benjamin, which is sometimes drawn from the dregs of the flour; it affords a very good scent, and may be used in wet compositions.". Sources: Jones, pp.10,11; Simienowicz, pp.120,121; Brock, *History of Fireworks,* p.190.

Bettings *O.E.D.* sb2 BEAT "A bundle of flax or hemp made up ready for steeping."; *O.E.D.* vbl. sb. obs. BEETING "The action of making good; mending, repair; making (a fire), kindling.". "Bettyngs" are recorded at Coventry and they complemented "puddyngs" as fuel in cressets. "Bettyngs" were clearly different from "puddyngs" and seem to have consisted of bundles of hemp or flax and used to kindle or re-kindle the "puddyngs" or "cressyt lyght". Presumably, loosely-bundled "bettyngs" would ignite more quickly than the densely-packed fibres of rope that constituted the "puddyngs". "Bettyngs" at Coventry were fuelled by pitch and rosin. Lucar offers the following recipe in respect of "cressyt lyght" that may well have functioned in the manner of the Coventry "bettyngs": "THrust lynnen ragges into oyle of hempsede, and after dippe them in melted tallowe, then putting them into Cressets giue fire to them, & you shall see that they all burne and giue a great light.". Sources: Lucar *Appendix,* p.84; *REED:Coventry,* pp.115, 118, 127, 129, 157; Sharp, p.187.

Bitumen See **Asphalt**. Sources: Bate, pp. 63,64; Lucar *Appendix*, p.81; Simienowicz, p.121.

Black powder The descriptions "gunpowder" and "blackpowder" are synonymous. The latter term has largely superseded the former in order to clarify the distinction between it and other more recent types of explosives. Sources: Guttmann, I, p.176; Crocker, *Gunpowder Industry*, p.10; Crocker, *Gunpowder Mills Gazetteer*, p.2; Percival, p.31; Patterson, pp. 1,9; Lancaster, p.29; Shimizu, pp.30,174.

Bombast [bombax, bumbast, bumbase]. *O.E.D.* 1. BOMBAST "The soft down of the cotton-plant; raw cotton; cotton wool.". Bate gives the following recipe to make "Compositions for Starres" for use in rockets: "Take a quarter of a pinte of *aqua vitae*, and dissolue therein one ounce, and a halfe of camphire, and dip therin cotten bumbast, and afterwards roule it up into little balles; afterwards rowle them in powder of quick brimstone, and reserue them for use.". Sources: Bate, p.61; Lucar *Appendix*, pp.81,82,84; Partington, pp.48,56,59.

Calamite [callamita] *O.E.D.* 2. *Min.* CALAMITE "A variety of tremolite (white-horn blende) occurring in crystals sometimes reed-like.". Bate makes use of "callamita" in a recipe to create "a Composition that will kindle with the water.". The function of the ingredient is unclear. Sources: Bate, p.64; Partington, p.163.

Camphor ($C_{10}H_{16}O$) [camphir,camfor] Camphor is a whitish, translucent, crystalline substance with a penetrating odour and pungent taste. It is volatile and readily evaporates at room temperature, hence the several warnings to keep the substance well covered when not in use. It boils at 204°C. Today camphor is distilled from Camphore officinarum (Laurus camphora) and purified by sublimation. According to Jones, the wood and roots of this tree were cut into small pieces, heated in large copper vessels that were filled with straw and covered:

> the camphor is raised in form of a white downy matter, and retained among the straw; when the process is over, they shake it out of the straw, and knead it into cakes. These cakes are not very compact, but easily crumbled to pieces;

Simienowicz similarly regarded camphor as "very Combustible, will even burn in Water, and is very Odoriferous:". Although responses to the smell of camphor vary, there are no discrepancies as to the quality of light it produced when ignited. Simienowicz sums up the effect as: "White, Pale, or Milky-Colour Fire.". Sources: Jones, pp.7-10, 36; Lucar, p.72; Lucar *Appendix*, pp.80,81; Hyll, C5^{r}; Serlio, f.26^{v}.; Bate, pp.61-65, 71; Babington, pp.11,41,42,56,57; Simienowicz, pp.121,168; Church, p.90; Ruggieri, pp.77-78; Ellis, p.49; Best and Brightman, p.95,n.48; *REED:Shrewsbury*, I, p.184; *The Accounts*, XII, p.404.

Canes Depending on the length and diameter, canes appear to have been used for different purposes. Larger canes were used as "coffins" or "truncks" to contain slow mixtures and used as suggested by Norton in his "canes of fire" recipe. Thinner canes were inevitably used as sticks for rockets. Canes were further used in short lengths for use in "swevels". Sources: Norton, pp.152,155; Bate, pp.76-77; Babington, pp.16-17; *Malone Collections*, VII, p.201; Simienowicz, pp.154-155; *The Accounts*, VII, p.357.

Cannon powder See **Corned powder**

Canvas [Poldavid cannavas] The use of canvas is recorded for two main purposes: one was to make small balls for use on fire arrows and the other was to make fire balls. *The Accounts* record payment for "fyftein ellis of Poldavid cannevas at ijs. vjd. the ell xxxvij s. vj d." for use at the *Baptismal Celebrations*. Sources: Lucar *Appendix*, p.80; Babington, pp.41,60; Bate, pp.63,86; *The Accounts*, XII, pp.404,405; *The Accounts M.W.,* II, pp.89-92; A.H.Johnson, p.115,n.2.

Cartoush One of the names given to strengthened-paper or parchment cases that contained firework mixtures. Sources: de Malthe, passim; Ruggieri, p.94.

Charcoal [coal, coledust] *O.E.D.* sb.1 CHARCOAL "The black porous pulverizable substance, consisting (when pure) wholly of carbon, obtained as the solid residue in the imperfect combustion of wood, bones, and other vegetable or animal matter." Although charcoal is one of the three constituents of gunpowder, it does not appear in the appropriate accounts with the same frequency as saltpetre and sulphur. A possible reason for this condition is linked to the relative ease with which charcoal is produced; it is capable of being made in situ. Charcoal was made more or less exclusively from indiginous hardwoods. Biringuccio warned of the inappropriate production of charcoal: "If one should make charcoal and make it of softwood, it would not serve well when there was need of a strong and enduring fire.". Bate is quite precise about the production of charcoal: "The best Coales for use are the sallow, willow, hazel and beech; onely see they be well burnt.". Whitehorne suggests the following technique for making charcoal:

> they vse to take yong hasell of a yeare olde, cut in shorte peeces, and they putting them into a greate yearthen potte, or other vessell of yron, or brasse, they shutte it and couer it close, and lute it, or daube it very well aboute, so that it cannot breathe: and then they make fire rounde aboute it and vpon it, till suche time as it maye bee thoughte that the heate is well entred in through all, and that the wood that is within is very well fired: and without firebrandes, or flame, burned onely through suche heate: and then they take the fire from the potte and let it coole, and so they finde the same wood become cole.

Charcoal is capable of performing several functions within a gunpowder mixture. As a fuel to the composition, charcoal produces considerable heat and gas in its reaction with saltpetre. The fuel also possesses the capacity to change the burning rate of mixtures as well as alter ignition conditions; it is also the means of creating an explosive force. The ability to produce sparks or fire dust together with the property to change the intensity of flame are other characteristics of charcoal within a mixture. Even if these specific functions were not required, charcoal would operate as a combustion agent. Sources: Whitehorne, ff.28ᵛ-29ʳ; Lucar, pp.69-71,73; Lucar *Appendix*, p.81; Biringuccio, p.174; Hyll, B4ᵛ; Bate, pp.55,58,59,62,63,64,86; Babington, pp.14,63; Jones, p.6; Lancaster, p.33; Shimizu, p.117.

Cod liver oil See **Oils**.

Coffins Another term for the case of a firework. See **Cartoush**. Sources: Bate, passim; Babington, passim.

Colophone [colofone, Greek pitch, rosin] Colophone or rosin is produced as a residue when turpentine is distilled with water. Rosin is composed of a relatively high proportion of carbon and is capable of being reduced to powder form. Rosin is capable of burning with a bright flame but also tends to produce much smoke. Rosin should not be confused with resin. The distinctions are made clear by Kentish: "Rosin is soluble in alcohol, and is therefore a resin; rosin and resin, however are not synonymous; all rosin is a resin; but all resins are not rosin. Rosin has been tried in pyrotechny, but is of no use: a solution of it in spirit will bind stars; but it renders them white and smoky.".*The Accounts* record payment for "roset" and "twa unce of colophone xii d." at the *Baptismal Celebrations*. Similar payments were made for "Rosine" and "xij ˡ of pytche" together with other firework ingredients at Maidstone in 1589. *The Accounts M.W.* record the following payments for rosin at the *Birthday Celebrations*:

For xx pond wecht of rossen	liii s. iiii d.
...	
For xii pond of rosen	xxx s.
...	
For xxviii pond of rosen	xlii s.
...	
For 5 pond of rosen	vii s. vi d.
...	
For ten lib. of rosen	xv s. vi d.

The large quantity of rosin recorded here may well have been used in fire ball construction, for rosin, like tallow, was used in mixtures to coat fireballs. Pitch was also mixed with rosin and used to coat fireballs. Rosin was also a constituent ingredient in the operation of cressets and used in the production of torches. Sources: Biringuccio, p.438; Lucar *Appendix*, pp.80-82,83; Bate, pp.63,95; Babington, pp.41-43,55,56,57,60; Simienowicz, p.126; *The Accounts*, XII, pp.403,404,406,407; *The Accounts M.W.*, II, pp.89-92; Kentish (1878), p.175; Wright, *Churchwardens' Accounts*, p.3; *Malone Collections*, VII, p.201; Lancaster, p.39.

Cord See **Marline**

Cork [tampions] Used for stopping the ends of firework cases. Sources: *The Accounts M.W.*, II, p.89.

Corned powder [corn powder, lump powder, cannon powder] This powder is one of the two varieties of gunpowder, the other being "mealed powder". The process of "corning" gunpowder was developed in response to the frequently inconsistent behaviour of mealed powder caused by the separating out of ingredients. Corned gunpowder consisted of larger granules and was produced by sieving the mixture. Whitehorne outlined the following technique:

> The maner of corning all sortes of pouder, is with a Seeue made, with a thicke skinne of Parchemēt, full of little round holes, into the whiche Seeue the pouder muste be put, while it is dancke, and also a little bowle, that when you sifte, it maie roule vp and doune, vpon the clottes of pouder, to breake them, that it maie corne, and runne throughe the hooles of the Seeue.

It was important that the mixture was moist so that the corned powder would adhere to form larger granules. The rolling ball would both help to form the granules and push them through the sieve. The sieved mixture was allowed to dry and the resultant properties were consequently different from those of mealed powder. Corned powder created rapid combustion and possessed increased strength. It was able to perform in this way because the air space between the granules was more evenly distributed. It was said that 2lb of corned powder could do the work of 3lb of serpentine [mealed] powder. The choice between these forms of gunpowder was therefore critical to the function required. Mealed powder was initially used in heavy guns while corned powder was used in medium-sized guns, harquebuses, and pistols. Biringuccio warned against the inappropriate use of powders:

> For, if you should use that for heavy guns in arquebuses and pistols, it would throw the ball scarcely ten *braccia* out of the barrel; and if you should use that made for arquebuses in heavy guns without great discretion, you might easily break them or spoil them for other uses...

This distinction did not continue to exist for the development of larger grained corned powder enabled its use in larger ordinance. Both forms of gunpowder were used in firework production to create different effects. See **Corned powder** and **Mealed powder**. Sources: Biringuccio, pp.412,413,413n; Lucar, p.79; Babington, p.11; Norton, p.145; Whitehorn, ff.27[v],28[r] [The account of sieving corned powder does not appear to have been plagiarised from Biringuccio]; Simienowicz, pp.158,159; *Malone Collections*, VII, p.196; *Malone Collections* XI, p.128; *REED:Devon*, pp.246,248; *REED:York*, I, pp.403, 409, 410, 414, 419, 445; *REED:Coventry*, p.391; *REED:Newcastle*, p.55; Hime, *Origin of Artillery*, pp.151-155; Partington, pp.154,174; Hodgetts, pp.28,29; Lynn White

Jr., *Medieval Technology,* pp.100,101,269 [White says that there is no evidence to suggest that corned powder was in use before 1429]; Crocker, *Gunpowder Industry,* p.19.

Cotton wick [cotton weeke, quickmatch, gunmatch, match, stouple] Used to prime or convey fire to a firework. The simplest recipe offered by the early pyrotechnists is that of de Malthe. He required that the "Cotton-wieke" be soaked in "faire water", wrung out and drawn through a gunpowder slurry created by mixing a little "faire water" with powder dust. Dry powder dust was then sprinkled over the "Cotton-wieke" and allowed to dry. Babington's recipe suggested that the "cotton wicke" be soaked in "oyle of Camphire", taken out, rolled in fine powder dust and left to dry. This recipe required that the "priming...must be kept close from ayre...otherwise the spirit of the Camphir will decay.". By this he means that the camphor will evaporate. Additional ingredients were included in Bate's recipe:

> Take cotten-week, such as the Chandlers use for candles, double it six or seuen times double, and wet it throughly in saltpeter water, or aqua vitae, wherein some camphire hath been dissolued, or, for want of either, in faire water; cut it into diuers peeces, rowle it in mealed gunpowder, or powder and sulphur; the dry them in the Sun, and reserue them in a box where they may lie straight, to prime Starres, Rockets, or any other fireworks.

The implication from Bate's recipe is that the use of "faire water" alone was adequate to its task and presumably employed in the manner suggested by de Malthe. The additional use of sulphur was no doubt intended to insure ignition. Storage of the "cotton-week" was similarly intended to inhibit evaporation. The rate at which the "match" burned presumably varied according to the composition of the powder, length of time in storage and atmospheric conditions. Sources: de Malthe, pp.22,23,84,86,91; Babington, pp.12,23,42; Lucar *Appendix,* pp.82,84; Bate, pp.65,72,86,92; Simienowicz, pp.123-126; Lancaster, p.184.

Cransis These are recorded for use at the *Baptismal Celebrations* and appear to be garlands or wreaths presumably formed by wreathing strands of opened-out rope around a former, covered in canvas, dipped in tar and set alight. Sources: *The Accounts,* XII, pp.406,407.

Cresset *O.E.D.* 1. CRESSET "A vessel of iron or the like, made to hold grease or oil, or an iron basket to hold pitched rope, wood, or coal, to be burnt for light; usually mounted on the top of a pole or building, or suspended from a roof. Frequent as a historical word; in actual use applied to a fire-basket for giving light on a wharf, etc.". Sources: Sharp, pl.9 opp. p.51; Hone, *Every-Day Book,* I, pp.416-417; Douce, *Illustrations of Shakespeare,* pp.264-265; Nicholl, *Ironmongers,* p.62; J.R.Green, *Short History,* III, p.992; Caspall, *Fire and Light,* p.257.

Cresset light The term was sometimes used to refer to the light produced, but more frequently to the fuel of the cresset. Lengths of rope smeared or impregnated with combinations of rosin, pitch and tallow were coiled around the central spike of the cresset and set on fire. Sources: *REED:Coventry*, pp.115, 157, 168, 169, 176, 180, 184; *REED:Devon*, pp.90, 94, 366, 370; *REED:Herefordshire Worcestershire*, p.403; *REED:Cambridge*, I, p.163; *REED:Norwich*, p.101; *Malone Collections*, III, xvi-xvii,p.15; *Malone Collections*, XI, p.129; Nicholl, *Ironmongers*, p.64, Appendix, xviii; Chambers, *Elizabethan Stage*, II, p.543 n3; W.J.Lawrence, *Light and Darkness*, p.13.

Fire arrows [fyr gannis] Both the longbow and the crossbow, sometimes referred to as the "slurbow", were used to drive fire arrows. Small canvas balls containing burning mixtures were fitted to conventional arrows. Norton describes the function of the fire arrow when used in a crossbow:

> charged with a Fire Arrow fitted therefore, with a Mixture proper thereunto, by the Barbes on the Arrow heads, it will hang where it strikes, and by the vents made of purpose, it will fire whatsoeuer combustible matter shall bee neere it, especially Sayles, dry Timbers, or Pitch and Tarred places: the effect of this Instrument was well experimented at the Siege of Ostend and else-where, taking great effect. The like may be done with a long Bowe, but that the Arrow must be longer,...

Payment for materials to equip fire arrows is recorded at the *Baptismal Celebrations*: "Item for nyne littill girthis (hoops) quhairof was maid balles coverit with canevas iijs.". Another payment in the same accounts records payment for "auchttein girthis of haisill (hazel) vjs.". These payments are connected with an adjacent payment: "Item for ane dosone of lang fedderit arrowis xxiiijs.". The hoops of hazel created the frames for the balls that were subsequently covered with canvas, filled with a burning mixture, primed and sewn up. Sources: Biringuccio, p.435; Whitehorne, f.43ʳ; Norton, pp.137,157; de Malthe, pp.20-24; Sayle, after p.105; *The Accounts*, XII, p.405; *The Accounts*, VII, p.357; Hime, *Origin of Artillery*, p.139.

Fire balls Typically, the fire ball was made out of a canvas case, filled with a gunpowder mixture, primed and sewn up. In order to reinforce the ball, marling cord was wrapped tightly around the surface and coated in mixtures of pitch, rosin, tallow and tar. Occasional references exist to wooden fire balls. Sources: Lucar *Appendix*, p.80; Bate, pp.63,86,97; Babington, pp.41,55-56,60; Simienowicz, p.252; *The Accounts*, III, p.395; V, p.47; VIII, p.450; Mill, pp.184,325-326.

Fire boxes Boxes of metal plate used to contain fire. Sources: Feuillerat, *Revels...Edward VI and Queen Mary*, p.108; Lancashire, p.146.

Fire pans Portable pans to contain fire. Sources: *The Accounts*, III, p.384; *The Accounts*, XII, pp.405,406,408

Fire pumps [trunk of fire] Although some artillery was capable of firing fire balls, the principal means of projecting them was from the fire pump.*The Accounts* record payment for fire pumps at the *Baptismal Celebrations*: "twa peices of treis [trees] to mak fyre pompis and bearing of thame to the hous ix s. iiij d." Fire pumps were effectively the large-scale precursors of "roman candles". The balls were filled with different mixtures in order to produce varying effects. Both mealed and corned powder was layered inside the pump; the mealed powder effectively acted as a slow fuse and the corned powder provided the propulsive force to fire the ball. Sources: *The Accounts*, XII, p.405; Babington, pp.41-42, after p.43.

Fire spears [fyr sparris, fyre speris] It is likely that fire spears were in flame when held aloft or thrown. Rags or tow impregnated with tallow, pitch or rosin and fastened tightly to the spear would have fulfilled the task. Sources: *The Accounts*, IV, pp.490,493,495; *The Accounts*, VI, p.454.

Flambeantis [flambrantis?] The identity of "flambeantis" is unclear. See **CHAPTER 6** for discussion of these objects. Sources: *The Accounts*, XII, pp.405,406.

Frankinsense [white frankinsense] *O.E.D.* 1. FRANKINSENSE "An aromatic gum resin, yielded by trees of the genus Boswellia, used for burning as incense;... 2. Resin resembling this, obtained from firs or pines...". Together with frankinsense, other gum resins such as gum sandarac and mastick are recorded in recipes by Lucar, Bate and Simienowicz. Such resins are capable of reacting with oils to produce different kinds of varnish. A number of recipes include varnish. Bate includes all three gum resins in his recipe for a "composition that will burne, and feed upon the water":

> TAke masticke halfe a pound, white Frankincense, gum sandrake, quickelime, brimstone, bitumen, camphire, and gunpowder, of each one pound and a halfe, rosin one pound, saltpeter fowre pounds and a halfe, mixe them all together.

Sources: Lucar *Appendix*, pp.81-82,86; Bate, pp.63,64,71; Hyll, C6^r, C7^v; Serlio, f.26^v; Babington, p.42; Simienowicz, pp.121-122,126; Church, pp.54, 97-107.

Fuse *O.E.D.* sb.2 1. FUSE "A tube, casing, cord, etc., filled or saturated with combustible material, by means of which a military shell, the blast of a mine, etc. is ignited and exploded.".

Fusée Some difficulty arises in the translation of this French term. According to Stuart Carlton in his translation of Ruggieri, the term "fusée" refers to the empty case of the firework and the firework itself when filled with a composition or mixture of flammable materials. Some dictionaries define "fusée" as a rocket, which it clearly is under Carlton's definition. Sources: *The Accounts*, XII, p.407; Ruggieri, p.94.

Glass Used in powdered form in the same manner as iron filings and sawdust to produce reflective glitter effects. Simienowicz suggested the following advice: "If you would have them [rockets] make an Appearance in the Air like *Fire Rain*, or like a Cloud of *Fiery Sparks*, or like long and broad *Rays* darting downwards: You must mix your *Compositions* with a little of Glass coarsely powdered, of Filings of Iron, or Sawdust of Wood.". Sources: Simienowicz, p.168.

Goose quills Used to contain mixtures for different purposes. They are recorded in *Il quaderno...* to contain a mixture of sulphur and aqua ardens to be blown over coals. Babington requires goose quills in his recipe "The manner of making silver and gold raine". Sources: *Il quaderno....*, p.52; Babington, p.14.

Greek Pitch See **Colophony**.

Gum arabic [gume of arabye, acacia gum] It is obtained from various species of acacia tree. Lancaster describes its appearance as "roundish or ovoid pieces of various sizes and varies in color from colorless or pale yellow to brown.". Kentish suggests that to make a gum solution for sticking purposes "as much water as will just cover the gum will be sufficient; but, for damping stars, or for making quickmatch, dissolve 1¼ ounce of gum in a pint of water.". Sources: *The Accounts*, XII, p.404; Simienowicz, p.125; Jones, pp.62,63; Kentish, (c.1976) p.10; Weingart, p.11; Brock, *History of Fireworks*, p.196; Lancaster, pp.37,85,184.

Gum sandarac [gum sandrake] See **Frankinsense**. *O.E.D.* 2. SANDARAC "In full gum sandarac. A resin which exudes from the tree Calitris quadrivalvis, native of N.W.Africa; it is used in the preparation of spirit varnish and pounce.". Lucar *Appendix*, p.81; Bate, p.63; Simienowicz, p.121; Church, p.54; Kentish, (c.1976), p.191.

Gum tragacanth [gum dragant] *O.E.D.* 1. TRAGACANTH "A 'gum' or mucilaginous substance obtained from several species of *Astragalus* (see 2), by natural exudation or incision, in the form of whitish strings or flakes, only partially soluble in water;". Sources: Bate, pp.62,71; Simienowicz, p.126; Jones, p.62; Church, p.68.

Gunmatch See **Cotton wick**

Gunpowder [gun poulder, black powder] See **Corned powder** and **Mealed powder**. Gunpowder is capable of producing both light and sound in the form of fire and explosion; its explosive properties also enable it to act as a propellant. By the fourteenth century the use of gunpowder in various kinds of ordinance was well established. The military use of gunpowder contributed towards a greater understanding of the behaviour of its constituents. Indeed by the end of the sixteenth century government had started to regulate the production of gunpowder. Recommended proportions of saltpetre, sulphur and charcoal in gunpowder mixtures vary among the writings of early pyrotechnists. Principal gunpowder mixtures existed under such names as corned powder, lump powder, cannon powder, culverin powder, serpentine powder and mealed powder. Particular caution needs to be exercised when attempting to determine the use of gunpowder for celebratory purposes. In some accounts gunpowder may be recorded for use in firearms or muskets; its use does not automatically imply firework production. Gunpowder was used for a variety of theatrical and celebratory purposes, although its use in the mystery plays appears to have been negligible. Sources: An extensive range exists and therefore the following is a selection; All *REED* volumes, see indexes; *Malone Collections*, III, pp.3,6,12,46; VII, pp.188,191,198; IX, p.9; XI, pp.101,128,145; Lucar, p.69; Lucar, *Appendix*, p.83; Bettey, pp.10,11; Bate, pp.54,58,59,62,63,65; *The Accounts*, XII, pp.403,404,406; Stowe's *Annales* 1615, p.282; Crawford, p.339; Chambers, *Mediaeval Stage*, II, p.375; Blewitt, p.138; Nicholl, *Ironmongers*, p.91; Platte, p.52.

Hards [hardis, hardin] *O.E.D.* sb.pl. HARDS "The coarser parts of flax or hemp separated in hackling.". Used as a combustible material. Sources: *The Accounts*, I, p.233; XII, p.404; *The Accounts M.W.*, II, pp.90,91.

Hemp *O.E.D.* sb.2. HEMP "The cortical fibre of this plant [sb.1], used for making cordage, and woven into stout fabrics.". Used as a combustible material. Sources: Lucar, *Appendix*, p.87; *The Accounts*, VII, p.357.

Iron Filings See **Glass**. The particles produced by the action of filing iron. Ruggieri suggests that "The most suitable iron filings are those which are produced by a coarse file; and iron which is rusty must not be used. The greater the length of the filing, the more it produces beautiful sparks which open out and form brilliant rays like those of the sun....The effect of iron filings is to produce white sparks mixed with red.". Sources: Lucar, *Appendix*, p.90; Bate, pp.54,59; Norton, p.151; Simienowicz, pp.126,168; Ruggieri, p.71; Brock, p.154.

Lances These were small tubes filled with mixtures and arranged in such a way as to create desired patterns or shapes. The lances were often connected by quickmatch so as to communicate fire quickly around the image. Faces, animals and lettered messages provide examples of the technique. Babington refers to the method as follows:

> HAving considered of what largenesse you will have your letters
> or figures, make them of pastboard, leaving a hollow to put in
> small quils, (which shall be filled with a cleare and strong mixture)
> then put in your quils, and glue them fast in;

The "quils" were from 2¹/₂ inches to 4 inches in length and filled with a slow mixture. The "quils" or lances were placed and glued around the periphery of the shaped pasteboard. Quickmatch was used to link and ignite the "quils" in different parts of the depicted shape, so that it could take fire rather more quickly than if it had been fired from just one place. Sources: Babington, pp.27,49; de Malthe, p.103; Bate, p.75; Kentish, (c.1976), pp.117-122; Weingart, pp.23,142-147,230.

Lead (Pb) Used to provide stability to fire balls when placed under water. Sources: Lucar, *Appendix,* p.80; Bate, pp.63,98; *The Accounts,* XII, p.405.

Lime (Ca) See **Quicklime** (CaO) Sources: *The Accounts,* XII, p.405; *The Accounts M.W.,* II, p.92.

Lime-pot [lem pottis] See **Quicklime**.*O.E.D.* LIME-POT "a pot or furnace in which limestone is burnt;". Sources: Bate, p.57; *The Accounts,* XII, pp.404,406.

Lint [lynt, lunt] *O.E.D.* 2. LINT "(Chiefly *Sc.*) Flax prepared for spinning. Also, the refuse of the same, used as a combustible.". Sources: *The Accounts,* VII, p.357; *The Accounts M.W.,* II, p.90.

Lumbard paper Good quality writing paper originally made in Lombardy. Used to make firework cases. Sources: *The Accounts,* VIII, p.450; XII, p.404; *The Accounts M.W.,* II, pp.70,90; Anna J.Mill, p.184.

Lycopodium *O.E.D.* 2. LYCOPODIUM "The fine powder formed by the ripe spores of species of *Lycopodium,* known as 'vegetable brimstone' from its inflammability.". When shaken or blown through a tube across a flame it produces a billowing eruption of flame. Sources: Ruggieri, pp.78,227-228; Weingart, p.213; Rees, p.144; Gilbert, p.30.

Marline [marling cord, merlin cord] *O.E.D.* sb. MARLINE "Small line of two strands, used for seizings.". An *O.E.D.* example of 1627 offers further clarification: "Marling is a small line of vntwisted hemp, very pliant and well tarred, to sease the ends of Ropes from raueling out...". It is most frequently recorded in the binding of fire balls. Sources: *The Accounts,* XII, p.405; *The Accounts M.W.,* pp.89,90,91.

Mastic [mastick, masticke] *O.E.D.* sb. 1. MASTIC "A gum or resin which exudes from the bark of *Pistacia Lentiscus* and some other trees (see 2). It is known in English commerce in the form of roundish, oblong or pear-shaped tears, transparent, and of a pale yellow or faint greenish tinge. Formerly much used in Medicine. Now used chiefly in the manufacture of varnish.". As such, it is combustible. Sources: Lucar, *Appendix,* p.86; Simienowicz, pp.121,122,126; Church, p.54.

Mealed powder [serpentine powder, powder dust, fine powder, weak powder] The grain texture of meal or mealed gunpowder was very fine and saltpetre, sulphur and charcoal were incorporated into a loose mixture. One of the problems with this kind of amalgamation was that the ingredients could separate out from each other, thus making for inconsistent reactions. The combustion properties of this kind of composition, when used in ordinance, were referred to as "slow and irregular, and much gas escaped through the vent, so that a low velocity was imparted to the shot, with the result that the gunners made but poor practice.". The solution to this problem was found in corning powder. See **Gunpowder** and **Corned powder**. Sources: Lucar, p.79;

222

Biringuccio, p.412; Babington, p.11; *Malone Collections,* XI, p.128; *REED, Devon,* pp.246,248; Hime, pp.151-155; Lynne White, Jr., *Medieval Technology,* pp.100-101; Crocker, *Gunpowder Industry,* p.19; Hodgetts, p.28.

Oakum *O.E.D.* 1. "The coarse part of the flax separated in hackling; hards, tow; also, clippings, trimmings, shreds.". 2. Loose fibre, obtained by untwisting and picking old rope...".

Oils [oyle of almonds, oil of camphire, oyle of benedick, linseed oyle, oyll linget, oyle of linne, oil of benjamin, fische oyll, cod liver oil, oyle of hempseed, oil of egg yolks, oil of mace, oil of juniper, oil of spike, oil of spike-lavender, oil of spikenard, oyle of spicke, oil of laurel, oleum laurinum, oil of bayes, walnut oil, wannat ule, vermillion oil, vermenioun ule, olive oil, ule de olive, oyle of petrole, petriol oyle, oyle of peeter, oyle of niter, rock oil, oil of saltpetre, oil of turpentine, oyle of tile, brick oil, oil of naptha, oil of sulphur, oyle of brimstone] Oils tend not to be used in firework manufacture of today because of their limited efficacy, although the variety presented here indicates something of the reliance placed upon them in the sixteenth and early seventeenth centuries. Brock suggests that oils were often included in firework compositions as a means of ensuring the inflammability of mixtures. A function required of some ingredients within a pyrotechnic mixture was considered to be that of "binding" the mixture. Various oils were used for this purpose. A typical need for binding mixtures existed in the production of stars to be ejected from aerial fireworks. Such compositions were rolled up into small balls, kept discrete from other mixtures and allowed to dry. Babington recommended "oyle of Almonds, or such like oyle" to bind a mixture "for starres". In this recipe the "oyle of Almonds" was mixed with camphor in a brass mortar and the resultant liquid was known as oil of camphor. Simienowicz explained that "The Oil of Camphire,...is made by adding a little Oil of Sweet Almonds, and grinding them together in a brass Mortar, with a Pestle of the same Metal, till all of it be turned into an Oil of a greenish Colour.". Oil of camphor was also used to make "quickmatch". See **Cotton wick.** A recipe for "A water ball which shall shoot forth many reports" contained a mixture bound by "oyle of benedick" and "linsed oyle". The specific identity of "oyle of benedick" is not clear, although "linseed oyle" was used for a number of purposes. Linseed oil went under other names such as "oyll linget" and "oyle of linne". Lucar recommended "oyle of Lynseed" to moisten a mixture used for "An other fireworke which will burne in water, and consume armor, wood, and euery other thing that it shall fall on.". Bate similarly required "linseed oyle boyled" to moisten a mixture to be placed in a canvas ball "that will burne underwater.". Babington suggested that "Linseed oyle" be incorporated in a mixture for rockets consisting of rochpetre, sulphur, camphor and fine powder dust. Jones required linseed oil to "preserve Steel or Iron Filings" that were included in some fireworks to create sparks. If stored for too long iron filings would otherwise rust and produce "a number of red and drossy sparks.". *The Accounts* for the *Baptismal Celebrations* record "ane quart of oyll linget xxiiij s." along with "half ane galloun of fische oyll xiij s. iiij d." among other firework ingredients. Oil of hempseed was used to impregnate cotton wicks for candles. In his recipe, "To make a light or Candle to indure burning without going out by any winde so long as the substance endureth.", Hyll requires the candle wick to be "soked in the oyle of hempseed, and after dipped into molten Tallowe,...". Biringuccio describes the process of producing oils from seeds:

> The oil of seeds is obtained by softening them with warm moist fumes and by pressing them. In this way that of mustard seed is extracted, while that of grain is made by burning it on a red-hot iron. In like manner the oil is extracted from egg yolks, almonds, nuts, flaxseed, sesame, hempseed, as well as from aromatic things, nutmeg, mace, and the like.

Oil of juniper was required by Lucar to perform two different tasks: one was to moisten a mixture to be contained in a "fireworke which will burne in water..." and the second was to wet "a little of bumbase or cotton wool" in order to ensure ignition between mixtures in a fire "truncke". Biringuccio outlines a method of producing oil of juniper:

> The oil of juniper, larch, fir, and every tree that produces a gum is made by means of a vessel similar to an earthenware pot, perforated on the bottom with many very small holes. Another is placed underneath as receiver, and in the one on top is put as much finely cut wood of the kind from which you wish to extarct oil as it will contain, and it is covered and well luted so that it may not breathe. A pit is made in the ground and both the pots are buried there, leaving only about four *dita* of the higher one uncovered. The fire is lighted above, it is heated, and the gummy liquor that the materials contain is made to run down in this way.

Oils produced from woods that do not produce gum were created in a different way. The wood was finely chopped and heated in a curcurbit in a furnace. The resultant oil was obtained as the distillate. "Oil of spike" or "spike-lavender" or "oil of spikenard" was produced in this way. Babington required "oyle of spicke" to moisten a mixture to create "starres of a blew colour, with red.". Babington also uses "oyle of spike" along with other oils to bind a mixture for use in a "water ball, which shall burn on the water, with great violence.". One of the oils contained in *The Accounts* concerning the *Baptismal Celebrations* is "oleum laurinum" or oil of laurel. The same oil is sometimes referred to as oil of bayes. Lucar requires "oyle of Bayes 24 partes" to help bind a mixture in his recipe: "To make a fireworke which will burne stones and yron.". The list of firework materials recorded in *The Accounts* between 1538 and 1541 contains a requirement for "wannat ule" or walnut oil. The same list includes "vermenioun ule" or vermillion oil. Although it is possible that both these oils were used to bind mixtures it is just as likely that the "vermenioun ule" was intended to be used as a colour-producing agent. A third oil contained in this list that is likely to have been used in binding mixtures is "ule de olive" or olive oil. De Malthe involves "oyle of petrole" as part of a mixture containing saltpetre and brimstone in the production of "fiery arrowes". The "oyle of petrole" is also required as a moistening agent in a mixture of saltpetre, brimstone and powder dust in de Malthe's recipe: "The manner how to make Starres". Lucar also used "petriol oyle" in a number of his recipes. Payment is recorded for "half ane unce quarter and half quarter of oyle petrole with ane glas, price iij s. iiij d." in *The Accounts* concerning *The Baptismal Celebrations*. In the list of "expensis maid upone the munitioun eftir the quenis grace hame cumming..." [Entry of Marrie of Lorraine], payment is made for "ule petroll" along with other firework materials. Sometimes "oyle of peeter" was known as "oyle of niter" but today is known as rock oil. It has been suggested that "oile of peter" was used "as an extra assurance of inflammability" in Bate's recipe for stars. Babington makes a similar requirement for the oil in his "Compositions for starres". Biringuccio recommends that oil of saltpetre should be created "by means of calcinations [reduction by fire to produce a "calx" or friable powder] put into solution in the wet way.". Oil of turpentine was produced by heating the waxy turpentine in a curcurbit, in the manner suggested for spike-lavender and letting the oil be distilled. Brick oil or "oyle of Tile" as recommended by Lucar and Bate was produced by mixing powdered brick with linseed oil. Oil of naptha was required by Simienowicz in a recipe for a "certain Artificial Water, which burns upon the Palm of the Hand without doing any Hurt.". Different methods of producing oil of sulphur are suggested by Biringuccio and Lucar. Biringuccio required oil of sulphur to be made " by boiling with strong lyes made of ashes and lime," or by " burning the sulphur itself under a bell that is open and engulfs all the fume and, by dripping it through the alembic, distills it into the receiver.". Lucar proposed another method of distillation in his recipe, "To make oyle of Brimstone for Firewoorkes":

> Melte Brimstone in a potte ouer a fire, and taking a sufficient quantitie of the eldest redde brickes that may be gotten, beate them into peeces so bigge as beanes: This done, put into the melted Brimstone so many of those small peeces as will drinke vp all the same melted Brimstone: And after you haue so done, distill them in a Limbecke, for that which shall come out of the saide peeces of brickes thoroe the Limbecke, is oyle of Brimstone which will serue for Firewoorkes.

Sources: Babington, pp.11,12,22-23,55,56-57; Simienowicz, pp.120,123; Bate, pp.61,63,64,65; Jones, pp.9-10,11,83,84; de Malthe, pp.21,83,91; Porta, p.283; Lucar, *Appendix*, pp.80,81,84,86,96,97; Hyll, A5^V-A6^V; Biringuccio, pp.350-352; Gessner, pp.120-121; *The Accounts*, VII, p.357; XII, pp.404,405; *The Accounts M.W.*, I, p.233; II, p.89; Brock, *History of Fireworks*, p.195; Church, pp.54,89.

Orpiment (As_2S_3) [arsenic trisulphide] *O.E.D.* ORPIMENT "A bright yellow mineral substance, the trisulphide of arsenic, also called Yellow Arsenic, found native in soft masses resembling gold in colour; also manufactured by the combination of sulphur and arsenious oxide; used as a pigment under the name of King's Yellow.". Orpiment (As_2S_3) should not be confused with realgar, the disulphide of arsenic (As_2S_2) which is also used as a firework ingredient in the production of yellow smoke. Orpiment is frequently used in the production of white stars. See **Realgar.** Sources: Bate, p.66; Lucar *Appendix,* p.81; Hyll, C5^r and C6^v; Porta, p.301; Brock, A *History of Fireworks,* p.153; Weingart, p.9; Lancaster, p.29; Shimizu, pp.132-134.

Packthread [packthreid, thread] *O.E.D.* PACKTHREAD "Stout thread or twine such as is used for sewing or tying up packs or bundles.". Frequently recorded for tying or "choaking" firework cases. Sources: Lucar, *Appendix,* p.80; *The Accounts M.W.,* I, p.233; II, pp.89,90,92; *The Accounts,* XII, pp.404,405; *Malone Collections,* VII, p.201; XI, p.128.

Pasteboard *O.E.D.* sb.1. PASTEBOARD "A substitute for a thin wooden board made by pasting sheets of paper together; *esp.* a board of a book so made. 2. As a material: A stiff firm substance made by pasting together, compressing, and rolling, three or more sheets of paper." de Malthe required the use of thin pasteboard to form cases or "cartoushes" in his recipe "How to make fierie Lances." The most commonly recorded uses of pasteboard are those for the thicker variety that required it to be cut to shape to form a framework or baseboard to take fireworks in the form of lancework. Sources: de Malthe, pp.103.104; Serlio, f.26^v.; *Malone Collections,* VII, p.201; XIII, pp.22,27,51,57,64,77,92; *The Accounts M.W.,* pp.89,91.

Petard *The Accounts* record the purchase of "half ane hundreth pettaratis" for use at the *Baptismal Celebrations.* The petard as used for celebration purposes was intended to explode, like its military counterpart, and yet not expected to impart the same kind of damage as the military kind. The design, however, was essentially the same. According to Lucar, the conical petard "which will bloe vp Walles, Towers, Fortes, and such like thinges,..." was made of "plates of yron, a vessell of eyght or ten feete in length". The recipe offered by Bate is of a scale capable of being produced by paper or parchment:

> You must make the coffins for them either of white yron, or else
> of paper, or parchment rowled upon a Former for the purpose,
> and afterwards fitted with a couer, which must be glewed on:
> these coffins must be filled with whole gunpowder, and peirced in
> the midst of the broad end, and primed thereat with prepared
> stouple; the paper ones must be couered all ouer with glew, and
> the[n] peirced.

Although there is a marked difference in scale between Lucar's petard and that of Bate, even smaller versions such as ones made of "an empty Walnut shell or 2 filld with powder" or "Armed loaded nutshell" are recorded by Norton. The term "armed" as used here refers to reinforcement of the shell with materials such as packthread or marling cord. Sources: Lucar, *Appendix,* p.92; Bate, pp.73,74; de Malthe, pp.55-58; Norton, pp.152,155; *The Accounts,* XII, p.407.

Pitch Pitch is produced as a residue in the distillation of tar. It is brittle when hard yet viscous when heated. Pitch is recorded as one of the fuels used in the Coventry "bettings" and was one of the substances used to coat, and thus seal, fire balls. Sources: Lucar, *Appendix*, pp.80,81,82; Babington, pp.41,42,43; *Malone Collections*, VII, pp.201,209; Blewitt, p.138; *The Accounts*, XII, pp.406,407; *The Accounts M.W.*, II, pp.89,90, 91,92.

Pokkis The name given to the cases made of Poldavid canvas for fire balls at the *Baptismal Celebrations*. *The Accounts* record: "Item payit to ane tailyeour of Leyth for making and sewing of thre dosone lang pokkis, threttye round pokkis, twelf bodomit [bottom] pokkis,....". In this case it appears that the terms "lang", "round" and "bodomit" refer to physical appearance as well as function. It is most likely that the "pokkis" were fired by the "fyre pompis" since that was their principal function. The "round" and "bodomit pokkis" may well have contained stars of the kind carried by rockets. The term "bodomit" refers to the position of the ball within the "fyre pompis" and may well have contained a distinctive mixture that was different from other balls placed higher up in the pump. Babington offers a possible explanation as to the significance of the term "lang":

> This ball may bee made somewhat cillindricall, in regard of the length of the rockets to be placed in it, as you have made this for to cast forth once, so you may make another to cast forth twise,...

The "lang pokkis" may have contained stickless rockets of the kind normally used at ground level and ignited, like equivalent stars, at the zenith of the trajectory. See **Fire pumps** and **Canvas**. Sources: Babington, p.63; *The Accounts*, XII, p.406.

Poldavid canvas [poldavid cannevas] See **Canvas**. Sources: Johnson, Drapers, 2, p.115; *The Accounts*, XII, p.404.

Pyle powder *O.E.D.* sb.1 PILE "A dart; a shaft; (?) an arrow.". Gunpowder used on fire arrows. Sources: *Malone Collections*, XI, p.128.

Quicklime (CaO) [calcium oxide] *O.E.D.* sb. QUICKLIME " Lime which has been burned and not yet slaked with water; calcium oxide, CaO.". At the *Baptismal Celebrations* payment is recorded for "ane bourding of unbrunt lyme furth of Cousland ij s.". An apparently greater quantity of lime is recorded for use at the *Birthday Celebrations* in 1617: "To a man that brocht lyme xxiiii s.". Lime, of itself, does not possess any combustible properties, so its purpose as an ingredient for pyrotechnic use is not immediately clear. However, when lime is burned the product becomes quicklime (Calcium oxide, Cao) and this is of use in pyrotechnic compositions. *The Accounts* that refer to the *Baptismal Celebrations* also record payment for "alevin lem pottis of sindry sortis vj s. v d." and "for bearing doun of all the saidis lem potis from Edinburgh to Leyth viij d.". Although the term "lem pot(t)is" used here may refer to the material of which the pots were made, it is more likely that these, or some of them, were the pots in which lime was burned to produce quicklime. Lucar requires quicklime as part of a mixture to make a "fireworke which will burne in water.". Bate makes a similar requirement in a recipe for a "composition that will burne, and feed upon the water.". Both Biringuccio and Bate require quicklime in their recipes for purifying saltpetre. Simienowicz includes quicklime in his recipe "to prepare the common Sort of Match.". A relatively simple pyrotechnic reaction takes place when quicklime is mixed with an inflammable material like sulphur. It is possible that such a mixture would spontaneously ignite if sprinkled with water, due to the large amount of heat produced by hydration of the quicklime. There are many early references to this chemical phenomenon. Sources: Lucar, *Appendix,* pp.81, 97; Bate, pp.57,63,64,65,66; Simienowicz, p.123; Biringuccio, p.406; Hyll, C8^r and D1v; Partington, pp.6-10,47,50,58,84,149,165,240,264; Hime, p.33; Best and Brightman, pp.95-96; *The Accounts,* pp.404,405,406; *The Accounts M.W.,* II, p.92.

Quickmatch See **Cotton wick**. Sources: Lucar, *Appendix,* p.82; de Malthe, p.91; Simienowicz, pp.125,126; Lancaster, p.184.

Quicksilver (Hg) [mercury] Partington suggests that "Mercury as an addition to gunpowder is useless, although it long continued to be specified.". de Malthe seems to have been one of the first pyrotechnists to denounce the value of quicksilver in pyrotechnic compositions. Sources: Lucar, p.72; Lucar, *Appendix,* p.86; Bate, p.63; de Malthe, preface; Partington, p.149; *The Accounts,* VII, p.357; XII, p.404.

Realgar (As$_2$S$_2$) When ground to a fine powder, realgar may be used to produce white fires and/or yellow smoke. The production of realgar occurs by sublimation when arsenopyrite is roasted. Sources: Lancaster, p.29; Weingart, p.9; Shimizu, pp.132-133.

Resin *O.E.D.* sb.1 RESIN "A vegetable product, formed by secretion in special canals in almost all trees and plants, from many of which (as the fir and pine) it exudes naturally, or can be readily obtained by incision; various kinds are extensively used in making varnishes or adhesive compositions, and in pharmacy.". See **Rosin** for the distinction between it and **Resin**. Sources: Lancaster, pp.36-39.

Roche petre [rochpeter, saltpetre in roche] *O.E.D.* "Native saltpetre, occurring as an effloresence on rocks.". The term "roche" refers to the crystalline form. See **APPENDIX 2C** for "saltpetre in roche". Sources: Babington, pp. 22,42,56,57; Bate, pp.54,57,64; Norton, p.143.

Rosin [roset, rossell, rosene] *O.E.D.* 1 = Resin sb; spec.,"this substance in a solid state obtained as a residue after the distillation of oil of turpentine from crude turpentine.". See **Collophone** and **Resin**. A further definition by Lancaster reads:"Rosin is the residue of the distillation of turpentine oil from the crude oleoresin obtained from the pine trees, principally from Pinus Palustrus and Pinus Carbea.". Sources:Babington, pp.41,56,57; Bate, pp.63,95; Simienowicz, p.126; Kentish, (1878), p.175; *Malone Collections,* VII, p.209; XIII, pp.64,78,84,104,110,116,121; *The Accounts,* XII, p.403; *The Accounts M.W.,* pp.89,90,91,92; Lancaster, p.39.

Sal ammoniac (NH$_4$Cl) [salt armoniacke, salmoniakill, ammonium chloride]. Brocks says of Ruggieri: "He is the first writer to make use of metal salts in the production of coloured flame – apart, that is, from the isolated use by Hanzelet [Henzelet] of verdigris. He also introduced sal ammoniac (ammonium chloride), which, by volatilizing the metal, greatly asisted colour production.". However, sal ammoniac is recorded in earlier lists of firework ingredients than those of Ruggieri. Sal ammoniac is listed among other firework materials in *The Accounts* for the years 1538-1541. The purpose of the ingredient in the list is likely to have been that of a colour- producing agent in a pyrotechnic reaction. Sal ammoniac produces a green flame. It is difficult to imagine or understand any other pyrotechnic function that sal ammoniac might have fulfilled. Sources: *The Accounts*, VII, p.357; Lucar, p.72; Lucar, *Appendix*, pp.81,82; Simienowicz, pp.123,168; Serlio, f.26^V; Brock, *History of Fireworks*, p.155.

Saltpetre (KNO$_3$) [saltpeter, sal nitre, sal niter, potassium nitrate]. One of the three ingredients of gunpowder. Saltpetre provides the necessary oxygen for combustion and charcoal and sulphur act as fuels. In a somewhat fanciful account Bate describes the ingredients of gunpowder thus: "Saltpeter is the Soul, the Sulphur the Life, and the Coales the Body of it.". Recipes contained in the writings of Roger Bacon, Albertus Magnus and Marcus Graecus make use of saltpetre and indicate understanding of the explosive properties of gunpowder. Before the appearance of such recipes, there existed incendiary mixtures known as "Greek Fire" or "Flying Fire", that consisted of charcoal, sulphur and other ingredients. These mixtures were not capable of producing explosion. Biringuccio said of saltpetre:

> saltpeter is a mixture composed of many substances extracted with fire and water from arid and manurial soils, from that growth which exudes from new walls or from that loosened soil that is found in tombs or uninhabited caves where the rain cannot enter.

The "manurial soils" referred to by Biringuccio contain nitrates which are merely the raw material for the production of saltpetre. An ordinance of 1573 at York authorized "therle of Warwik, Maister of the Common Ordynaunce" or his appointed deputies:

> to dig and breake ground in bearnes, stables and other places convenient for salt peter within this realme, as well in the late suppressed abbayes and howses of religion, olde castles, or ells where, bothe within francheses and liberties and withowte, for the makyng of Salt peter for the Queenes ordynans was nowe redde; wherapon it was aggreed that the said deputie and deputies shall digge and breake ground in all places within this Citie and suburbs for the said salt peter except onely in halls, parlours and shoppes; and also they to spare litle howses of poore men there.

Biringuccio offered a detailed description of the purification of saltpetre. The process required freshly dug earth to be mixed with quicklime and wood (oak) ash and boiled in water. The resultant liquid was filtered and saltpetre was obtained in solution from which it was evaporated and allowed to crystallize. The product was sometimes known as Rochepetre. Calcium nitrate $(Ca(NO_3)^2)$ produced by the interaction of decomposed organic matter in the earth and quicklime was converted into potassium nitrate by the reaction with the wood ash that contained potasium carbonate (K_2CO_3). Sources: Bate, pp.54,55,57,64; Biringuccio, pp.404-409; Whitehorn, f.23^V [This version is an unacknowledged translation of Biringuccio]; Agricola, pp.561-564,561n.9; Babington, pp.22,42,56,57; Norton, p.143; *REED:Shropshire*, I, p.184; *The Accounts*, III, p.332; XII, p.404; *The Accounts M.W.*, I, p.233; Mill, pp.53,183-184,325-326; Hime, Chpts.II,III,VII; Partington, Chpt.II,323-329; Lalanne, pp.749-757; Cutbush, *Greek Fire*, pp.302-315; Raine, VII, p.80; Hodgetts, pp.180-181,185,201,213,219,220,228-229,235,244,246-247,251,252; Hunter, pp.381-382; Burtt, pp.68-75; Tout, pp.666-702.

Sawdust See **Glass** and **Iron Filings**. Sources: Simienowicz, p.168.

Serpentine powder See **Mealed powder**. Sources: *REED:Devon*, p.246; *Malone Collections*, XI, p.128.

Starch $(C_6H_{10}O_5)$ [**CHAPTER 3**]. Starch comes as a glutinous rice form or as wheat starch. When powdered, it will burn when scattered over flame. It is most frequently used today as a binding agent in star compositions. Sources: Shimizu, pp.157-162; Lancaster, pp.48,249.

Stuppa [stupe, stuppum] *O.E.D.* sb.1. STUPA. Tow, hards, oakum.

Sulphur [brimstone, brunstane, bristane] Ease of ignition points to the importance of sulphur as one of the constituents of gunpowder. A relatively low ignition temperature of 223°C in the air enables easy firing and secures the use and value of this element in firework compositions other than gunpowder ones. Although sulphur is used in gunpowder mixtures, it is capable of burning independently and doing so with a blue flame. The preparation of sulphur required natural sulphur to be melted and separated from other impurities before it could be solidified into a mass and subsequently powdered. The element exists as dense, pale yellow powder and is considered by pyrotechnists to be safe to handle. See Serlio's use of sulphur to produce lightning in **CHAPTER 3**. This method of producing flame was also employed with powdered rosin and later, lycopodium dust. Lucar recommended sulphur "To make Rockettes or Squibbes...". Babington required sulphur for "Divers Compositions for starres.". Bate made use of sulphur in recipes for both rockets and stars. *The Accounts* for 1512 record payment for "xj stane brunstane for gune powder; price stane viij s.; summa...iiij li. viij s.". Sulphur in the form of "brunstane" is recorded among the list of "expensis maid upone the munitioun eftir the quenis grace hame cumming..." [*Entry of Marrie of Lorraine*]. *The Accounts* record the use of "bristane" among other firework ingredients between 1538 and 1541. See **CHAPTER 1**. At New Romney, Kent, payments for firework materials including "brymstone" are recorded in the *Chamberlains' Account Book* for 1560:

It' pd for ij ^{li} of glewe   viij ^{d}
It' pd for ij ^{li} of brymstone   viij ^{d}

...

It' pd for di li of rosset   iiij ^{d}

...

It' pd for di li of vardegrese   xvj ^{d}

...

It' payd for a realme of the best whyte pap   iiij ^{s} iiij ^{d}

...

Itm' payd to m^r Baylif iij ^{d} of three
iij ^{d} of pytche & rosen j ^{d} ob of glewe iij ^{d}

Sources: Lucar, p.69,70; Lucar *Appendix*, pp.81,83; Babington, pp.11,41,56,57; Serlio, f.26^v; Bate, pp.54,55,58-66; Simienowicz, p.168; Hyll, A3^r; A7^r; B4^v; C6^v; C6^v-C7^v; C8^r, D1^v; D1^r; D4^v; *The Accounts*, VII, p.357; XII, pp.403,404; *The Accounts M.W.*, I, p.233; II, pp.89,90,91; *Malone Collections*, VII, p.209; Mill, p.209.

Tallow [talloun] Bees-wax and tallow [animal fat] were the two main fuels used in candle production. The combustible properties of tallow enabled a wider use of the substance beyond that of candle production for it was frequently used in other pyrotechnic processes such as the construction of fireballs "as wel for service in warre, as for pleasure or triumph,...". *The Accounts* for 1538-1541 record payment for "talloun" among other firework ingredients for use in the production of "xv fyre ballis" and other works of fire. *The Accounts* itemise "twa stane and ane half of talloun at xviij s. the stane xlvs." and "mair for talloun ij s. viij d." among firework materials at the *Baptismal Celebrations*. The possibility of this tallow being used in fire ball construction is supported by an eye-witness account concerning the "fort haldin in Striueling besyid the kirk-yaird, quhairin wes artailzerie, schote fyre ballis, fyre speris, and all vtheris thingis plesand for the sicht of man.". Three separate payments for "talloun" are recorded in *The Accounts M.W.* concerning the *Birthday Celebrations*:

For four pond of talloun   xvi s.

...

For 8 pond of talloun   xxxii s.

...

For four pund of talloun   xvi s.

Although such quantities of tallow may have been used in the production of fire balls, it is equally possible that the tallow was used to create light. When used for lighting purposes the mutton variety of tallow was considered to produce the clearest light and least smoke. A mixture of mutton and beef tallow was sometimes used as a means of improving the quality of light produced by the beef variety. Pork tallow was generally avoided since it produced poor light and thick, acrid smoke. However, tallow did not create the brighter flame associated with beeswax. Candles composed of tallow created more smoke than those made of bees-wax. Tallow was also used in the production of rushlights. Sources: Lucar *Appendix*, p.84; Babington, pp.41,56-57,60; Hyll, A5ᵛ, A5ʳ; *The Accounts*, VII, p.357; XII, pp.405,406; *The Accounts M.W.*, II, pp.89.91; White, *History of Selborne*, pp.180-183; Cobbett, pp.144-145; Thwing, pp.97-99; Jekyll, pp.101-107; Ellis, p.279; O'Dea, p.213; Eveleigh, p.7.

Tampions See **Cork**.

Tar *O.E.D.* sb.1. "A thick, viscid, black or dark-coloured, immflamable liquid, obtained by the destructive distillation of wood (esp. pine, fir, or larch), coal, or other organic substance; chemically, a mixture of hydrocarbons with resins, alcohols, and other compounds, having a heavy resinous or bituminous odour, and powerful antiseptic properties; it is much used for coating and preserving timber, cordage, etc.". Sources: *The Accounts*, XII, pp.404,405,406,407; Blewitt, p.138.

Toureantis [tourteantis?] The identity of "toureantis" is unclear. See **CHAPTER 6** for discussion of these objects. Sources: *The Accounts*, XII, pp.405,406,407.

Tow [towe, towis] *O.E.D.* sb.2. "A rope. Chiefly *Sc.*". Rope was a serviceable material and used in different ways. *The Accounts* record the following payment concerning preparations for the *Baptismal Celebrations*: "payit to twa men for fetching furth of the castell of sum auld towis,...". The same accounts record payment for "oppinning out towis" to "Johnne Lamy and Henry Scherar, marinellis". Rope could be converted to fuel when, for instance, it was smeared with rosin or pitch and used in cressets. Old rope was suitable for this purpose. Similarly, rope could be smeared or impregnated with any combustible material and shaped into any pattern or design, held on a frame and ignited. Today, such a technique is practised by soaking rope in paraffin, covering the rope with polythene (to avoid evaporation) and shaping into the desired form. The ability to unravel rope into thin starnds allowed a flexible means of creating objects such as fire wreaths. These objects were coated or dipped in pitch, tar or rosin and ignited. Sources: Lucar *Appendix*, pp.81,83; *The Accounts*, XII, pp.406,407; *The Accounts M.W.*, II, p.92.

Turpentine [terpentyne, torpentine, turpatyne] Turpentine, in its original state, is not a liquid but a waxy resinous secretion produced by different conifers. When turpentine is distilled, the distillate is oil of turpentine and the residue is a rosin known as collophone or Greek pitch. Turpentine, like other hydrocarbons ignites and burns. In *The Accounts* for the years 1538-1541, payment is made for "turpatyne" along with other firework ingredients. The precise use of these ingredients is uncertain although it seems that they were used in the production of "vj dosane fyr sparris [spears], twa dosane fyr gannis [arrows], xv fyre ballis, and viij fyre perkis [poles or stakes]...". *The Accounts M.W.* for 1538 record payment for "tarpentyne" and other firework materials for the *Entry of Marrie of Lorraine*. On this occasion pyrotechnic "set pieces" appear to have been employed in the form of "quheill rymmis" [wheel rims] containing fireworks. At the *Baptismal Celebrations* payment is made for "four unce of terpentyne with ane pig xij d.". Lucar employs turpentine in a number of his recipes. In one version he requires both "the oyle and gumme of Turpentine". Payment is recorded "For tua pond of tarpettyne xlviii s." at the *Birthday Celebrations*. See **Collophone, Rosin** and **Resin**. Sources: Lucar *Appendix,* pp.81,97; Simienowicz, p.123; *The Accounts,* VII, p.357; XII, p.404; *The Accounts, M.W.,* I, p.233; II, p.89; Kentish, (c.1878), p.175.

Varnish [vernis, vernish] When used in early pyrotechny, varnish could refer to any resin or gum resin such as gum sandarac, mastic or frankinsense. Normally it was used in powdered form and included in mixtures because of its capacity to ignite quickly. Isacchi suggests the technique of blowing powdered varnish over flame to produce a billowing fire effect. Serlio also required similar use of varnish to produce lightning. Porta refers to the same technique [See **CHAPTER 3**]. Sources: Isacchi, pp.109-111; Serlio, f.26^v; Porta, p.301; Lucar, pp.81,82; Babington, p.42; Bate, pp.64,71; Simienowicz, p.121; Best and Brightman, p.110.

Verdigris [vardegrese] See **Sal ammoniac** and **Sulphur**. Verdigris is a blue/green salt produced by the action of acetic acid on copper: it it thus an acetate of copper. According to Ruggieri the salt was rarely used since it was considered too dangerous to handle. Sources: *Malone Collections,* VII, pp.207,209; Hyll, A4^r; Ruggieri, p.77; Brock, *History of Fireworks,* p.155.

Vermillion [vermenioun] As a pigment, vermillion was used in painting and the creation of red sealing wax. It is recorded in the composition of an oil, "vermenioun ule", among a list of firework ingredients in *The Accounts* for the years 1538-1541. Presumably its function was to operate as a colour-producing agent in a firework mixture [**CHAPTER 1**]. Vermillion has also been used in the production of red smoke [See **APPENDIX 3B**]. Sources: *The Accounts,* VII, p.357; T.L.Davis, p.122.

Vinegar The properties ascribed to vinegar in pyrotechnic compositions were often innapropriate or over emphasised. Lucar recommended vinegar to moisten "balles of fire which will burne in water" and in another recipe required that "The Saltpeeter in this composition must bee sodde in strong vineger, and well dried before you doe beate it among the other things to powder.". Biringuccio suggested that ordinary water would have performed the task required of vinegar during incorporation. The following payment is recorded in the *Chamberlains' Account Book* of Rye, Sussex, for 1448/9: "Paid for a quart of vinegar to test the saltpetre 1^1/₂d.". The purpose and outcome of this reaction is referred to by Albertus Magnus: "And when Saltpetre is put in a vessel, and vinegar upon it, it will boil or seethe mightily without fire.". Sources: Lucar *Appendix,* pp.80,81; Bate, p.55; Hyll, A3^r; Biringuccio, p.413; Simienowicz, pp.121,123,125; *The Accounts M.W.,* pp.89,90,91; Partington, pp.5,28-29,88,163,318; Victoria History-*Sussex,* II, p.237.

Bibliography

Adams, Jon. *The Fireworks Manual*. St.Hellier, Jersey: The Pyrotechnic Press, 1992.

Adrian, Gertrude. *Die Bühnenanweisungen in den englischen Mysterien*. Inaugural-Dissertation zur Erlangung der philosophischen Doktorwürde der Philosophischen und Naturwissenschaftlichen Fakultät der Westfälischen Wilhelms-Universität zu Münster. Bochum-Langendreer: Heinrich Pöppinghaus, 1931.

Ady, Thomas. *A Candle in the Dark*. London: Robert Ibbitson, 1655.

Agricola, Georgius. *De Re Metallica*. Basel:1556; rpt. trans. New York: Dover Publications, 1950.

Alessio, [Don Alessio Ruscelli]. *The Secrets of the Reverende Maister Alexis of Piemovnt. Translated out of Frenche into English by Wyllyam Warde*. London: Iohn Kingstone for Nicolas Inglande, 1558. The First Boke.

— *The second part of the Secretes of Maister Alexis of Piemont, by hym collected out of diuers excellent aucthours*. London: Rovland Hall, for Nicholas Englande, 1563.

Anderson, J.J. ed. *Records of Early English Drama: Newcastle upon Tyne*. Toronto: University Press and Manchester University Press, 1982.

Anderson, Robert. *The Making of Rockets...Experimentally and Mathematically Demonstrated*. London: Robert Morden, 1696.

Anglo, Sydney. *Spectacle, Pageantry, and Early Tudor Policy*. Oxford: Oxford University Press, 1969.

Anon. *The Birth of Hercules* in W.W.Greg ed. *Reprints*. Oxford: The Malone Society, 1911.

Anon. *Grim The Collier of Croydon* in John S.Farmer ed. *Five Anonymous Plays*. London, 1908; facs. rpt. 1966.

Anon. *Hocus Pocus Junior. The Anatomy of Legerdemain*. London: G.Dawson, 1654.

234

Anon. 'The Scenic World'. *Cornhill Magazine* 53, pt.1 (1886): 281-96.

Anon. *The Second Maiden's Tragedy* in Hazlitt ed. *Reprints*. Oxford: The Malone Society, 1910 (for 1909).

Anon. *Two Noble Ladies* in W.W.Greg ed. *Reprints*. Oxford: The Malone Society, 1930.

Axton, Richard and Stevens, John eds. *Medieval French Plays*. Oxford: Basil Blackwell, 1971.

Ayalon, D. *Gunpowder and Firearms in the Mamluk Kingdom: A Challenge to a Mediaeval Society* . London: Vallentine, 1956.

Babington, John. *Pyrotechnia Or, A Discovrse Of Artificiall Fire-works...* London: Thomas Harper for Ralph Mab, 1635.

Balfour-Paul, Sir James ed. *Accounts of the Lord High Treasurer of Scotland*. Edinburgh: H.M.General Register House, 1902-8.

Baker, Donald C., Murphy, John L. and Hall, Louis B. eds. *The Late Medieval Religious Plays of Bodleian MSS Digby 133 and E Museo 160*. The Early English Text Society. OS 283. Oxford: Oxford University Press, 1982.

Bakere, Jane A. *The Cornish Ordinalia: A Critical Study*. Cardiff: University of Wales Press, 1980.

Barbour, Richard T. *Pyrotechnics in Industry*. New York: McGraw-Hill, 1981.

Baskerville, C.R. *The Elizabethan Jig and Related Song Drama*. Chicago: Chicago University Press; rpt. New York: Dover Publications, 1965.

Bate, John. *The Mysteryes of Natvre and Art: The Second Booke, Teaching most plainly, and withall most exactly, the composing of all manner of Fire-works for Triumph and Recreation*. London: Ralph Mab, 1634; facs. rpt. Amsterdam: Theatrum Orbis Terrarum, 1977.

— *The Third Booke Of Drawing, Limming, Colouring, Painting, and Graving*. London: Ralph Mab, 1634; facs.rpt. Amsterdam, Theatrum Orbis Terrarum, 1977.

Battisti, Eugenio and Battisti, Giuseppa Saccaro. *Le Macchine Cifrate Di Giovanni Fontana*. Milano: Arcadia Edizioni, 1984.

Beadle, Richard ed. *The York Plays*. London: Edward Arnold, 1982.

Beaumont and Fletcher.*The Maid's Tragedy* in Fredson Bowers ed.*The Dramatic Works of Beaumont and Fletcher Canon* II. Cambridge: Cambridge University Press, 1970.

— *Four Plays or Moral Representations in One* in A.R.Waller ed.*The Works of Francis Beaumont and John Fletcher* X. Cambridge: Cambridge University Press, 1912.

— *The Triumph of Time* in A.R.Waller ed.*The Works of Francis Beaumont and John Fletcher* X. Cambridge: Cambridge University Press, 1912.

Beckmann, John. *A History of Inventions, Discoveries, and Origins*. London: Henry G.Bohn, 1846.

Bell, C.F. 'The Artificial Lighting of the Court Scene'. in C.H.Herford, Percy and Evelyn Simpson eds. *Ben Johnson* X. Oxford: Clarendon Press, 1950, 413-20.

Bentley, Gerald Eades. *The Jacobean and Caroline Stage*. 7 vols. Oxford: Clarendon Press, 1941-68.

Berger, Sydney E. *Medieval English Drama: An Annotated Bibliography of Recent Criticism*. New York/London: Garland Publishing, Inc., 1990.

Bergeron, David M. 'Venetian State Papers and English Civic Pageantry, 1558-1642'. *Renaissance Quarterly* XXIII (1970): 37-47.

— *English Civic Pageantry 1558-1642*. London: Edward Arnold, 1971.

Bergman, Gösta M. *Lighting in the Theatre*. Stockholm: Almqvist & Wiksell International, 1977.

Bernheimer, Richard. *Wild Men in the Middle Ages*. Cambridge, Mass.: 1952; rpt. New York: Octagon Books, 1970.

Best, Michael R. and Brightman, Frank H. eds.*The Book of Secrets of Albertus Magnus*. London: Oxford University Press, 1973.

Bettey, Joseph ed. 'Two Tudor Visits to Bristol' in Patrick McGrath ed. *A Bristol Miscellany*. Bristol: Bristol Record Society Publications XXXVII (1985), 3-12.

Bevington, David. *Medieval Drama*. Boston: Houghton Mifflin, 1975.

Biringuccio, Vannoccio. *De la Pirotechnia*. Venetia: Venturino Roffinello, 1540; trans. Cyril Stanley Smith and Martha Teach Gnudi eds. *The Pirotechnia of Vannoccio Biringuccio*. New York: Basic Books, Inc., 1942; rpt. 1959.

Blackstone, Mary. 'A Survey and annotated bibliography of records research and performance history relating to early British drama and minstrelsy for 1984-8'. *Records of Early English Drama Newsletter* XV, 1 and 2 (1990): 1-104 and 1-104.

Blewitt, D.W. 'Records of Drama at Winchester and Eton 1397-1576'. *Theatre Notebook* XXXVIII, 3 (1984): 135-43.

Bibliography

Bourne, William. *Inventions or Devices*. London: Thomas Woodcock, 1578.

Briscoe, Marianne G. and Coldewey, John C. eds. *Contexts for Early English Drama*. Bloomington and Indianapolis: Indiana University Press, 1989.

British Library Additional MS 70518.

Brock, Alan St.Hill. *Pyrotechnics: the Art and History of Firework-making*. London: Daniel O'Connor, 1922.

— *A History of Fireworks*. London: George G.Harrap & Co., 1949.

Brock, James Wilson. *A Study of the Use of Sound Effects in Elizabethan Drama*. Unpublished PhD thesis. Evanston, Illinois: Northwestern University, 1950.

Bruhl, Frederick. *The Art of Making Fireworks, Detonating Balls etc.*. London: W.Brittain, 1844.

Bull, George ed. *Lives of the Artists*. 2 vols. London: Penguin, 1965; rpt. 1988.

Burtt, Joseph. 'Extracts from the Pipe Roll of the Exchequer, 27 EDW. III. (A.D.1353), relating to the Early Use of Guns and Gunpowder in the English Army.'. *Archaeological Journal* XIX (1862): 68-75.

Butterworth, P. 'Gunnepowdyr, Fyre and Thondyr'. *Medieval English Theatre* 7:2 (1985): 68-76.

— 'The Baptisme of Hir Hienes Darrest Sone in Stirviling'. *Medieval English Theatre* 10:1 (1988): 26-55.

— 'Hellfire: Flame as Special Effect' in Clifford Davidson and Thomas H.Seiler eds.*The Iconography of Hell*. Early Drama, Art, and Music
Monograph Series, 17, Medieval Institue Publications. Kalamazoo: Western Michigan University, 1992. 67-101.

— *Fire and Flame as Special Effects in the Medieval and Tudor Theatre*. Unpublished PhD thesis. Leeds: School of English, University of Leeds. 1993.

— 'The Light of Heaven: Flame as Special Effect' in Clifford Davidson ed.*The Iconography of Heaven*. Early Drama, Art, and Music Monograph Series, 21, Medieval Institute Publications. Kalamazoo: Western Michigan University, 1994. 128-145.

— 'Royal Firework Theater: The Fort Holding'. *Research Opportunities in Renaissance Drama* XXXIV (1995): 145-166.

— 'Royal Firework Theater: The Fort Holding, Part II'. *Research Opportunities in Renaissance Drama* XXXV (1996): 17-31.

— 'Stage Directions in the Towneley Play of Jacob'. *The National Arts Education Archive Occasional Papers* 6 (1996): 1-8.

— 'Comings and Goings: English Medieval Staging Conventions'. *The Early Drama, Art, and Music Review* 18:1 (1995): 25-34.

Calderwood, David. *The History of the Kirk of Scotland*. 8 vols. Edinburgh: The Wodrow Society, 1842 -9.

Calender of State Papers, Domestic Series, of the reigns of Edward VI, Mary, Elizabeth. 7 vols. eds. Robert Lemon [vols. 1-2], Mary Anne Everett Green [vols. 3-7]. London: Longmans, 1856-71.

Calender of State Papers and Manuscripts, Relating to English Affairs, existing in the archives and collections of Venice and in other libraries of Northern Italy. 38 vols. eds. Rawdon Brown [vols. 1-6], R.Brown and G.Cavendish Bentinck [7], Horatio Brown [8-12], Allen B.Hinds [vols. 13-38]. London: Longmans (H.M.S.O.), 1864-1947 [for 1940].

Campbell, Lily B. *Scenes and Machines on the English Stage during the Renaissance. A Classical Revival*. Cambridge: Cambridge University Press, 1923.

Cannell, J.C. *The Secrets of Houdini*. London: Hutchinson, 1931; rpt. New York: Dover Publications, 1973.

Carthew, G.A. 'Extracts from Papers in the Church Chest of Wymondham'. *Norfolk Archaeology* IX (1884): 121-152.

Caspall, John. *Fire & Light in the home pre-1820*. Woodbridge: Antique Collectors' Club, 1987.

Chambers, E.K. *The Mediaeval Stage*. 2 vols. London: Oxford University Press, 1903; rpt. 1967.

— *English Literature at the Close of the Middle Ages*. Oxford: Clarendon Press, 1945; rpt. 1971.

— *The Elizabethan Stage*. 4 vols. Oxford: Clarendon Press, 1923; rpt. 1974.

Chancellor, Gary Lynn. *Stage Directions in Western Drama: Studies in Form and Function*. Unpublished PhD thesis. University of Wisconsin-Madison, 1980.

Chapman, George. *Bussy D'Ambois* in *Old Plays, being a continuation of Dodsley's Collection*. 6 vols. III. London: Rodwell and Martin, 1816.

— *Caesar and Pompey* in *The Comedies and Tragedies of George Chapman Now First Collected with Illustrative Notes and A Memoir of the Author in Three Volumes* III. London: John Pearson, 1873.

Cheales, Henry John. 'On the Wall-Paintings in All Saints' Church, Friskney, Lincolnshire'. *Archaeologia* LIII (1893): 427-433.

Christopher, Milbourne. *The Illustrated History of Magic*. London: Robert Hale, 1975.

Church, A.H. *The Chemistry of Paints and Painting*. London: Seeley and Co., 1890.

Clark, A. 'Maldon Records and the Drama'. *Notes and Queries*, Tenth Series VII, January-June (1907): 181-83, 342-3, 422-3; VIII, July-December (1907): 43-44.

Clephan, Robert Coltman. *An Outline of the History and Development of Hand Firearms, from the Earliest Period to about the End of the Fifteenth Century*. London: Walter Scott Publishing Co., 1906.

Clopper, Lawrence M. ed. *Records of Early English Drama: Chester*. Toronto: University Press and Manchester University Press, 1979.

Cobbett, William. *Cottage Economy*. London, 1822; rpt. Oxford: Oxford University Press, 1979.

Cockle, Maurice J.D. *A Bibliography of English Military Books up to 1642 and of Contemporary Foreign Works*. London: Simpkin, Marshall, Hamilton, Kent and Co., 1900; rpt. *A Bibliography of Military Books up to 1642*. London: The Holland Press, 1957 and 1978.

Cohen, Gustave. *Le Livre De Conduite Du Régisseur et Le Compte Des Dépenses pour le Mystère De La Passion joué à Mons en 1501*. Paris: Honoré Champion, 1925.

— *Histoire De La Mise En Scène Dans Le Théâtre Religieux Francais Du Moyen Age*. Paris: Honoré Champion, 1926.

Coleman, R. 'On the Manufacture and constituent Parts of Gunpowder. Read before the Askesian Society May 1801'. *The Philosophical Magazine* IX (1801): 355-65.

Coletti, Theresa. 'The Design of the Digby Play of Mary Magdalene'. *Studies in Philology* LXXVI, 4 October (1979): 313-333.

Collier, John Payne. *Household Books of John Duke of Norfolk and Thomas Earl of Surrey ; Temp. 1481-1490*. London: Roxburghe Club, Shakespeare Press, 1844.

Conkling, John A. *Chemistry of Pyrotechnics: Basic Principles and Theory*. New York: Marcel Dekker Inc., 1985.

Cook, David ed. 'Dramatic Records in the Declared Accounts of the Treasurer of the Chamber'. *Collections* VI. Oxford: The Malone Society, 1961 (1962).

Coulton, G.G. *Life in the Middle Ages*. 4 vols. Cambridge: Cambridge University Press, 1928-30.

Cox, Charles, J. *Churchwardens' Accounts* [Chelmsford]. London: Methuen, 1913.

Craig, Hardin. *English Religious Drama*. Oxford: Oxford University Press, 1955; rpt. 1968.

— ed. *Two Coventry Corpus Christi Plays*. The Early English Text Society. ES 87. London: Oxford University Press, 1957.

Craigie, Sir William A. *A Dictionary of the Older Scottish Tongue From the Twelfth Century to the End of the Seventeenth*. London: Oxford University Press, 1938 -.

Crawford, Anne (ed.). *Howard Household Books*. Stroud: Alan Sutton, 1992.

Crocker, Glenys. *The Gunpowder Industry*. Aylesbury: Shire Publications, 1986.

— *A Guide to the Chilworth Gunpowder Mills*. Surrey Industrial Group, 1985 ; rpt. 1990.

— *Gunpowder Mills Gazetteer*. Occasional Publication 2. London: Gunpowder Mills Study Group, The Wind and Watermill Section, The Society For the Protection of Ancient Buildings, 1988.

Crombie, A.C. *Robert Grosseteste and the Origins of Experimental Science 1100-1700*. Oxford: Clarendon Press, 1953.

Culver, Max Keith. *A History of Theatre Sound Effects Devices to 1927*. Unpublished PhD thesis. Urbana-Champaign: University of Illinois, 1981.

Cutbush, James. 'Chinese Fire'.*American Journal of Science* VII (1823): 118-40.

— 'On the Properties and Composition of Greek Fire'. *American Journal of Science* V (1822): 302-15.

Cutts, Cecilia. 'The Croxton Play: An Anti-Lollard Piece'. *Modern Language Quarterly* V (1944): 45-60.

Davenport, Robert. *A New Tricke to Cheat the Diuell*. London: John Okes, for Humphrey Blunden, 1639.

Davidson, Clifford. *Technology, Guilds, and Early English Drama*. Early Drama, Art, and Music Monograph Series, 23. Medieval Institute Publications. Kalamazoo: Western Michigan University, 1997.

Davies, Richard. *Chester's Triumph in Honour of Her Prince* III. Manchester: Chetham Society, 1844.

Davies, Robert. *Extracts from the Municipal Records of the City of York during the Reigns of Edward IV, Edward V, and Richard III*. London: J.B.Nichols, 1843.

Davis, Norman ed. *Non-Cycle Plays and Fragments*. The Early English Text Society. SS 1. London: Oxford University Press, 1970.

Davis, Tenney Lombard. *The Chemistry of Powder and Explosives*. New York: John Wiley & Sons, Inc., 1943; rpt. Hollywood: Angriff Press,1970.

Dawes, Edwin A. *The Great Illusionists*. New Jersey: Chartwell Books Inc. and David & Charles, 1979.

Dawson, Giles E ed. 'Records of Plays and Players in Kent 1450-1642'. *Collections* VII. Oxford: The Malone Society, 1965.

Dean, Henry. *The Whole Art of Legerdemain, or Hocus Pocus In Perfection*. London: H.Dean, 1722.

De Beer, E.S. 'The Early History of London Street-Lighting'. *History* XXV (1941): 311-24.

Deimling and Mathews eds. *The Chester Plays*. 2 vols. The Early English Text Society. ES 62. ES 115. London: Oxford University Press, 1892 and 1916; rpts.1968.

Dekker, Thomas and Webster, John. *Northward Ho* in Fredson Bowers ed.*The Dramatic Works of Thomas Dekker* II. Cambridge: Cambridge University Press, 1955.

— *If this be not a Good Play, the Devil is in it* in Fredson Bowers ed.*The Dramatic Works of Thomas Dekker* III. Cambridge: Cambridge University Press, 1958.

— *The Virgin Martyr* in Fredson Bowers ed.*The Dramatic Works of Thomas Dekker* III. Cambridge: Cambridge University Press, 1958.

Del Villar, Mary. 'Some Approaches to the Medieval English Saint's Play'. *Research Opportunities in Renaissance Drama* XV-XVI (1972-73): 83-91.

— 'The Staging of the Conversion of Saint Paul'. *Theatre Notebook* XXV, 2 (1970-1): 64-68.

Denny, Neville ed. *Medieval Drama*. London: Edward Arnold, 1975.

Dessen, Alan C. 'Interpreting Stage Directions: Elizabethan Clues and Modern Detectives' in G.R.Hibbard ed.*The Elizabethan Theatre* IX. (1981), 77-99.

— *Elizabethan Stage Conventions and Modern Interpreters*. Cambridge: Cambridge University Press, 1984.

241

A Diurnal of Remarkable Occurrents that have passed within the Country of Scotland since the death of King James the Fourth till the year M.D.LXXV. Edinburgh: Bannatyne Club, 1883.

Douce, Francis. *Illustrations of Shakespeare, and of Ancient Manners: with dissertations on the Clowns and Fools of Shakespeare; on the collection of popular tales entitled Gesta Romanorum; and on the English Morris Dance.* London: Thomas Tegg, 1839.

Douglas, Audrey and Greenfield, Peter eds. *Records of Early English Drama: Cumberland, Westmorland, Gloucestershire.* Toronto: Toronto University Press, 1986.

Dunlap, William. *The Life of George Frederick Cooke.* 2 vols. London, 1815.

Durand, W.Y. 'Palaemon and Arcyte, Progne, Marcus Geminus, and the Theatre in which they were acted, as described by John Bereblock (1566).'. *Publications of the Modern Language Association of America* XX, New Series XIII (1905; rpt. 1961): 502-28.

Dussauce, H. *A Practical Treatise on the Fabrication of Matches, Gun Cotton, Colored Fires and Fulminating Powders.* Philadelphia: Henry Carey Baird, 1864.

Eamon, William. 'Technology as Magic in the Late Middle Ages and the Renaissance'. *Janus* 70 (1983): 171-212.

— *Science and the Secrets of Nature*: *Books of Secrets in Medieval and Early Modern Culture.* Princeton: University Press, 1994.

Eccles, Mark. *The Macro Plays.* The Early English Text Society. OS 262. London: Oxford University Press, 1969.

Ellern, Herbert. *Modern Pyrotechnics: Fundamentals of Applied Physical Pyrochemistry.* New York: Chemical Publishing Co., 1961.

Ellis, Oliver C.de C. *A History of Fire and Flame.* London: The Poetry Lovers' Fellowship, 1932.

England and Pollard eds. *The Towneley Plays.* The Early English Text Society. ES 71. London: Oxford University Press, 1897; rpt. New York: Kraus Reprint Co., 1975.

Etten, Henry van. *Mathematical Recreations.* London: T.Cotes for Richard Hawkins, 1633.

Eveleigh, David J. *Candle Lighting.* Aylesbury: Shire Publications, 1985.

Fairholt, Frederick W. *Early English Poetry, Ballads, and Popular Literature of the Middle Ages.* London: Percy Society, 1843.

Faraday, Michael. *Chemical History of a Candle: A Course of Six Lectures*. London: The Scientific Book Guild, 1960.

Ferguson, John. *Bibliographical Notes on Histories of Inventions and Books of Secrets*. Glasgow: Glasgow University Press, 1883.

— *Bibliographical Notes on Histories of Inventions and Books of Secrets. Part III., Part IV., Part V.* in *Transactions of the Glasgow Archaeological Society.* New Series-Volume I. Glasgow: James Maclehose & Sons, 1890.

—*Bibliographical Notes on Histories of Inventions and Books of Secrets. First Supplement* in *Transactions of the Glasgow Archaeological Society.* New Series-Volume II. Glasgow: James Maclehose & Sons, 1896.

—*Bibliographical Notes on Histories of Inventions and Books of Secrets. Second Supplement and Third Supplement* in *Transactions of the Glasgow Archaeological Society.* New Series-Volume III. Glasgow: James Maclehose & Sons, 1899.

— 'Some Early Treatises on Technological Chemistry'. *Proceedings of the Philosophical Society of Glasgow* 19, (1888): 126-59; 25, (1894): 224-35; 43, (1911): 232-58; 44, (1912): 149-81.

Feuillerat, Albert. *Documents Relating to the Office of the Revels in the time of Queen Elizabeth*. Louvain: A.Uystpruyst, 1908; rpt. New York: Kraus Reprint Ltd., 1963.

— *Documents relating to the Revels at Court in the time of King Edward VI and Queen Mary*. Louvain: A.Uystpruyst, 1914; rpt. New York: Kraus Reprint Ltd., 1963.

Fletcher, J. and Massinger P. *The Prophetess* in V.A.R. Waller ed. *The Works of Francis Beaumont and John Fletcher*. Cambridge: Cambridge University Press, 1907.

Foakes, R.A. and Rickert, R.T. eds. *Henslowe's Diary*. Cambridge: Cambridge University Press, 1968.

Forbes, R.J. *A Short History of the Art of Distillation*. Leiden: E.J.Brill, 1948.

Fouquet, Jean. *The Hours of Etienne Chevalier*. London: Thames and Hudson, 1972.

Frank, Grace. 'The Genesis and Staging of the Jeu D'Adam'. *Publications of the Modern Language Association of America* LIX (1944): 7-17.

Froissart, *The Chronicle of Froissart*. 6 vols. trans. Sir John Bourchier, Lord Berners. London: David Nutt, 1901-3.

Furnivall, F.J. ed. *The Digby Plays*. The Early English Text Society. ES 70. London: Oxford University Press, 1896 ; rpt. 1967.

Furedi, Frank. *Culture of Fear: Risk-Taking and the Morality of Low Expectation*. London: Cassell, 1997.

Gage, Thomas. *The English-American his Travail by Sea and Land: or, A New Svrvey of the West-Indies, containing A Journall of Three thousand and Three hundred Miles within the main Land of America*. London: R.Cotes for Humphrey Blunden, 1648.

Galloway, David and Wasson, John eds. 'Records of Plays and Players in Norfolk and Suffolk 1330-1642'. *Collections* XI. Oxford: The Malone Society, 1980.

Galloway, David ed. *Records of Early English Drama: Norwich 1540-1642*. Toronto: Toronto University Press, 1984.

Gayley, Charles Mills. *Representative English Commedies*. 4 vols. New York: The Macmillan Company, 1903.

George, David ed. *Records of Early English Drama: Lancashire*. Toronto: University Press, 1991.

Gesner, Conrad. *The newe Iewell of Health, wherein is contayned the most excellent Secretes of Phisicke and Philosophie, deuided into fowyer Bookes*. London: George Baker, 1576.

Gilbert, Douglas. *American Vaudeville:Its Life and Times*. Whittlesey House: 1940; rpt. New York: Dover Publications, 1963.

Goffe, Thomas. *The Couragious Turk* in David Carnegie ed. *Reprints*. Oxford: The Malone Society, 1968 (1974).

Grafton's Chronicle [A Chronicle at Large]. London, 1569; rpt. 2 vols., 1809.

Grant, William and Murison, David D. eds. *The Scottish National Dictionary*. Edinburgh, 1931-1990.

Grantley, Darryll. 'Producing Miracles' in Paula Neuss ed.*Aspects of Early English Drama*. Cambridge: D.S.Brewer, 1983, 78-91.

Graves, R.B. 'Stage Lighting at the Elizabethan and Early Stuart Courts'. *Theatre Notebook* XXXVIII, 1 (1984): 27-36.

— 'Elizabethan Lighting Effects and the Conventions of Indoor and Outdoor Theatrical Illumination'.*Renaissance Drama* XII (1981): 51-69.

— 'Daylight in the Elizabethan Private Theatres'. *Shakespeare Quarterly* XXXIII, pt.I (1982): 80-92.

Green, J.R. *A Short History of the English People*. London: Macmillan and Co., 1893.

244

Greene, Robert. *Alphonsus King of Aragon* in W.W.Greg ed.*Reprints*. Oxford: The Malone Society, 1926.

Greene and Middleton. *Friar Bacon and Friar Bungay* in John S.Farmer ed.*Old English Drama*. London: 1914.

Greg, W.W. ed. 'The Academic Drama at Cambridge: Extracts from College Records'. *Collections* II, pt.II. Oxford: The Malone Society, 1923.

Grose, Francis and Astle, Thomas eds. *Antiquarian Repertory*. 4 vols. London: Jeffery, 1807-9.

Grove, Sir George. *A Dictionary of Music and Musicians (AD 1450-1889)*. London: Macmillan, 1899-1900.

Guttmann, Oscar. *The Manufacture of Explosives*. 2 vols. London: Whittaker and Co., 1895.

Gwei-Djen, Lu and Needham, Joseph and Needham, Dorothy. 'The Coming of Ardent Water'. *Ambix* XIX, pt.2 (July 1972): 69-112.

Hall, Bert. *Weapons and Warfare in Renaissance Europe: Gunpowder, Technology, and Tactics*. Baltimore: The John Hopkins University Press, 1997.

Hall, Trevor H. *A Bibliography of Books on Conjuring in English from 1580 to 1850*. Lepton: Palmyra Press, 1957.

— *Old Conjuring Books*. London: Duckworth, 1972.

Halle, Edward. *Hall's Chronicle; containing The History of England During The Reign of Henry The Fourth And The Succeeding Monarchs To The End of The Reign of Henry The Eighth*. London, 1548 ; rpt.1809.

Halliday, F.E. *The Legend of the Rood*. London: Gerald Duckworth & Co., 1955.

Harbage, Alfred. *Annals of English Drama 975-1700*. Revised by S.Schoenbaum. London: Methuen & Co., 1964.

Hardison, O.B. *Christian Rite and Christian Drama in the Middle Ages*. Baltimore: The John Hopkins Press, 1965; rpt. 1969.

Hartshorne, Charles H. 'Bills of Medicines Furnished for the Use of Edward I. 34 and 35 EDW.I., 1306-7'. *Archaeological Journal* XIV (1857): 267-71.

Hardy, W.J. *The Manuscripts of Lord Kenyon* [A calendar]. Historical Manuscripts Commission, 14th Report Appendix, pt.4. London: H.M.S.O., 1894.

Harris Markham ed. *The Cornish Ordinalia: A Medieval Dramatic Trilogy.* Washington D.C.: The Catholic University of America Press, 1969.

Harris, Mary Dormer. 'The "World" in the Doomsday Mystery Play'. *Notes and Queries* CXLIX (October 3, 1925): 243.

Harris, Max. *The Dialogical Theatre: Dramatizations of the Conquest of Mexico and the Question of the Other*. London: The Macmillan Press, 1993.

— 'Parachicos at Chiapa'. *Intergrad* (Summer, 1972):1-5.

— 'Muhammed and the Virgin: Folk Dramatizations of Battles Between Moors and Christians in Modern Spain'. *The Drama Review* 38 (Spring, 1994): 45-61.

Hart, William Henry. *A Short Account of the Early Manufacture of Gunpowder in England*. London: W.H.Elkins, 1855.

Herford, C.H., Percy and Simpson, Evelyn eds. *Ben Jonson*. 10 vols. Oxford: Clarendon Press, 1925-52.

Hewitt, Barnard ed. *The Renaissance Stage - Documents of Serlio, Sabbattini and Furtenbach*. Coral Gables, Florida: University of Miami Press, 1958; rpt. 1969.

Heywood, John. *The Play of Love* in John S.Farmer ed.*The Tudor Facsimile Texts*. London: T.C. and E.C.Jack, 1909.

Heywood, Thomas. *The Golden Age* in *The Dramatic Works of Thomas Heywood, Now First Collected with Illustrative Notes and a Memoir of the Author in Six Volumes* III. London, 1874; rpt. New York: Russell and Russell, 1964.

— *The Silver Age* in *The Dramatic Works of Thomas Heywood, Now First Collected with Illustrative Notes and a Memoir of the Author in Six Volumes* III. London, 1874; rpt. New York: Russell and Russell, 1964.

— *The Brazen Age* in *The Dramatic Works of Thomas Heywood, Now First Collected with Illustrative Notes and a Memoir of the Author in Six Volumes* III. London, 1874; rpt. New York: Russell and Russell, 1964.

— *Ivpiter and Io* in *The Dramatic Works of Thomas Heywood, Now First Collected with Illustrative Notes and a Memoir of the Author in Six Volumes* VI. London, 1874; rpt. New York: Russell and Russell, 1964.

Hime, Henry William Lovett. *Gunpowder and Ammunition: their origin and progress*. London: Longmans, Green and Co., 1904.

— *Origin of Artillery*. London: Longmans & Co., 1915.

Hodges, C.Walter.*The Globe Restored*. London: Ernest Benn, 1953.

Nashe, Thomas. *Summer's Last Will and Testament* in Robert Dodsley ed.; rpt. W.C.Hazlitt ed. *A Select Collection of Old English Plays* VIII. London: 1744; rpt. London: 1874.

Nelson, Alan H. ed. *Records of Early English Drama: Cambridge*. 2 vols. Toronto: Toronto University Press, 1989.

— *Early Cambridge Theatres: college, university, and town stages, 1464-1720*. Cambridge ; Cambridge University Press, 1994.

Neuss, Paula ed. *Aspects of Early English Drama*. Cambridge: D.S.Brewer, 1983.

— *the Creacion of the World - A Critical Edition and Translation*. New York and London: Garland Publishing, Inc., 1983.

Nicholl, John.*Some Account of the Worshipful Company of Ironmongers*. Second edition. London, 1866.

Nichols, John. *The Progresses and Public Processions of Queen Elizabeth*. 3 vols. London: John Nichols and Son, 1823.

— *The Progresses, Processions, and Magnificent Festivities of King James the First*. 4 vols. London: J.B.Nichols, 1828.

Nichols, John G. *Literary Remains of King Edward the Sixth*. 2 vols. London: Roxburghe Club, 1857.

— ed. *The Diary of Henry Machyn, Citizen and Merchant-Taylor of London, From A.D. 1550 to A.D. 1563*. London: Camden Society, 1848.

Nicoll, Allardyce.*The Development of the Theatre*. London: George G. Harrap & Company Ltd., 1927; rpt. 1966.

Nightingale, Pamela. *A Medieval Mercantile Community: The Grocers' Company and the Politics and Trade of London, 1000-1485*. London: Yale University Press, 1995.

Norris, Edwin. *The Ancient Cornish Drama*. 2 vols. Oxford: Oxford University Press, 1859; rpt. New York/London: Benjamin Blom, 1968.

Norton, Robert. *The Gvnner Shewing The Whole Practise Of Artillerie: With all the Appurtenances therevnto belonging. Together with the making of Extraordinary Artificiall Fireworkes, as well for Pleasure and Triumphes, as for Warre and Seruice*. London : A.M. for Hvmphrey Robinson, 1628; facs. rpt. Amsterdam: Da Capo Press Theatrvm Orbis Terrarvm Ltd., 1973.

Nye, Nathanael. *The Art of Gunnery*. London: William Leake, 1648.

O'Dea, William T. *The Social History of Lighting*. London: Routledge and Kegan Paul, 1958.

Oglesby, Lloyd Scott. *Glitter:Chemistry &Techniques*. Dingmans Ferry: American Firework News, 1983; rev. rpt. 1989.

Ormerod, George. *History of the County Palatine and City of Chester*. 3 vols. London: Routledge, 1882.

Partington, J.R.*Origins and Development of Applied Chemistry*.London: Longmans, Green and Co., 1935.

— *A History of Greek Fire and Gunpowder*. Cambridge: W.Heffer & Sons, 1960.

Paterson, Morton. 'The Stagecraft of the Revels Office during the Reign of Elizabeth' in *Studies in the Elizabethan Theatre*. Shoe String Press, Inc., 1961, 1-52.

Paton, Henry M. ed. *Accounts of the Masters of Works for Building and Repairing Royal Palaces and Castles 1529-1615* I. Edinburgh: H.M.S.O., 1957.

Patterson, Edward M. 'Gunpowder Terminology and the Incorporation Process in the Manufacture of Gunpowder and the History of the Associated Explosions', *Faversham Papers* XXVII (1986):1-32.

Pearson, Karl. *The Chances of Death and Other Studies in Evolution*. London: Edward Arnold, 1897.

Peele, George. *The Old Wives Tale* in W.W.Greg ed. *Reprints*. Oxford: The Malone Society, 1908.

— *The Battle of Alcazar* in W.W.Greg and Frank Sidgwick eds. *Reprints*. Oxford: The Malone Society, 1907.

Penzel, Frederick. *Theatre Lighting Before Electricity*. Middletown, Connecticut: Wesleyan University Press, 1978.

Percival, A.J. 'The Faversham Gunpowder Industry and its development'. *Faversham Papers* IV. Third edition (1986):1-36.

Pevsner, Nikolaus. *The Buildings of England: London* I. London: Penguin, 1973.

— and Wedgewood. Alexandra.*The Buildings of England:Warwickshire*. London: Penguin, 1966.

— *The Buildings of England: North Somerset and Bristol*. London: Penguin, 1958; rpt.1979.

Pfister, Manfred. *The Theory and Analysis of Drama*. Trans. John Halliday. Cambridge: Cambridge University Press, 1988.

Philip, Chris. *A Bibliography of Firework Books*. Winchester: St.Paul's Bibliographies, 1985.

Philp, Brian. *The Dartford Gunpowder Mills*. Dover, Kent: Archaeological Rescue Unit, 1984.

Philopyrphagis Ashburniensus. *The Gentleman's Magazine and Historical Chronicle* XXV (1759): 59.

Platte, Hugh. *The Jewell House of Art and Natvre*. London: Peter Short, 1594.

Plimpton, George. *Fireworks: A History and Celebration*. New York: Doubleday & Company Inc., 1984.

Pollard, Alfred W. ed. *English Miracle Plays, Moralities and Interludes*. Oxford: Oxford University Press, 1890; rpt. 1973.

Porta, John Baptista. *Magia Naturalis*. Naples:1558; English translation, *Natural Magick*. London: Thomas Young and Samuel Speed, 1658; facs. rpt. of English translation Derek J.Price ed.*Natural Magick*. New York: Basic Books, Inc., 1957.

Purnell, E.K. *Report on the Pepys Manuscripts preserved at Magdalene College, Cambridge*. Historical Manuscripts Commission. London: H.M.S.O., 1911.

Rabelais, Francois. *Gargantua and Pantegruel*. Trans. J.M.Cohen. London: Penguin, 1955.

Raine, Angelo ed. *York Civic Records*. Record Series, I-VIII. Wakefield/York/London: The Yorkshire Archaeological Society, 1939-1953.

Rees, Terence. *Theatre Lighting in the Age of Gas*. London: The Society For Theatre Research, 1978.

Ridd, S.[S.R.]. *The Art of Ivgling or Legerdemaine*. London: George Eld, 1614.

Robertson, J. and Gordon, D.J. eds. 'A Calendar of Dramatic Records in the Books of the Livery Companies of London 1485-1640'. *Collections* III. Oxford: The Malone Society, 1954.

Romocki, S.J.von. *Geschichte der Explosivstoffe: Geschichte der Sprengstoffchemie, der Sprengtechnik und des Torpedowesens bis zum Beginn der neuesten Zeit*. Berlin: Robert Oppenheim (Gustav Schmidt), 1895.

Rossiter, A.P. *English Drama From Early Times To The Elizabethans: Its Background, Origins and Developments*. London: Hutchinson, 1950; rpt. 1962.

Rovenzon, John. *A Treatise of Metallica*. London: Thomas Thorp, 1613.

Rowley, William. *The Birth of Merlin*. London: 1662; facs. rpt. Wing R 2096, 1800/475.

Royal Commission on Historical Manuscripts. *Fifth Report of the Royal Commission on Historical Manuscripts. Report and Appendix*. London: H.M.S.O., 1876.

Ruggieri, Claude-Fortune. *Principles of Pyrotechnics*. Trans. Stuart Carlton. Buena Vista, California: MP Associates, Inc., 1994.

Runnals, Graham A. 'Le Mystère de la Passion à Amboise au Moyen Age: représentations théâtrales et texte'. *Le Moyen Francais* XXVI (1990): 7-86.

Sabbatini, Nicolo. *Pratica di Fabricar Scene E Machine Ne' Teatri*. Ravenna:1638; facs. rpt. Roma: Carlo Bestetti, 1955.

Sachs, Edwin. *Sleight of Hand: A Practical Manual of Legerdemain for Amateurs and Others*. London: L.Upcott Gill, 1885.

Salter, F.M. *Mediaeval Drama in Chester*. Toronto: Toronto University Press, 1955; rpt. New York: Russell and Russell, 1968.

Sauzay, A. *Marvels of Glass-Making in All Ages*. London: Sampson Low, Son, and Marston, 1870.

Sayle, R.T.D. *Lord Mayors' Pageants of the Merchant Taylors' Company in the 15th, 16th and 17th Centuries*. London:1931.

Schneideman, Robert Ivan. *Elizabethan Legerdemain and its Employment in the Drama 1576-1642*. Unpublished PhD thesis. Northwestern University:1956.

Schoenbaum, S. *Shakespeare's Lives*. Oxford: Oxford University Press, 1970.

Scottish Record Office, *SRO MS E23/3/45*.

Sellers, Maud.*York Memorandum Book*. 2 vols. CXX, CXXV. London: Surtees Society, 1912 [for 1911], 1915 [for 1914].

— *The York Mercers and Merchant Adventurers 1356-1917*. CXXIX. London: Surtees Society, 1918 [for 1917].

Serlio, Sebastiano.*The Five Books of Architecture: An Unabridged Reprint of the English Edition of 1611*. New York: Dover Publications, 1982.

Sharp, Thomas. *A Dissertation on the Pageants or Dramatic Mysteries anciently performed at Coventry*. Coventry: Merridew and Son, 1825; facs. rpt. Wakefield: EP Publishing, 1973.

Sheingorn, Pamela. *The Easter Sepulchre in England*. Early Drama, Art, and Music Reference Series, 5, Medieval Institute Publications. Kalamazoo: Western Michigan University, 1987.

Shergold, N.D. *A History of the Spanish Stage from Medieval Times until the end of the Seventeenth Century* . Oxford: Oxford University Press, 1967.

Shimizu, Takeo. *Fireworks:The Art, Science and Technique*. Tokyo: Takeo Shimizu, 1981.

Shirley, Frances Ann. *Shakespeare's Use of Off-Stage Sounds*. Lincoln: University of Nebraska Press, 1963.

Shirley, Henry. *The Martyrd Soldier*. London: I.Okes and are to be sold by Francis Eglesfield, 1638.

Shirley, James. *The Doubtful Heir* in *The Dramatic Works and Poems of James Shirley*. 6 vols. London: Murray, 1833.

Simienowicz, Casimir. *The Great Art Of Artillery Of Casimir Simienowicz, Formerly Lieutenant-General of the Ordnance to the King of Poland. Translated from the French, By George Shelvocke, Jun.Gent.*. London: J.Tonson, 1729.

Simmons, W.H. *A Short History of the Royal Gunpowder Factory at Waltham Abbey*. London: Royal Ordnance Factories, 1963.

Simon, Eckehard. *The Theatre of Medieval Europe - New Research in Early Drama*. Cambridge: Cambridge University Press, 1991.

Sismondi, J.C.L. Simonde De. *Historical View of the Literature of the South of Europe*. 2 vols. London: Bell, 1872-77.

Smith, F.M. *A Handbook of the Manufacture and Proof of Gunpowder, as carried on at the Royal Gunpowder Factory, Waltham Abbey*. London: H.M.S.O., 1870.

Smith, Lucy Toulmin ed. *The Maire of Bristowe is Kalendar, by Robert Ricart, Town Clerk of Bristol 18 Edward IV*. London: Camden Society, 1872.

— *York Plays*. Oxford: Clarendon Press, 1885; rpt. New York: Russell and Russell, 1963.

Somerset, J.Alan B.Somerset ed. *Records of Early English Drama: Shropshire*. Toronto: University of Toronto Press, 1994.

Somerset, J.A.B. 'Local Drama and Playing Places at Shrewsbury: New Findings From the Borough Records'. *Medieval and Renaissance Drama in England* II. AMS Press (1985): 1-31.

Sorrell,W.J. *The Amateur's Hand-Book*. London: Thomas Hailes Lacy, 1866.

Southern, Richard. 'the stage groove and the thunder run'. *Architectural Review* LXXXXV (May 1944):135-6.

— *The Medieval Theatre in the Round*. London: Faber, 1957.

— *Changeable Scenery*. London: Faber, 1952.

Spector, Stephen ed. *The N-Town Play: Cotton MS Vespasian D.8*. 2 vols. The Early English Text Society. SS 13 SS 14 Oxford: Oxford University Press, 1991.

Sprague, Arthur Colby. 'Off-Stage Sounds'. *University of Toronto Quarterly* XV (1945-6): 70-75.

Stokes, Whitley ed. *Gwreans An Bys: The Creation of the World, A Cornish Mystery*. Berlin: A.Asher & Co., 1863; London and Edinburgh: Williams and Norgate, 1864.

— *The Life of Saint Meriasek, Bishop and Confessor*. London: Trübner and Co., 1872.

Stow, John. *The Annales of England, Faithfully collected out of the most authenticall Authors, Records, and other Monuments of Antiquitie, lately corrected, encreased, and continued, from the first inhabitation vntill this present yeare 1601*. London: Ralfe Newbery, 1601.

Stratman, Carl J. *Bibliography of Medieval Drama*. 2 vols. New York: Frederick Ungar Publishing Co., 1972.

Streitberger, W.R. 'Jacobean and Caroline Revels Accounts, 1603-1642'. *Collections* XIII. Oxford: The Malone Society, 1986.

Strong, R.C. and van Dorsten, J.A. *Leicester's Triumph*. Leiden/London: University Press and Oxford University Press, 1964.

Studer, Paul ed. *Le Mystère D'Adam*. Manchester: Manchester University Press, 1918; rpt. 1928.

Thompson, Daniel V. *The Materials of Medieval Painting*. London: George Allen & Unwin, 1936.

Thomson, S.Harrison. 'The Texts of Michael Scot's Ars Alchemie'. *Osiris* V (1938): 523-559.

Thorndike, L. *History of Magic and Experimental Science*. 8 vols. New York: Columbia University Press, 1923-58.

Thwing, Leroy. *Flickering Flames: A History of Domestic Lighting through the Ages.* The Rushlight Club. Rutland, Vermont: Charles E. Tuttle Company, 1958.

Toole Stott, Raymond. *A Bibliography of English Conjuring 1581-1876.* 2 vols. Derby: Harpur & Sons, 1976 and 1978.

Tout, T.F. 'Firearms in England in the Fourteenth Century'. *English Historical Review* XXVI (1911): 666-702.

Trease, G.E. 'The Spicers and Apothecaries of the Royal Household in the Reigns of Henry III, Edward I and Edward II'. *Nottinghamshire Medieval Studies* III (1959):19-52.

Tydeman, William. *The Theatre in the Middle Ages.* Cambridge: Cambridge University Press, 1978.

— *English Medieval Theatre 1400-1500.* London: Routledge & Kegan Paul, 1986.

Venn, Thomas. *Military and Maritime Discipline in three books....* London: E.Tyler and R.Holt for Rob.Pawlet, 1672.

Victoria History of the Counties of England [The-]. Sussex. 7 vols. in 9. London: Constable, 1905-87.

Vitale-Brovarone, Allessandro. *Il quaderno di segreti d'un regista provenzale del Medioevo: Note per la messa in scena d'una Passione.* Alessandria: Edizioni Dell'Orso, 1984.

Vitruvius, *The Ten Books on Architecture.* Trans. Morris Hicky Morgan. New York: Dover Publications, 1960.

Walker, James. *Remarks on the Safe Conveyance and Preservation of Gunpowder.* London: J.Darling, 1814.

Wanley, Nathaniel. *The Wonders of the Little World: Or a General History of Man in Six Books.* London: T.Basset and J.Wright, 1678.

Ward, Richard ed. (See Isaacson, R.F. Gen. ed.).

Warrack, Alexander. *A Scots Dialect Dictionary.* London: Chambers, 1911.

Wasson, John M. ed. *Records of Early English Drama: Devon.* Toronto: Toronto University Press, 1986.

— 'Types and Analysis of Records'. *Proceedings of the First Colloquium.* Joanna Dutka ed. Toronto: Records of Early English Drama, 1979.

Weingart, George W. *Dictionary and Manual of Pyrotechny*. New Orleans: Copyright New Orleans, 1937.

— *Pyrotechnics*. New York: Chemical Publishing Company, Inc., 1947.

Whetstone, George.*The Historie of Promos and Cassandra* in Geoffrey Bullough ed. *Narrative and Dramatic Sources of Shakespeare* II. London: Routledge, Kegan & Paul, 1958.

White, Gilbert. *The Natural History of Selborne*. London: 1878-9 ; rpt. London: Penguin, 1977.

White, John. *A Rich Cabinet,with variety of inventions....* London: W.Gilbertson, 1651.

White, Lynn Jr. *Medieval Technology and Social Change*. London: Oxford University Press, 1962.

— *Medieval Religion and Technology*. Berkley, Los Angeles, London: University of California Press, 1978.

Whitehorne, Peter. *Certaine wayes for the ordering of Soldiours in battleray, and setting of battayles, after diuers fashions, with their maner of marching: And also Fugures of certayne newe plattes for fortification of Townes: And more ouer howe to make Saltpeter, Gunpouder, and diuers sortes of Fireworkes or wilde Fyre, with other thinges appertayning to the warres*. London: VV.VVilliamson, 1573.

Wickham, Glynne. *Early English Stages 1300-1660*. vol.I, 1300-1576, 1959; rev.rpt. 1980; vol. II, pt. I, 1576-1660, 1963; vol.II, pt.II, 1576-1660, 1972; vol.III, 1981. London: Routledge & Kegan Paul.

Wilson, C.Anne. 'Philosophers, *Iosis* and Water of Life'. *Proceedings of the Leeds Philosophical and Literary Society* XIX, pt.V (1984): 45-93.

Wilson, F.P. *The English Drama 1485-1585*. Oxford: Clarendon Press, 1969.

Wilson, Jean. *Entertainments For Elizabeth I*. Woodbridge, Suffolk: D.S.Brewer, 1980.

Withington, Robert. *English Pageantry*. 2 vols. Cambridge: Harvard University Press, 1918.

Wright, Louis B. 'Juggling Tricks and Conjury on the English Stage Before 1642'. *Modern Philology* XXIV (1926-7): 269-284.

Wright, Thomas. *Churchwardens' Accounts of the Town of Ludlow in Shropshire, from 1540 to the end of the Reign of Queen Elizabeth* . London: Camden Society, 1869.

Yallop, H.J. 'The Lacemaker's Globe'. *The Report and Transactions of the Devonshire Association* 123 (1991): 189-193.

Young, Karl. *The Drama of the Medieval Church*. 2 vols. Oxford: Clarendon Press, 1933.

Young, William Donald. *Devices and Feintes of the Medieval Religious Theatre in England and France*. Unpublished PhD thesis. Stanford University, 1959.

Index

White, John – xx, 71, 72, 77
Whitehorn, Peter – xviii
Wildmen – 3, 10, 21, 24, 25, 100, 103, 104, 115
Woodhousys (see Wildmen) – 21, 24, 26
Woodmen (see Wildmen) – 21
Woodwards (see Wildmen) – 21, 24
Wymondham , Norfolk – 15, 60